Beyond the Baton

Beyond the Baton

WHAT EVERY CONDUCTOR
NEEDS TO KNOW

Diane Wittry

OXFORD
UNIVERSITY PRESS

OXFORD
UNIVERSITY PRESS

Oxford University Press, Inc., publishes works that further
Oxford University's objective of excellence
in research, scholarship, and education.

Oxford   New York
Auckland   Cape Town   Dar es Salaam   Hong Kong   Karachi
Kuala Lumpur   Madrid   Melbourne   Mexico City   Nairobi
New Delhi   Shanghai   Taipei   Toronto

With offices in
Argentina   Austria   Brazil   Chile   Czech Republic   France   Greece
Guatemala   Hungary   Italy   Japan   Poland   Portugal   Singapore
South Korea   Switzerland   Thailand   Turkey   Ukraine   Vietnam

Published by Oxford University Press, Inc.
198 Madison Avenue, New York, New York 10016

www.oup.com

First issued as an Oxford University Press paperback, 2011

Oxford is a registered trademark of Oxford University Press

Library of Congress Cataloging-in-Publication Data
Wittry, Diane.
Beyond the baton : what every conductor needs to know /
Diane Wittry.
p.   cm.
Includes bibliographical references and index.
ISBN-13 978–0–19–977393–0
1. Conducting—Vocational guidance. I. Title.
ML3795.W54 2007
781.45—dc22   2005037782

Printed in the United States of America
on acid-free paper

Acknowledgments

Special thanks to: The Gates Family Foundation for their ongoing support of enriching my knowledge; The Thyll-Dürr Foundation for providing a wonderful place to write this book; The American Symphony Orchestra League for their Leadership Academy; Ellen Rienstra and Steve Menke for their tireless efforts in proofing and editing; Cindy Ovens and Sue Kong for their research; and Richard Peckham, my husband, for the graphics, and for always believing it could be done.

Contents

Resources

Beyond the Baton

Music Director's Job Posting

Duties and Responsibilities:

The Music Director will serve as a leader, both on stage and in the community. The Music Director is responsible for developing and enhancing the artistic vision and quality of the orchestra. He/She is responsible for musical decisions including the planning and supervision, preparation, programming, rehearsing and conducting of all scheduled concerts. He/She will also be involved in the hiring of guest soloists to perform with the orchestra. The Music Director is responsible for functioning within the orchestra's policies and procedures for selecting new players, disciplining players, and determining seating within sections.

The Music Director will also participate in fundraising and promotional activities in the community to help encourage business and individual support. He/She will guide and help to expand the educational outreach initiatives of the orchestra. It is important that the Music Director establishes a vital presence in the cultural community.

Requirements:

Exceptional musicianship and conducting skills; innovative and thoughtful programming style; strong skills in interpersonal relations, leadership, and communication.

Prologue

"So—You Want to Be a Conductor? It Starts with *You*"

Conducting: *"The art of leading and coordinating a group of instrumentalists and/or singers in a musical performance or rehearsal."*

The New Harvard Dictionary of Music

Many of us will spend our lives trying to perfect this art form, but what truly makes one conductor great, and another conductor just good? People used to say that conductors were born, not taught; that you had to already possess the "right" personality from birth to assume this leadership role; that, if the first time you ever stepped on the podium, you didn't have the mysterious "it," you never would. I do not believe this is true. I believe that anyone who is passionate about music-making, and who is willing to work hard and learn, can become a conductor. There are many areas that must be studied and mastered to make this a reality. Beyond the musical skills that must be learned, you must master the essential ingredient that makes the difference between a good conductor and a great one. That quality is *leadership.*

A conductor makes no sound, and yet they are responsible for the quality of the music-making. Much can be accomplished through their expertise as musicians, yet it is in the transference of this knowledge that many conductors fall short. In essence, all of their work is done through other people. It is the ability to work with people to achieve a common goal that raises the good conductor into the "great" category. There are many conductors with perfect pitch, impeccable knowledge of harmony, excellent baton technique, and fluent understanding of musical styles who are not successful on the podium.

The ability to work with others is essential to being successful as a conductor, but the word *conductor* deals mostly with what is happening on the stage and with the orchestra. What about the growing list of other responsibilities that a conductor must assume, off the podium? Over the past twenty years, the role of the conductor with American orchestras has changed dramatically. No longer are the self-centered, egotistical "maestro" personalities able to be effective. The structure between unions, musicians, and management has shifted to that of a cooperative organization in which a teamwork approach is much more emphasized. This is not to say that these constituents are not without their disagreements, but they are looking for conductors to do more than just show up, "wave their arms," and tell others what to do. In order to function in this new environment, conductors need multiple arrays of skills—skills that go beyond identifying whether the second trombone is out of tune in the V^7 chord; skills that are centered on leadership and vision.

To Change an Organization, You Must *Change* the Leader

All orchestras require leaders to move them forward on their institutional paths. Because of our current training system, young conductors do not always have the necessary background and experience to enable them to lead effectively. They lack the vision of what the organization could become and the knowledge of how to move it forward. We must teach and improve our conductors through changing their leadership style. Therefore, when I say "change" the leader, I do not mean get a new leader; I mean that leadership starts from within the individual. To be an effective artistic leader, you must learn new ways of communicating and new ways of looking at yourself. Your view of the world cannot just center on your personal needs and wants; it must encompass the desires of many individuals and a community. Whatever you can imagine, you can become. By bettering yourself, you can better serve the organization for which you work.

To be truly effective, not simply as a conductor but as a music director with an American orchestra, you must become an artistic leader for the entire organization. You must be fully involved with helping to set the artistic vision and able to empower the various groups within the organization to work toward common goals. Truly great orchestras have exceptional music directors, not just great conductors. Through this book, I hope to show you how you can move from being a *good* conductor to a *great* conductor; from being an adequate music director to being an exceptional music director; from performing a series of concerts to changing a community through your music.

We are conductors because we want to perform quality music with excellent musicians, but this enjoyment is not half as fulfilling as when we share this music with others. Our music-making should affect thousands of people. It should be the focal point of the community that supports it. Through achieving the artistic goals of an organization that is larger than ourselves, we truly can make a difference in a community through our music.

Chapter 1

Preparing for Success

So you have decided that you want to be a conductor. You have probably been involved with music for the majority of your life. Most people who study conducting are very well trained in the musical components of the job. It is common to attend college as a music major focusing on a specific instrument, and then to study conducting in a master's degree program. Even with this extensive preparation, there will still be gaps in your overall knowledge. As you make decisions about your future, understand that the choices you make early on will greatly affect your career path. Here are some of the steps you might consider as you begin your career as a conductor.

Formal Musical Training

Schools and Teachers

FSU?
Dr. Jimenez

The conducting world is a very close-knit community. As you select where you want to study, carefully evaluate the conducting teacher with whom you will be studying and the amount of podium time that will be available. It is very important that you have a good orchestra to work with on a regular basis. Do not just attend the school that will give you the largest scholarship. You should consider carefully the professor's national reputation as a teacher and their involvement with the professional field as you narrow down your choices. You also should consider their personal teaching style. Some teachers are nurturing, and others are like drill sergeants. You will know what type of motivation works for you. *whiplash?* Take the time to talk to some of their previous students and ask them about their experiences. You want to study with a teacher who has a track record of excellent ✓ students that are getting placed in good jobs. Choosing the right teacher is one of the most important decisions you will make. If you choose someone who is well respected nationally, many doors will open for you later on when you are applying for conducting positions. A good teacher also can help provide feedback regarding the types of positions for which you might be ready. A conducting teacher should be a mentor and friend for you during your entire career.

Summer Festivals and Seminars

In addition to your main teacher, you should attend music festivals and conducting workshops to help round out your training. Many of these are offered throughout the United States and Europe. Attending summer music festivals is recommended for many reasons:

1. You are able to study with someone else and get a new opinion on conducting technique and style;
2. You can interact with other conductors to share experiences and ideas;
3. You will work with other orchestral musicians who will become familiar with your name and your work;
4. This is an opportunity to be "seen," which might lead to other doors opening for your career; and
5. You have something new to put on your résumé.

When you are attending a conducting workshop or festival, sometimes the new ideas presented will conflict with other concepts you have been taught or other theories you believe. When this happens, it is best to keep your opinions to yourself and to be open to new learning experiences. Try to do exactly what the teacher requests and try to absorb every bit of information that you can. You will have plenty of time later for further reflection. After the festival is over, you can decide what you want to incorporate into your style and what you choose to discard. It is only by being open to new ideas that you can make progress and define what is important, and true, for you.

After attending these types of programs, try to stay in touch with your new colleagues. They will be your network for programming ideas, recommendations, and feedback in the future. A list of festivals and conducting programs is available in the Resource section.

Instrument Training

In your early training, you will probably have studied an orchestral instrument or piano, or both. As a conductor, you do not need to be proficient playing every instrument in the orchestra because you will usually defer to the individual expertise of your musicians. There are some specific areas, however, where a more in-depth knowledge is necessary for your success.

Piano

It is necessary for anyone studying to be a conductor to study and master basic piano technique. Proficiency at score-reading at the piano is a requirement. If you are not fluent in this skill, I recommend a series of books, *Partiturspiel,* by Heinrich Creuzberg, to help you master this technique. The ability to read quickly through a new score will be a tremendous asset when you are faced with learning a lot of music in a short amount of time.

Strings

Studying a string instrument is very helpful when dealing with string sound as it relates to bowings. How the player draws the bow across the string and how they use different parts of the bow can change the sound produced dramatically. As a conductor, you will want to establish your own concept of orchestral sound. Understanding string bowing is essential to achieving the sound you want. Spend some time talking with the concertmaster of an orchestra near you and see what choices they make in bowing a part and why. Have them explain and demonstrate the basic concepts of bowing so that your ear will be familiar with the types of sound colors that can be produced.

Percussion

Because this family of instruments is so diverse, it is useful to know more about the variety of instruments available. This is especially important if you conduct new music. More and more composers are expanding the list of what is considered a *percussion* instrument. A good reference book for clarifying percussion instruments is *A Practical Guide to Percussion Terminology* by Russ Girsberger. It is also worthwhile to spend some time with a percussionist and have them explain some of the peculiarities of their instruments, demonstrate specific playing techniques, and give examples of their favorite mistakes that conductors make.

Other instruments

You will be most successful with your orchestral musicians if you are aware of the strengths and weaknesses of their individual instruments. You should know what notes are difficult to play in tune, which tend to play sharp, which instruments play flat, and where the limits are for range, speed, and dynamics. Some of this can be learned from a basic orchestration book; other more specific details can be learned from speaking with orchestra members and asking them questions. By keeping their instrumental limitations in mind, you will not put yourself in a position in which you push your musicians too hard on a musical passage when they are dealing with "instrument" peculiarities. This can help avoid a backlash from the players during rehearsals.

Orchestration

Once you have a better idea of how the instruments function individually, you will probably need more information about how they function together. Norman Del Mar's book *The Anatomy of the Orchestra* is excellent for this purpose. It gives you insights into the individual peculiarities of each instrument and showcases how this is reflected in the orchestral repertoire. Another excellent book is Samuel Adler's *The Study of Orchestration*. Knowledge of how individual composers combine their instrumental sounds will help you to know which voice to bring out in specific passages. The blend of your musicians' individual sounds also will affect how you balance your chords. A lifetime can be spent analyzing orchestration and individual tone color.

Languages

Because the standard conducting repertoire is drawn mostly from central Europe, you can never overestimate the advantages of studying and becoming fluent in German, French, and Italian. This will help you immensely as a conductor, especially in a Mahler score, in which almost every bar has written instructions in German. A working knowledge of Russian and Spanish is also helpful. With Russian, you also might want to learn the Cyrillic alphabet. This will help you to pronounce titles correctly because many of the characters do not translate. To learn languages early in your career will save you a lot of time later, especially if you want to conduct opera or if you want to study conducting in another country. *The International Vocabulary of Music*, by Stephen Dembski, is a good resource to help translate musical terms from different languages.

When you are conducting a composition, make sure you translate all of the instructions and be ready to answer any questions the orchestra might have regarding these translations. They look to you as the expert and you will lose all credibility if you have not done your preparation with the translations in the score. When performing a vocal piece, do not rely on the standard English translation that may be printed in the score. Instead, you should retranslate the text from the original language so that you truly have a concept of which words and meanings go with which harmonic and melodic movements in the music.

Harmony, Composition, and Ear Training

As a college student, you will probably study harmony, composition, and ear training. A deep knowledge of these is essential. Often, the courses required for the basic music degree are not as in-depth as the knowledge you will need to be effective as a conductor. Do not hesitate to take additional courses or to do more reading in this area. A good book for reviewing theory is *Harmony and Voice Leading* by Edward Aldwell and Carl Schachter. The most important area to work on, and perhaps the most difficult to practice on your own, is ear training. Many schools have ear training computer programs that are helpful. You also can tape examples and play them back to yourself to practice aural dictation. It is critical that you continue to practice and refine your skills in this area throughout your career.

Music History and Repertoire

A good conductor must understand intimately the progress of musical style throughout the ages. You must feel comfortable with the music "languages" of a vast number of composers because you will be asked to conduct many different pieces as you begin your career. Your general knowledge will later be refined as you broaden your repertoire. As you prepare for your concerts, take the time to research every piece that you conduct. You should be familiar with the composer's personal life, when the piece was written, and other pieces that the composer wrote around the same time. You also should know the circumstances for which the piece was composed, and what other events were taking place in the world. Composers such as Shostakovich and Prokofiev were greatly affected by political events around them, whereas others, such as Dvořák and Bartók were influenced by the folk music of their countries. Understanding these relationships will help tremendously in interpreting the music, and also provide more depth for your preconcert talks. Do not try to learn everything overnight. Most of your knowledge will accumulate over time. The popular music history text *A History of Western Music* by Donald Jay Grout is still one of the most comprehensive in the business. One of my favorite sources, however, for research information from a "humanized" view of musical history is *Music in the Western World: A History in Documents*, selected and annotated by Piero Weiss and Richard Taruskin.

Conducting Technique

Obviously, one could write volumes on conducting technique. For the purpose of this book, however, I am going to assume that you have already been well trained in this area. A clear, effective technique that communicates tempo, inflection, dynamics, and energy is essential to being a successful conductor. Your body type also must be taken into consideration as you learn the most effective ways to communicate the music to your players. Conductors that are tall with long arms will use a slightly different technique than conductors who have short arms. Through studying with a variety of teachers, you will be able to assimilate the basic gestures that work for you. *The Grammar of Conducting* by Max Rudolf is still a treasure in the field, and every conductor should be familiar with it. Another book with a different approach that you may want to investigate is *The Saito Conducting Method* by Hideo Saito (Saito was the teacher of Seiji Ozawa, former music director of the Boston Symphony). Basic conducting technique is important and critical to communicating your musical ideas, but it is only the tip of the iceberg when it comes to becoming a great conductor and eventually a great music director.

Informal Musical Training

Much of your study of conducting will be on your own, and it will last a lifetime. Throughout your career, always try to videotape yourself at rehearsals and concerts. Continual growth is dependent on being able to see what you are doing so that you know when you are effective, and you can see what needs to be improved. Try to get permission to record every rehearsal for study purposes. If you review the recording after each rehearsal, you will be able to keep yourself from developing bad habits. Orchestra musicians should be encouraged by your quest to grow continually as a conductor; don't let your ego get in the way of asking permission to record for your own study. They already know that you are not perfect.

As you continue your musical growth, you must expose yourself to films, videotapes, and DVDs of past conductors to study their baton techniques and rehearsal styles. More and more of these are becoming commercially available. You also should plan on attending rehearsals whenever possible. This is very educational and should be continued throughout your career.

Identify conductors that you respect musically and see if you can pinpoint what makes them special. It is usually a musical spark, a sense of energy, passion, or a commitment to the musical phrase that evokes an emotion in the listener. So much of conducting is the ability to interpret and convey emotions, yet how does one learn to do this effectively? How does one learn to feel, to understand, and to communicate? Exposure to a wide array of the arts and to the diversity in the world will help you to bring depth to your musical performances. If you want to be a conductor, you must have something musical to say! Take time to travel, meet people, and exchange ideas. Do not be afraid to explore the depth and variety of your emotions. One must know love to communicate love. How can you conduct the "Liebestod" from *Tristan and Isolde* until you have truly experienced love? Don't be afraid to feel, and don't be afraid to let those feelings show. This openness to emotion will be a tremendous asset in bringing focus and universality to your music-making.

CHARACTER DEVELOPMENT

Attributes

One of the most important things that you can do as you prepare for a career as a conductor is to work on *you*: who you are, how you present yourself, how you relate to people, how you set your goals, and how you can get where you want to go. Here are some of the more important personality traits for being successful not only as a conductor but also in anything you do in life.

Positive Outlook

Have you ever thought about how you greet the world? Do you approach people positively, with a smile on your face, or are you forever looking at the negative sides of life? It has been proven that positive people are more successful in meeting their goals than others. People with positive attitudes tend to inspire positive attitudes in others.

As a conductor, you are constantly working through others to accomplish your goals. If you were a member of an orchestra, would you prefer to work with someone who was positive and smiling, or someone who was overbearing and pessimistic? Your attitude on the podium can inspire or demoralize the entire ensemble. Understand that negative thoughts will affect your ability to communicate the music. If something is bothering you, on or off the podium, learn how to control your emotions and your reactions to stressful situations so that they don't affect the way you respond to others. You are completely responsible for your feelings and how you relate to people.

As you work with your orchestra, be generous with your praise. Everyone wants to feel needed and appreciated. Draw your musicians into your circle with positive dialogues and treat them as you would treat members of your family. When correcting mistakes at a rehearsal, use constructive comments rather than destructive ones to convey your concerns. As you converse with the orchestra members outside of rehearsals, refrain from gossip and discourage these types of conversations among the musicians and staff members. Following this rule consistently will help to create a stimulating and positive work environment for everyone. There are times when you will need to disagree openly with people with or for whom you work. When this happens, try to position your response so that you can say "no" without being negative or difficult. It is even better if you can help them discover why something will not work without you actually saying "no."

As you follow through with your positive attitude, always expect the best from yourself and realize that you are capable of wonderful things. Then, apply the same philosophy to those with whom you work. If you set a high standard of expectations within a nurturing environment, people will always rise to the expected level. Often, they just need someone to believe in them. You can be that supportive presence in their lives.

Integrity

Integrity is the cornerstone for being a successful leader. People gravitate toward someone whom they can trust, someone who is consistent, and someone who always seems to do the "right" thing. Maintaining integrity in thought, word, and deed—both to your players, staff, and board members as well as to the composer of the music you conduct—will lead to a fulfilling and successful life. It is crucial that you respect the score and always search for the intent of the composer. Historically, the conductors who were loved and respected by their musicians demonstrated high levels of musical integrity as well as personal integrity. In your role as a music director, do not try to be everything to all people because this might require compromising your values. Decide first what is important to you and to the organization, and stick with it. Be honest and truthful in everything you do and make sure that you follow through with whatever you promise. In your decision-making process, it is important that you are both loyal and fair and consistent with your colleagues and orchestra members. As you develop your style as a leader, your personal integrity is your most valuable asset. Honor it and let it guide you in your decision-making process.

Humility

For a conductor, humility seems like a contradiction because they are so accustomed to the expectation of the "Great Maestro" personality. Humility does not mean that you are not assertive. Assertiveness is a wonderful trait, and it is necessary to help achieve your goals. But humility gives you the ability to relate to people and to recognize that you are not, nor will you ever be, perfect. Accept the fact that as you make artistic decisions, you will make mistakes. Be willing to accept the blame when you are wrong and then quickly decide how you will solve the problem. You also must recognize that your orchestra members are not perfect, even though you continually try to motivate them toward perfection. Acceptance of where they are and encouragement toward the goal is necessary to empower the people you lead. Dealing with people in this fashion will help you to build trust within your followers.

As you work together to become a great orchestra, everyone should focus on what is good for the entire organization. When you do come up against differences of opinions or beliefs, try to put yourself in the other person's shoes. Just because their view varies from yours does not mean that either of you are right or wrong. Remember, the world is not black or white. There are few right answers. Humility will enable you to accept everyone as they are.

Discipline

Discipline and the art of delayed gratification are factors that contribute to success. Luckily, these are taught early with music, as one learns to practice a single phrase over and over with the hope that it will be totally mastered for the recital that might be three months away. Just the task of practicing every day creates a routine of discipline that is deeply engrained in all musicians. This discipline must be applied to everything you do. Scores must be studied slowly over the course of months and years, not crammed into one's head in a week or two. The discipline to prepare thoroughly is essential for a conductor. Often, the result of this preparation is not evident until much later. As a conductor, you cannot afford to procrastinate. Train yourself to complete your high-priority work first and to stay on schedule with learning your scores. If you have bad habits that are getting in the way of your success, identify them and develop a systematic way of eliminating these habits from your life. Carefully set your goals regarding what you want to accomplish and have the discipline to finish what you start. You are the only person who can hold yourself accountable for your own actions. Remember, you are *always* preparing for success.

Persistence

Even if you already possess each of the personal attributes described earlier, the additional quality you need to be successful as a conductor is *persistence*. The longer you stay in the field, the more you are able to learn and improve. At the same time, the longer you are active, the more you will see other people dropping out, or finding other easier or more stable occupations. The conducting field will continue to shrink as time passes. Keep in touch with your contacts and your professional network, and keep knocking on those doors. Eventually, you will have the musical experience, knowledge, and connections to fulfill your goals. If you really want to be a conductor, you can. Just take the time to envision your dreams and never, ever give up!

Presenting Yourself

Assertiveness and Assurance

Assertiveness is taking ownership and responsibility for your thoughts and feelings. It also involves accepting other people's thoughts, feelings, and actions without blame or judgment. Assertive actions should be incorporated into your everyday relationships with people. For most conductors, these actions are second nature. Actions such as using a firm handshake, looking people directly in the eyes, and listening attentively will go far toward strengthening your relationship with your peers, colleagues, and orchestra members.

Assurance is the quiet confidence that accompanies success. Through focused patience and perseverance, one always will accomplish more. Learn to see the big picture and to distinguish between problem situations and annoying issues. The confidence of knowing what is really important is what allows one to truly be a leader. People gravitate toward people who they feel are grounded. Empower yourself with an assured personality that does not obsess over insignificant matters. This will help you in your leadership role as a conductor.

Physical Appearance

No matter how hard you try to convince yourself otherwise, your daily appearance does make a difference in how you are perceived by other people. People make their first-impression decision about you unconsciously, within the first ten to fifteen seconds of meeting you. The common phrase "Dress for the job you want, not the job you have" is true.

For a conductor, deciding on an image is a little more difficult than most professions. You don't really want to be perceived as a "businessman," and yet often the people you are meeting with and trying to impress (the orchestra's board and the community) are businessmen. If you are to be successful in their eyes, they expect you to look like them. By comparison, orchestra members often dress "down." They come to rehearsals in T-shirts and jeans. For rehearsals, you don't want to dress so much more formally than the orchestra that you lose contact with the people whom you work with daily. When you are dealing with the general public, you might be considered "artsy." Avoid dressing in such a manner that leads people to not take you seriously. Dressing in an artsy manner is probably the least effective way to make an impression as a conductor.

The best approach is to tailor your dress to the occasion: business attire for business meetings, fund-raising, and public talks, and trim, ironed shirt/blouse and slacks for rehearsals. Shoes used in rehearsals by women should have very low heels, and all shoes should be polished. You might discover that some members of the orchestra are extremely dress-conscious and will keep track of what you wear. Even if you are traveling with very few clothes, be careful not to wear the same clothes for too many rehearsals in a row. Not only will the orchestra notice it, but also it will become a topic of conversation among the players. Perception is reality, and how you dress will define how people perceive you. Always put your best foot forward and dress for the job you want.

CHOOSING THE PATH

Once you have developed your basic knowledge and refined the personality traits to be a conductor, you also are going to need experience. You have studied hard for this occupation, yet when you graduate and apply for jobs it is as though you are applying for the CEO position with a major company. Who is going to hire a conductor without experience? And how do you get experience if no one will hire you?

There are many routes you can travel once you have finished your degree and begun your path to becoming a professional conductor. There is no proven right route. It is an unpredictable field. Some of the possible routes and choices that you might face are described here. The industry has some stereotypes regarding some of these choices, but I have always believed that you should take the position that is put in your path. If you do everything you can to be successful at your job, then you will achieve your goals. Hard work breeds success; success breeds more success; and, eventually, the "cream always rises to the top."

In deciding a career path, you must first assess your personal tolerance for stress. You also must recognize your strengths and weaknesses. This is not to say that you will not improve in your weak areas over time but, rather, to encourage you to focus on what you do well and to use that as your starting place on your career path. It is also important that you have a clear idea of where you want to go. What type of orchestra would you ideally like to work with in the future?

To put this in perspective, consider the following scene from *Alice in Wonder-*

land: Alice, lost, approached the Cheshire Cat and asked, "Which way ought I to go?" The Cheshire Cat replied, "First I must know which way you want to go." Alice said, "Oh, I don't know. It doesn't really matter." The Cat wisely answered, "Then it doesn't really matter which way you go."

One of the big decisions you will have to make is whether to become an assistant conductor first, or to become a music director with a community level orchestra (youth, adult volunteer, or semiprofessional). If you enjoy working with young people and want to have an opportunity to try new things, you might try starting as a conductor of a youth orchestra. If you feel you need to observe more conductors, are interested in major repertoire, and not so interested in specific conducting time, you would be better off auditioning to be an assistant with a major orchestra.

Each job has its advantages and disadvantages. We all see the world differently. What may be perceived by one person as a disadvantage might be perceived as an advantage to someone else. Here is an introductory list of some possible working situations for a conductor, and an overview of some of the possible advantages and disadvantages.

Assistant Conductor

Local Orchestra (Volunteer or Per-Service)

ADVANTAGES. You will have the opportunity to watch numerous rehearsals; sometimes you also might play in the orchestra. As a first job, this will provide some résumé material. Occasionally you will have an opportunity to conduct perhaps one piece on a concert or an entire children's concert. This type of position will provide an opportunity for feedback.

DISADVANTAGES. Your actual conducting time will be limited. The learning level will be directly related to the professional quality level of the music director. You might be faced with widely varying levels of musical abilities in orchestra. The pay will be part-time or volunteer.

Mid-Size Professional Orchestra

ADVANTAGES. You will be able to learn extensive amounts of repertoire and watch many rehearsals, often with the same conductor. There will be opportunities to conduct children's concerts, runout concerts of standard repertoire, and pops concerts. This position provides an opportunity to learn about the other staff positions within the organization. A concert you conduct might get reviewed. This position could pay enough to live on very modestly.

DISADVANTAGES. Usually, the music director will not be there to see you conduct. You can get overloaded with learning new repertoire. Sometimes this will make you sacrifice quality for quantity. The repertoire you conduct will often be assigned to you, not chosen by you, and you will have very little rehearsal time to prepare the concerts. Because of this, it is often hard to win the respect of the orchestra. Usually, these positions require you to move.

Major Professional Orchestra

ADVANTAGES. You will have an opportunity to network with the top people in the industry and you will see how things are done at the top level of the field. This job requires learning (understudying) a lot of repertoire. You will be able to watch many rehearsals. Other staff members will see your work and will be excellent references for future jobs. You might get reviewed. This is usually a full-time position with benefits.

DISADVANTAGES. Often, you will not have much "quality" podium time. Your actual conducting will usually be for children's concerts, or pops and family concerts. With this type of job, you will have very little rehearsal time and is very hard to win the respect of the orchestra. The music director will probably not see your work and sometimes it is difficult to get constructive feedback. You may have to relocate or have a second residence in the city where the orchestra performs.

Opera Orchestra

ADVANTAGES. This is a great starting position if you are a pianist. This job will help you master languages and will allow you to observe vocal coaching and stage direction. Opera companies usually provide an assistant with conducting opportunities in a controlled environment. You will find yourself conducting piano rehearsals with vocalists, or off-stage chorus and small ensembles. Usually the musicians in the orchestra are all professional and of a high caliber. Salary ranges from part-time to full-time, depending on the size of the organization.

DISADVANTAGES. You will have limited opportunities to conduct the orchestra in an entire production. This is a very difficult job to get unless you are an excellent pianist. The best of these positions would require moving to Europe. You will have no input on repertoire, and you will probably only be exposed to opera repertoire. Because of this, you might become stereotyped as an opera coach/conductor.

Ballet Orchestra — *Not a bad sounding gig*

ADVANTAGES. You will learn about dancers and the quirks of ballet repertoire. You will master consistency of tempo that is required by the dancers. You will be able to study and perform standard orchestral repertoire that is used in ballet performances. Usually, the orchestra members are well-qualified professionals. You might have the opportunity to conduct multiple performances. Salary ranges from part-time to full-time, depending on the size of the ballet company.

DISADVANTAGES. You might have to conduct hundreds of performances of *The Nutcracker*. You may become stereotyped as a ballet conductor. You will have to limit your musical interpretation to tempos that work for the dancers. You will have very little rehearsal time with either the dancers or the orchestra.

Music Director

Youth Orchestra Conductor

ADVANTAGES. You will have an opportunity to learn and experiment in a protected environment. You will have control over the repertoire. Local reviewers might attend your concerts. You will have substantial conducting time. Your orchestra will be composed of young people who are passionate about music.

DISADVANTAGES. You might be limited by the technical ability of your players. You might find yourself 80 percent teacher and 20 percent musician (not necessarily a bad thing). In this position, it is easy to develop habits of overconducting. The quality of your players will vary tremendously. You will spend time dealing with parents, parental expectations, and community relations. This position usually requires a lot of time for part-time pay.

College Orchestra

ADVANTAGES. Most colleges are open to more diversity in programming than a professional or community orchestra. This position provides extensive conducting time. You will not have to worry as much about budgets, fund-raising, or audience development. The students will be committed to their music-making, and you will have continuity of orchestra members from rehearsal to rehearsal. You also will have your summers totally free. This is usually a full-time position with benefits.

DISADVANTAGES. You may have to spend additional time teaching other classes that may or may not be of interest to you. You will probably have other university administrative duties. The quality of your players will vary year to year, which will affect the repertoire you are able to program. Your overall quality level might be limited by the amount of scholarships available to attract excellent players. Your quality level also will vary depending on whether you are teaching at a music conservatory, a university school of music, or a liberal arts college.

Volunteer Community Orchestra

ADVANTAGES. This job will provide many hours of conducting time. You will be working with people who really want to play. If music is properly selected, you can produce quality musical performances. These orchestras usually have a positive energy. Some of the concerts might be reviewed by a local paper.

DISADVANTAGES. The limited technical ability of the group will affect which pieces you can program. Inconsistency of players from rehearsal to rehearsal might affect the quality of your concerts. Often, you will be more of a teacher and friend than a conductor. You will be expected to help with administrative duties. If your concert is reviewed, the reporter might talk more about the program notes than the actual performance. This is a part-time position.

Regional Per-Service Orchestra

ADVANTAGES. You will be in charge of selecting the repertoire, and you can help build the organization artistically. You will have a "general" consistency of players from rehearsal to rehearsal and concert to concert. You will be able to focus more on the music. You will have fewer overall rehearsals than a volunteer group, but your concerts will probably have a higher overall artistic quality. There will be opportunities to have concerts reviewed. Pay ranges from modest to full-time. Some orchestras might pay benefits.

DISADVANTAGES. You will need to travel or move to where the orchestra is located. This type of position is difficult to achieve. Most of these orchestras perform only five to ten concerts per year. The quality level is often limited by the orchestra's location. You might discover "deadwood" within the sections that could be difficult to address. It is easy to become stereotyped as a conductor for a certain budget level. Your ability to improve the orchestra might be limited by the musician's pay scale, the local economy, or how close you are to a major metropolitan area. You job will require a lot of community involvement and fundraising, which might take time away from your score study.

"Core" Professional Orchestra

ADVANTAGES. These orchestras usually have a higher quality of music-making because the "core" musicians are paid full-time. This type of orchestra will perform many concerts. You will conduct a variety of repertoire and you will have the ability to impact a community. This job will pay very well—full-time plus benefits.

DISADVANTAGES. You will need to know and feel comfortable conducting large amounts of repertoire with very little study time. Salaries for players might not be high enough to attract the best quality nationally. The orchestra will be dependent on the local economy. If large businesses move out of the area, or experience financial difficulty, this will have an impact on the orchestra's budget. The competition for this type of position is very daunting ("Don't call us, we'll call you"). You will need to be very involved in the community to help promote the orchestra and assist in the fund-raising efforts. This job might involve hours of travel if you do not already live in the area.

Opera Orchestra

ADVANTAGES. You will be able to influence the entire production, which is wonderful if you have a theatrical approach to music-making. You will be working with many people and sharing ideas. The orchestra musicians are usually good and very flexible. Salary ranges from part-time to full-time, depending on the size of the organization.

DISADVANTAGES. There are very few positions as music director for opera companies in the United States; you may have to move to Europe. You will have to commit weeks to each production, which may limit your other conducting. You will never have enough rehearsal time with the orchestra. You must be fluent in several languages. You will have to deal with difficult stage directors, lighting designers, and ballet and chorus masters. You might become classified as an opera conductor.

Ballet Orchestra

ADVANTAGES. You will conduct large, mainstream repertoire. You will work with professional musicians. There may be opportunities to collaborate with the choreographer on new productions. You will be able to conduct pieces for multiple performances. The salary ranges from part-time to full-time, depending on the size of the organization.

DISADVANTAGES. You might be involved with long touring productions, requiring weeks of travel. Different conductors might conduct the same pieces for multiple performances so you will never have a personal stamp on your music-making. Tempos will always be limited to whatever works best for the dancers. You will have very little rehearsal time, and sometimes none, if it is a standard piece.

New Music Ensemble

ADVANTAGES. Working with this type of ensemble allows you to be on the cutting edge of music-making. You can select your own repertoire. You will probably be working with excellent musicians. They will be committed to performing this type of music. You will probably conduct many world premieres and be able to work personally with many composers.

DISADVANTAGES. This type of ensemble will rarely perform the standard works—Mozart, Beethoven, Brahms, or Tchaikovsky. You will spend many hours researching new music. Every time you conduct a piece, it will probably be new for you and for the players. (This makes it hard to settle into an interpretation.) You risk being typecast as a "new music" person. The pay for this type of position will probably be part-time and very low.

Forming Your Own Orchestra   — just no

ADVANTAGES. You will be able to define how many concerts you perform each year, who will perform, and what you are going to play. You can experiment with repertoire and musical interpretations. You can develop excellent organizational skills and an ability to understand the organization as a whole. You will gain solid conducting experience to put on your resume. Your concerts might be reviewed.

DISADVANTAGES. When you form your own orchestra, you usually have to spend an excessive amount of time organizing and raising money. You will probably have to form a board of directors and become incorporated. This will take time away from your focus on the music. It is hard to raise money for organizations that are unknown. The repertoire will be defined by how much money you have available for hiring players or how many friends you can talk into playing for you. It is hard to gain credibility in the industry, because you have not been hired for this position. Often the orchestra folds when you leave. This type of orchestra pays very little, if anything.

Final Thoughts

As you review the different types of orchestral situations, try to match up the things that are important to you. You will have many different jobs throughout your career. Each one should change and enhance your approach to music making. Remember, there is no "right" path that works for everyone. Take the time to analyze what works for you.

Many believe that the surest path to the top is to attend the best-known schools (such as Juilliard or Curtis), participate in all the most famous summer festivals (Tanglewood and Aspen), become an assistant conductor with a major orchestra (such as Boston, Philadelphia, or Cleveland, for example), and become a music director of a "core" orchestra (the size of Fort Worth, Knoxville, or Buffalo). Then, you should go overseas and become music director of a European orchestra. In a few years, you eventually return as a music director for a major American orchestra. This is the basic path followed by Michael Tilson Thomas, Andrew Litton, Marin Alsop, and others. It is a path to the top that can work, and has worked very successfully for many conductors. Even so, it is not the right path for everyone. Many people have started out on this path with stars in their eyes, only to discover that they hit a glass ceiling, or that perhaps they were very happy working at a certain level that was not necessarily perceived as the "top." Remember, we need great conductors for *all* of the orchestras—in the United States and abroad.

Goal Setting

Often, an individual will take the first job offered regardless of if it is the "right" position to ensure success. A failure early on can be tremendously damaging, both personally and professionally. In order to avoid this mistake, try to plan your future by asking yourself the following questions:

> What are your greatest strengths? How can these be best put to use as you move forward?
> What are your weaknesses? How can you improve in these areas?
> What job are you ready for currently? What steps can you take to get that job?
> What goals would you like to accomplish in the next year?
> Where would you like to be in five years, and how do your strengths help you get there?
> What else do you need to learn, master, or experience in order to achieve this next level?

Ten years from now—Describe your life:

> What type of orchestra will you be conducting?
> What will you have accomplished that has made a difference in other people's lives?

How much money will you be making?

How will you spend your time?

As you work through these questions, take the time to really think them through. Write down your answers and reflect on your possible choices along the way.

We often are taught that the larger the budget is of the orchestra we conduct, the more successful we are, or the better we are as conductors. I challenge you to leave this viewpoint behind. There are more than a thousand orchestras in the United States, not counting ballet orchestras and opera orchestras. All of these orchestras need excellent conductors with exceptional leadership skills and a passion for the art form. Just because you are not conducting the New York Philharmonic does not mean that you are not making music of a high quality in a community where it is important. There are no small jobs, only small minds.

As you set your goals for the future, make sure that the goal is challenging but attainable, set a specific deadline for achieving the goal, and develop a list of what you need to do to accomplish what you want. This might include breaking each goal down into easily doable tasks, assigning a priority level to each task, and making sure that you address top-priority items first. Remember, life is often a self-fulfilling prophecy; you may not necessarily get what you want, but you usually get what you expect.

Chapter 2

PATH TO THE PODIUM

As I said before, there is no "one path" to success as a conductor. Each person somehow finds their own way to achieve their goals. I spoke with leading American conductors and discovered a variety of successes and frustrations that they experienced on their way to their current positions. Here are examples of their career paths and their words of advice.

INTERVIEW: LEONARD SLATKIN

"Right place at the right time —and prepared"
—*Leonard Slatkin*

- Juilliard School of Music, BM
- Assistant Conductor, Saint Louis Symphony
- Music Director, New Orleans Symphony
- Music Director, Saint Louis Symphony
- Festival Director, Cleveland Orchestra Blossom Festival

- Principal Guest Conductor, Royal Philharmonic
- Music Director, National Symphony
- Principal Guest Conductor, Los Angeles Philharmonic at the Hollywood Bowl

Path to the Podium: Leonard Slatkin

My career developed partly from being in the right place at the right time, but mostly from being prepared. I suppose one could say that I had a built-in advantage because my entire family were musicians; from the earliest possible age, there was music in the house constantly. I would say that from the age of about three or so, I already realized I would become a musician. There was really no choice.

When I got to the point in my studies of music, particularly in piano and composition, where my parents thought that I exhibited a degree of talent, they tried to explain to me how difficult the music profession was, and rather than encourage, they said "you have to be prepared to make sacrifices and work really hard." At one point, my mother actually locked the piano because I refused to practice. After three days of screaming and kicking to get it back, she gave in, and I understood what was expected. If you want to have a career in music, you have to be prepared to sacrifice a lot of your own personal life and your childhood because of practicing and studying.

I think it is different today then when I was a child in that today's young people are more aware of the world than my generation was. As I was growing up, it was easy to be isolated. I think it is important today for a young person to be aware of the variety of experiences that life offers, not just in music, but in everything. The music business still remains difficult, but if you look broadly, there are more choices. You can go into the pop end; conduct music for film or musical theater; or you can conduct church music, youth orchestras, regional orchestras, academic orchestras, or opera and ballet. There is plenty of work for a good conductor.

My interest in conducting was started by the fact that I was playing viola in a youth orchestra, and the conductor was called away to the phone. As he left, he threw the score down to me and said, "Here, you conduct." After that experience I began to pursue studies in conducting, although, at the time I was still intent on being a composer and pianist. It really wasn't until my college years, after my father (who had also been a conductor) died, that I felt the path open for me.

I attended Juilliard and I think a lot of my early success was because I would solicit the players to perform extra concerts. I would say to them, "Let's do this;

let's play that." I was always putting groups together and doing everything I could to conduct as much as possible.

Later, when I was a conducting student at the Aspen Music School, the music director there was Walter Susskind. During my third year in Aspen, he asked me to come to his new orchestra in Saint Louis as his assistant. After nine years of being an assistant conductor, acquiring a manager, and getting more experience through guest conducting dates, I was appointed music director of the New Orleans Symphony. Two years after that, I was invited to return to Saint Louis as the music director.

Here in Washington, D.C., the opportunity with the National Symphony happened because the president of the Kennedy Center and Bill Clinton attended a concert I conducted. I felt fortunate to have been in the right place at the right time. It doesn't happen to everyone, but I was there and I was ready. Being ready is the most important thing. Learn as much as you can; conduct as much as you can; go to many rehearsals and concerts; and always be ready.

Successes

At this point, the thing that satisfies me the most as a conductor is reaching someone who has never been to a concert or who is inexperienced, and feeling that you have made a connection with them. People will come backstage after a concert and tell you how much they enjoyed it, or in a pre or post-concert discussion they will talk about it being their first experience. I find it tremendously gratifying to be able to reach people. I have also enjoyed my work trying to help the education system. Although far from ideal, I know that I have made some inroads (though not nearly as many as I would like to); I have had some impact in terms of schools having to reinstate, or create music programs where none existed.

My relationships with the players from different orchestras throughout the world are important to me. I value these relationships. I value the friendships that I have, not just within the music community, but outside that area. I think I have grown more in the last ten years of my life than I did in the first fifty, because I expanded my own horizons. I became less obsessed with music as being the beginning and end of life. I initially learned this from Carlo Maria Giulini, but it took me a long while to really take it to heart. If you don't experience life, you have nothing to bring to your music, and doing it the other way around just doesn't work. You think it does, when you are young . . . "Oh, all I have is music, and music will shape my life." Well you do that, and you have a pretty boring life. If you go to a dinner party and you are only able to talk about one thing, it turns people off.

Skills Set

I always suggest to every conducting student that it is important to study a string instrument. The majority of your remarks during rehearsals will be to the string section. This doesn't mean that you have to play a string instrument fluently, but you must understand the mechanics of string playing, no matter how lousy you might be at the actual playing. Then what you say to the orchestra will be dictated by your experience of knowing that an up-bow and a down-bow are really two different things. Everything is as basic as understanding what the impact of the bow stroke is; from that you can go to everything else.

I also believe that even if you are a good pianist and able to read a score at the keyboard, you should not rely on the keyboard because you will get the sound of the piano in your head rather than the sound of the orchestra. You have to look at a score the same way a screenwriter or director looks at a script and envision in your mind what the sound will be. For me, the score is nothing more than a book in another language. The language happens to be circles and dots and lines and we translate that in our head to sounds. It is important to have the sound of the instruments themselves in your head, not the sound of the keyboard. Reading a score at the piano is a nice skill to have, but ultimately it is more important to be able to look at a score, hear it in your head, and understand it. So how do you do that? Most of it is through experience, I am afraid, but a lot of it is through imagination. Learn to read one or two lines at a time and imagine how they sound together, then gradually add another line, and another one. Eventually, you will read a score with ease.

I always suggest to every conductor to go to as many rehearsals of as many different conductors as possible. This is not so much to mimic their skill, but instead, to watch for their mistakes. If you watch for what a conductor *does not* achieve, you will learn more than watching what they do achieve. In other words, you need to learn how to avoid mistakes. We all make mistakes up there. I am the first one to acknowledge the ones that I make on a day-to-day basis. Learn how to avoid doing the things that don't work for a conductor and strive to not make the same mistakes. If you simply try to imitate the things that do work, you will be an imitation.

Another skill that is critical today, but might not have been a long time ago, is the ability to communicate to individuals, both socially, in rehearsal circumstances, and in every other way. Speaking has become more important for conductors and it is critical that you are able to communicate verbally to audiences and the media. I advise every young person to use the experience of doing radio in some way. This will help you learn to talk without huge pauses. If you are at a university, go to the local university station and do a couple of interviews. If you can get your own show, it is even better. Do whatever you can to gain speaking experience.

Social skills are more difficult to acquire but they are important to acquire at the youngest possible age. Understanding how to deal with boards of directors, fundraising issues, and public relations situations is essential. I know that these things are not directly related to conducting, but they end up being a large part of the job.

At one time, I was highly ineffective in communicating with others. I was terrible at it. I was nervous and I couldn't deal with people on a one to one basis, much less in a group. So what was I going to do? It meant sitting down very carefully and trying to find a way to improve this area. That is why I went into radio. I did three years of radio. There was nothing better for this shy introvert than sitting in a studio alone and talking to nobody. Eventually I was able to translate this skill to speaking in front of thousands of people and I am no longer afraid of public speaking.

The Conductor's Role

The world has changed and we are more conscious of our communication with others than we were before. The conductor now exists in many roles: you are a psychologist, you are a father-mother figure, you are a doctor, and you are also a spokesperson for the ensemble that you lead. In the role of spokesperson, you have to be able to communicate to many people in many different ways. You have to be aware of every function that your particular orchestra participates in, be it fund-raising, development, public relations, media, community outreach, or everything else; you have to be aware of your surroundings. In the past, it was fairly easy for a conductor to just come in, conduct and go home. They were the *maestro* and the organization didn't expect much more than that. Well today they do, especially in the regional, community, and smaller orchestras. They expect you to be a part of the community—to get out there, work in the schools and work with young people. You must develop relationships with the board of directors, attend meetings, and really establish communication. It doesn't matter whether you are from this country or from abroad, you have to find a way to be yourself and be outgoing enough to communicate, without being offensive. Demanding your way doesn't work anymore, either. You could be offensive in the past; you could pretty much do anything. Now you can't. You have to be careful what you say, and make sure you are always politically correct. Despite this, people still want you to be a little different. You still have to be the "Maestro." People like that. (I don't care for the term very much, but that is how it is.) Each person acquires their skills for these various roles in a different way. There is no one solution for it. A lot of it is simply understanding that you have to have interpersonal skills. This is a large part of the job these days.

National Conductors Institute

The Conductors Institute was designed to help bridge the gap between the conductors who are in university, community, or amateur circumstance who might be making their debut with a major orchestra or an orchestra that plays full time. I started this because I remembered that my first professional orchestra experiences, (even though I came from a musical household) were fraught with peril. The musicians of the orchestra knew far more than I did, and had played the repertoire many, many more times—what was I going to say to them? What was I going to bring to the Philadelphia Orchestra in a rehearsal of a Rachmaninoff Symphony, for instance? I wanted to address how to get past this intimidating gap and how to be successful. This idea turned into a conducting Institute where one week is about the conductor's relationship to every aspect of the musical organization administratively. How does a music director interact with the community? How can they reconcile a budget with their own artistic vision? How can they be a leader for the organization? These are things we talk about. The second week is watching me work with the orchestra, followed by a session where the orchestral musicians discuss the rehearsals, what was successful, what didn't work, and how we interacted with each other. Then in the third week, the conductors actually deal with the professional orchestra themselves. The National Conductors Institute strives to develop the skills you need to communicate to professional musicians. It is very intense and it is a program that I am very proud of. I am really pleased that most of our conductors have gone on to positions, either as assistant conductors, or music directors with orchestras worldwide. I think a lot of it is because after they finish the Institute's program, they have much more knowledge as to what is really expected of a music director.

Words of Advice

If I were to pass on words of advice, I would have to say:

1. Be prepared
2. Create your own opportunities
3. Conduct as much as possible

If you want to be a conductor, you have to conduct. Conduct any type of group, even if you hate it. It is important to get as much physical experience as you can. That is the rule for the first ten years of your conducting existence at least, so don't turn your nose up at anything. You must love *everything* when you are starting out and never turn anything down. Learn to read lead sheets, learn to accompany, and try to work with a band, a chorus, a jazz group, young people, and old people. Later on you can be selective, but when you are young, you cannot. I look back and think of all the things I did when I was starting out which I would never do again, but which I am really glad I did. For example, I conducted concerts with rock groups—I conducted the first performance of *Jesus Christ Superstar*. Would I do things like that now? No. But I learned so much from doing it. Strive to get as much experience as possible. Experience is the best way of learning anything. You don't need a teacher—experience teaches you.

INTERVIEW: ROBERT SPANO

"Dramatic Changes"—*Robert Spano*

- Oberlin Conservatory of Music, BM
- Curtis Institute of Music, MM
- Faculty Member—Bowling Green State University
- Faculty Member—Oberlin Conservatory
- Assistant Conductor—Boston Symphony
- Music Director—Brooklyn Philharmonic
- Music Director—Atlanta Symphony Orchestra

Path to the Podium: Robert Spano

I guess the first thing that occurs to me is that there is no set path. For every person, the path is different and it is valuable to trust your instincts. I know that along the way, in a sense, everything I did was wrong. For example, many people would say that if you want to conduct professionally, you should not take a university job. The first job I took was a teaching position at Bowling Green State University, but it was great for me. I learned so much conducting a university orchestra. Having to develop that orchestra and make them better made me develop my skills much more quickly, through necessity. So, it was a great thing for me to do, despite the common wisdom, so-called anyway, of that *not* being a good idea. So there is something about trusting your own intuition regarding what is going to be musically satisfying and what you need to do next for your own development that I think is worth paying attention to.

The other thing about "the path" is that things happen, not necessarily incrementally or gradually, but often *dramatically*. The first professional orchestra I ever conducted was the Boston Symphony. After I taught at Bowling Green University, I went on to teach at Oberlin. Then, I suddenly got the opportunity to audition for the BSO (Boston Symphony Orchestra) assistant conductor position. It surprised me because, before that, I had applied to Aspen and Tanglewood and had always been rejected. So, I guess you also have to be lucky. For me, the opportunity to audition for the BSO assistant conductor position, and then being able to take that position, was luck. It created a dramatic change in my conducting career. I guess I was ready for the next step, but I certainly didn't feel like it at the time.

My approach to my career was pretty simple-minded. I just wanted to conduct and if I got an opportunity to conduct, by God, I was going to do it. At the beginning I took everything that came my way. I loved teaching and I still do, but in a sense, the reason I took the teaching position initially, was so that I could have my own orchestra to conduct. That was always what I had wanted. So for me, it wasn't so much about "I want to conduct this orchestra—or that opera house." It was more, "I want to do this for a living." At the beginning, you do everything, but at a certain point, you get so busy that you have to start making choices about how you are going to spend your time so that you can continue to do your work well. Once you have been around a lot of orchestras, you know which ones you have better chemistry with than others and where you want to go back and what is most rewarding.

Management

After the BSO assistant conductor position, I spent three years as an itinerant conductor, guest conducting many different orchestras. I had a wonderful agent at the time, Mariedi Anders, who was getting me engagements all over. It was really a profound education to conduct so many orchestras in so many places. I don't know how anyone does anything without good management. I feel very dependent on them. If I had to promote myself, I would be recommending other people all the time. It is much easier to have someone else lobbying on your behalf. Even if you are so inclined to promote yourself, I think that nice things being said about you by other people is much more effective than saying them about yourself. The other thing about having a manager is the way that they can seek out opportunities that you might not even be aware of without that help. As a conductor, there is just so much musical work to do, that there is just no time. So I have felt very lucky and very well taken care of by good artist managers.

Successes

My greatest thrills have always been working with living composers. Recording Jennifer Higdon's Concerto for Orchestra and *CityScape*; or having John Adams here when we performed *El Nino* or working with him in Brooklyn when we were doing *Nixon in China*. David Del Tredici just finished *A Midnight Ride of Paul Revere*. He dedicated that to me and we will perform the premiere in Atlanta. These types of musical projects are peak experiences for me. For me there is no greater thrill than working with the composer and bringing the music to life.

Frustrations

When I was teaching, I was applying for other assistant conductor positions and things like that, and nothing was working out. All I got was a tremendous pile of rejection letters. I think it is important to have a thick skin about things like this. I remember how painful it was for me and I often wondered just how bad I really was. It is important to not let rejection get you down. Winston Churchill said, "Success was moving from failure to failure without losing your enthusiasm." I think that this is the most important part of it, not to get discouraged. Everyone gets rejected. I don't know of anyone who didn't have some things not work out the way they thought they wanted them to. Just keep applying and learning, sometimes things that don't work out the first time actually work out for the better. My university teaching feels that way to me. When I realize all that I learned during my first job, it was the greatest training that I could possibly have gotten— I don't think I really knew that at the time.

Skills Set

When you are talking about skill sets for conductors, obviously I think the foundation necessary to be a conductor and music director is to have really strong musical ideas and skills. Examples of this are: listening very well and very precisely; having great internal rhythm; and having the tools with which to effectively study scores, digest them, and own them. I also know how much I have learned from playing chamber music and accompanying singers, so becoming involved as a musician who is actually making sounds is also important. I know there are great conductors who didn't go through a lot of that, but I think they are the exceptions, not models. Most of us need "ears on" musical activities.

After these items, the range of skills needed beyond the musical is extraordinary. As music directors, we act as ambassadors for music in our cities and in our communities. Speaking skills are imperative, right down to the different ways that one handles stage behavior, to a television appearance, a radio interview, or a talk at a Rotary Club. I think each of these require a different approach. I remember that the first time I was on television I couldn't believe how broad everything seemed when I saw it played back. I was used to gesturing from a stage, where large gestures are appropriate, but with a television camera, the situation was entirely different. On TV, all gestures must be smaller and more direct. Throughout my career, I've learned many things by doing, but I have also hired consultants to help. I hired a director at one point to help me with television appearances. The first few times I spoke in public at the beginning of my career were horrifying. Now that I do it a lot, my neurosis level is much lower. I don't know of any way to train yourself for all the skills that you actually need as a music director, but public speaking is an incredibly important part of the role that we play.

Be Who You Are

I think the other more difficult and more personal aspect of being a public figure as a music director is to really trust in being one's self. To be a good conductor, first and foremost, you have to be who you are. In other words, I am not going to be more effective if I put on a fake accent—I am an American. I have to be that, because that is what I am. I think it is easy to say that a conductor is supposed to be certain things, when in fact, a conductor could be many, many different things. Many different kinds of personalities end up being conductors. If one's basic personality is kind of soft-spoken and gentle, that can be just as effective in its own way as a more extroverted personality who has lots of charisma. Both of these can work. You must strive always to be who you are. Friedrich Nietzsche's autobiography, written late in his life, is titled *How One Becomes What One Is*. I think that it is hard for us to trust ourselves because we have so many models that we think a conductor must be like. Perhaps twenty years ago, it may have been true that symphony boards were looking for a more specific model, but now it is a much different field. As we get more racial and gender diversity in the field, it is changing.

Understanding Priorities

In working with a board of directors, it is important to be sensitive to the concerns of a board which are very real and very important—like financial stability. I don't have to be an expert on those things, but I do have to be mindful of them and know how to understand what language they are speaking, what their priorities are, and what their needs and interests are. I attend board meetings when I am able to, and I spend time with board members individually. Even when I give speeches around the city, I try to encourage board members to attend. Giving speeches at Rotary Clubs and for other civic organizations requires knowing the priorities of each specific group. It is important that we express ideas that will appeal to their values, so that they will be interested in us. I think most of this is all about paying attention and listening to people.

Words of Advice

I have two things to say regarding words of advice for young conductors:

1. Know who you are
2. Know where you live and whom you live with

It is vitally important for you to live in the community where you are conducting. To me, what any orchestra needs to do in a given community has a lot to do with what is already going on there. I don't think there are universal solutions, although there might be universal principles, or paradigms, that will work from one place to another. Ultimately, it is about creating the orchestra that fits the needs of the place where you exist. Everything must be designed for that particular community. To me it is really not about my agenda, it is about music's agenda. I believe that great music needs to exist for a healthy society. It is part of being human. My job is to bring the music to the people and to help the organization find the best way to do this. I must find the artistic vision that is right for that specific place.

Interview: JoAnn Falletta

"Slow and Steady"—*JoAnn Falletta*

- Mannes College of Music, BM
- The Juilliard School, MM, DMA
- Music Director—Queens Philharmonic
- Music Director—Denver Chamber Orchestra
- Associate Conductor—Milwaukee Symphony
- Music Director—Women's Philharmonic
- Music Director—Long Beach Symphony
- Music Director—Virginia Symphony
- Music Director—Buffalo Philharmonic

Path to the Podium: JoAnn Falletta

I dreamed of being a conductor since I was eleven years old, long before I even knew what a conductor really did. I began my musical life as a classical guitarist when I was seven, but I soon fell in love with the orchestra and I tried to absorb everything I could about it. I feel very fortunate that I was able to study at the Mannes College of Music, where I received my bachelor's degree, and then attended the Juilliard School for a master's and doctorate. I think that the most fortuitous thing for me was that my conducting career developed slowly and steadily. I found myself in situations—whether as the associate conductor of the Milwaukee Symphony, or as the conductor of the Women's Philharmonic—that were challenging to me, but also allowed me to work with success and fulfill-ment. Because of this, I was always able to learn and develop. In looking back, I am sure that there were other career paths that I might have taken, but I am not sure if I knew what those were at the time. In this profession, we seem to create our own path, so my first job—working with a volunteer orchestra, the Queens Philharmonic—was a tremendous learning experience that worked for me. The Queens Philharmonic was already in existence when I became the music direc-tor, but I really had to rebuild it. The orchestra needed someone who was will-ing to work hard (without any financial compensation) and who had contacts with advanced music students in order to ask them to come and play. It was a great deal of work, but it was a wonderful way to learn. There might have been other paths—perhaps going to Europe to study, or working in an opera house, or becoming an assistant conductor in a large orchestra—but I took the oppor-tunities that were available to me. We all want that "big break" to happen right away—it didn't happen for me, and I feel that I am a much better conductor be-cause of that. Every step of my career path enabled me to grow; everything hap-pened slowly and at the right time.

Successes

During my career as a conductor, there have been many special moments—the night the Virginia Symphony made its debut in Carnegie Hall, or returning to Carnegie with the Buffalo Philharmonic, or my first recording with the Women's Philharmonic. All of these were wonderful experiences, but I think what really has meant the most to me is looking back over the years and seeing what we ac-complished as an organization, and realizing that a music director can help to make a difference. All the concerts are thrilling, but the sum is more than the con-certs. It is about helping a community begin to embrace an orchestra, to get to know them personally, and to consider them valuable to their quality of life. See-ing slow and important change in an orchestra is the most deeply satisfying ac-complishment. It is well worth those 7:30 AM breakfast meetings at the Rotary and the Lions' clubs to look back and you see that somehow you have helped to knit together an artistic vision for an organization, a vision that everyone can share. Of course, it comes with a price. As a music director of a regional orches-tra, you are always worried about challenges in addition to the music—ticket sales, personnel issues, fund-raising, managerial duties, and the relationship of the orchestra to its extended community. It is daunting and it takes a tremendous amount of work. Seeing that the hard work and time make a difference has really been a great satisfaction for me.

Frustrations

Our industry tends to foster two ideas that are unfortunate: the supposition that you have to have success early in life, and that the budget size of your orchestra is very important.

We have all been frustrated with questions like "What is our next career move?" and "Why aren't we conducting a bigger orchestra?" In the music business, we are conditioned to early success—the 12-year-old prodigy playing the violin or piano—so that if your conducting career doesn't happen right away, we think something is wrong. Sometimes young conductors are so focused on looking for the next step that they forget that they are actually doing what they always dreamed of doing—they are conducting an orchestra and they are enriching the artistic life of a community. In terms of conductors, it might be best if the career doesn't blossom right away. Too much repertoire for a young conductor can result in a lot of repertoire done badly; and too much pressure to increase your current orchestra's budget might lead to half-filled halls and financial instability for the organization. Take the time to learn and grow musically with your orchestra. Often, it is actually a disadvantage to work with a professional orchestra situation too soon. If you have a number of bad experiences because you are not ready, you might be actually setting your career back by many years.

Perseverance

Because of the critical nature of the field, every single conductor, at every level, has days, weeks, and even years, when he/she is depressed or confused about his/her career. There will be moments when you will feel as if you will never be in a situation where you can practice what you trained so diligently for. During these times, it is the love of music that keeps us going. We just can't give up. We keep on conducting and learning. That is why it is so important for each of us to try to understand that we must live in the moment. I believe that all of us must focus on how we can develop further as musicians. At a certain point, you will be very glad for all the study and for all the time you invested in every score and every professional training opportunity. You should never scatter your energy by wondering why and why not—it diffuses your concentration. Your energy should be targeted on what you are doing musically. In reality, the conductors that seem to spring out of nowhere, really have been putting in their time—often decades of study—before people decide that they are the next "hot" conductor. It is not a profession where you can graduate from the conservatory and be immediately successful as a conductor. Now, I no longer spend energy frustrated by what I can't control or by asking "What is next?" Instead, I have discovered wonderful music, wonderful colleagues, and wonderful experiences within the orchestra and within the communities. I try to live in the present. This has made a very positive difference in my life.

The Conductor's Role

Over the last twenty years, the conductor's role has changed dramatically. I think that our job is actually harder now. In the past, the conductor was completely in charge. Anything the maestro said or did was never questioned; decisions were arbitrary and sometimes made without any attention to the needs and desires of the musicians. Now we deal in a more collegial way with our orchestras, but at the same time, we still have the final responsibility for the results. We recognize that the work environment of the musicians with whom we work is critically important. I think this has added new challenges to what was already a very difficult profession, but in the end, our role is much more satisfying because the conductor is fully collaborating with the musicians in the music-making. We should think of conducting an orchestra as an expanded chamber music experience. When you are faced with making difficult decisions, you know that you are making them because they are best for the total organization. It should always be a question of "What is best for the orchestra?"

Orchestras are comprised of extremely talented and diverse people. I think that this aspect is quite challenging and rarely addressed in music school. In the conservatory you study music and occasionally preside over an orchestra of your colleagues and your friends. When you are in front of a professional or semiprofessional orchestra, you are in front of seventy-five to one hundred experts. If you add up the number of years the musicians have studied and the number of hours they have practiced, it is absolutely daunting. Many of these musicians never expected to be in an orchestra; they expected to be soloists. Somehow, you have to build them into a performing team and psychologically make it satisfying for these talented individuals. To be successful, you have to recognize the incredible artistic mosaic in front of you. You begin to realize that it is the human beings *behind* those instruments who are really making the music. Their music is directly influenced by their lives, their moods, their musical standards, tastes, and aspirations. Working with extraordinarily gifted artists in a situation that doesn't always allow for their personal satisfaction is, perhaps, the most difficult issue you will face as a conductor.

Residency

Another concept that has changed regarding the role of conductors is the fact of residency. I don't know when our current practice of a conductor spending only five to ten weeks in a community became the norm, or why orchestral associations accept this lack of commitment from their artistic leaders. The great conductors like Toscanini, Stokowski, Ormandy lived in the cities where they conducted. They went to dinner parties, attended social functions as a part of their normal life. They knew their community. Maestro Ormandy's yearly bill for flowers was $50,000! He knew so many people personally. If a supporter or a donor was ill, they received flowers from the Maestro; if someone had their first grandchild, they received flowers. This was a man who relished being a part of the community. It is critically important that you become a part of the community in which you conduct. To magically appear for each concert is not enough.

If you are a music director, the organization should come first, not your career. I get calls from people who have been offered their first job and they are already worried about what their next step will be: "Should I stay here three years? Should I try for something else?" I always remind them, "You were just entrusted with the incredible responsibility of this precious artistic entity. Don't worry about what you will do next. Worry about what you are going to do now for this orchestra." You may not be able to conduct the all the pieces you want to, or take the orchestra on tour, or hire expensive soloists. It is more important to make decisions that are best for the orchestra and the organization, not best for you or your ego. What is the point of being a conductor if you are just going to use the orchestra for your own interests—if you are not changing the orchestra for the better, if you are not building it, if you are not helping the members of the orchestra realize their potential as musicians? Your orchestral musicians are completely committed to the organization. Can the music director be anything less?

Fund-Raising

Conducting is about making music, and sharing ownership of that music in every public way that you can. If your time is well utilized, all of these extra involvements will have a positive impact on the organization and help with fundraising. After giving a speech at a local Rotary Club, you might discover that the president of the cement company in town happens to be an avocational cellist—perhaps he would love the opportunity of sponsoring Lynn Harrell as a soloist. Or that a wealthy patron has a daughter who is very interested in art, and would enjoy helping create the visual component of your concert that is focused on art.

Because of your access to this type of information, your role in fund-raising is strategizing and sharing information that you have collected from your interaction with the community. As the music director, you are the appropriate person to explain your artistic vision and to share your enthusiasm for specific projects. Why is it important to perform the Mahler Second Symphony on the seventy-fifth anniversary of the orchestra? Why is this particular guest artist so critical? Why do you need two more cellists in the orchestra? No music director, however, would be well used by going on every call and asking for small gifts. Your involvement should be focused on larger or sustained gifts, in communicating artistic vision, and in building long-term relationships.

Community Interaction

More and more demands are being made on conductors in the area of administration, and community interaction. I sometimes joke that being a music director could be a full-time job without the concerts; we could easily spend 100 percent of our time on our nonconducting responsibilities. In fulfilling these demands, good communication skills are critically important. You will write the columns for the newsletter; you will present preconcert talks; you will give speeches to countless civic organizations. Each of these encounters will require a different perspective. How do you communicate with people? In our society there are many who are curious about music but don't have a background in the arts. It is important that we are able to clearly express our thoughts about the repertoire we conduct. Many people tell me that while it is enlightening to hear a professor or music critic speak, they really enjoy hearing from the performer. The relationship is different. If the speaker then gives a performance of that piece, it gives immediate relevance to what they are saying. As a conductor and music director, you have to be able to communicate on many different levels—a talk for a third grade class, for a high school band, for an orchestra managers' conference. Few of us have formal training in areas such as public speaking and professional writing. Instead, we learn on the job. It is critical for conductors to be willing to become spokespeople for our art and ambassadors for the presence of music in a community.

Words of Advice

Here are my words of advice for conductors:

1. Enjoy studying the music
2. Be prepared for disappointment
3. Be persistent

I think that conductors need to be prepared to spend the rest of their lives studying music. You can never know enough and you can never learn enough. If you are not content with being on a sort of an endless journey, then you should really find a different profession. As much as you study a score and as many times as you perform it, there is always that feeling on the podium of "I want to know this better" or "I wish I could have spent more time with this score." It is an intensive process and there is always more to learn. There is no setting it aside and saying that "I'm finished." It is never at an end.

Secondly, conductors need to be prepared for disappointment. You will face many challenges and you will need to be as flexible as possible. I think that if you want to conduct for the right reasons—if you want to conduct because you are totally in love with the symphony orchestra, the idea of the symphony, and the musical repertoire—then you will find a way to do it. If there are other reasons why you want to conduct, it is probably not going to be a happy life for you. This is a profession where you create your own path, nothing is laid out clearly. As much as organizations have tried to put apprentice programs and training programs in place, essentially, the route of your professional development will be designed by you yourself. You need to relish the kind of a lifestyle where you are part entrepreneur, part musician, and part fundraiser. It can be deeply satisfying, but it is a full-time, full-life job.

Persistence in this field is critical. You would never continue in this profession if you didn't have courage, flexibility and persistence, combined with a thick skin, so that rejection, which always hurts, will not keep you from succeeding. At the core, you must have a firm belief in what you can do. This, I feel, is separate from ego. It is a belief that through your intense desire to make music, you will develop to a point where you will have something musically to say that is valid. You will need to care so deeply about this body of repertoire and this organization, the symphony orchestra, that you are willing to be persistent despite all discouragement. Sometimes it takes literally decades before things happen. You must be dedicated to the art form. Do not expect instant success, and always try to see the beauty in what you are doing, wherever you are. Through your efforts you can have a lasting musical impact on an entire community. Recognize the incredible beauty and the true value in raising musical consciousness.

Chapter 3

YOUR FIRST JOB

GETTING THE JOB

Once you have finished your formal training in conducting, in order to be a conductor, you have to first get a job. As I mentioned at the beginning of the book, "How can you get a job if they require experience?" and "How do you get experience without having a job?" Somehow, you have to figure out how to get your first step on the ladder.

If you have been out there working for a few years, you may want to move into a better position. This also requires applying for jobs. Most people assume that the longer they are in the field, the more experience they will have, and the easier it will be to get the next job. This is just not true. In the field of conducting, you are *always* paying your dues. When you move to the next level, you pay your dues there, and so on. No matter what, if you want to be successful, you will need to spend a lot of time, energy, and money applying for jobs.

Applying for Jobs

To get a job, you should follow up on every possible opportunity. There are job announcements in the Conductors Guild job bulletin and the American Symphony Orchestra League (ASOL) announcements that will cover most of the larger universities and the regional and professional orchestras in the United States. These are both organizations that you should join. They will provide you with many resources throughout your career. You also will want to check the *Chronicle of Higher Education.* This publication often lists jobs that do not show up on the other lists. This is especially useful if you are looking for a university position.

Take the time to send a personal letter to every orchestra in your area to let them know that you are available and interested in helping in any way they might need. Even better than a letter is taking the time to call and arrange a meeting with the music director, executive director, or a member of the staff. The orchestra might not have an opening at the moment, but if they like you, you might be the first person they think of when an opening occurs. Remember, people hire people they know—make sure they know who you are. Keep in touch with them and add them to your contacts list.

Keep your eyes and ears out for the unadvertised jobs. Many times, in the field of conducting, the jobs are filled from the inside or from a small list of names that are familiar to the organization. A press packet sent at the right time with the right reference names on it might get you on a short list, even if no official announcement has been made. When you hear that a person is leaving, make sure you contact the orchestra to see how their search will be handled.

Apply for everything. When you are starting out in the field, you can not afford to be picky. To be a good conductor, you need the experience of working with an orchestra—score study alone is not enough. If you are an experienced conductor, apply for anything that is more challenging than your current position. It is important for a conductor to work with a variety of orchestras. Whenever you apply for a job, don't be disappointed if you are cut from the next round. There are usually between two hundred and three hundred people applying for every single conducting job advertised in the country. Do not get discouraged; just send out more applications. The next one may be the right one for you, and, at worst, everyone is still becoming familiar with your name. By the law of averages, the more applications you send out, the better chance that one of them will work out.

Sometimes the jobs are not what they seem from the description. Apply even if you have concerns. These concerns can be worked out later, after you have been made an offer. Often, you will not progress far enough in the search to worry about it anyway. Some jobs that look less than attractive from their advertisements actually turn out to be wonderful. Others look great on paper, but when you get there, you might find out that there are huge personality or financial issues. When you apply, try not to judge the position—just put your name in the hat.

Becoming Known in the Field

One of the best ways to be moved up the list from the massive number of applicants for each job is to be well known. Establishing "name" recognition does not happen by accident. Name recognition comes from years of attending conferences, conducting workshops and master classes, and from following up with people whom you met at concerts and social events. Every conductor must be part "publicity agency" when they first start out. It is essential that you be a self-promoter and that people know you are looking for conducting positions. It is also important for you to be willing to do almost anything at the beginning of your career—and even into the middle of your career. Quite often, it is the small, off-stage conducting position for a community opera production that opens a door to a larger conducting opportunity; or it is the time you worked as a librarian in the summer for a major orchestra that eventually led to a guest conducting engagement for a children's concert series. People hire people they know. Work hard to become known.

Putting Your Best Foot Forward

Résumé, Photo, and Biography

It is essential when you apply for a job that you present yourself in a way that will get you into the finals. The overall look and quality of your press materials are critical. It is very important early on in your career to spend the money for good press photos. A conductor is a very visual person in a community, and people want a face that they can sell and that people will trust.

It is also important that your resume be organized in a professional manner. Even if you have very little experience, try to find a way to present it so it showcases what you are capable of doing. Above all, do not list every concert you have ever conducted, and do not put emphasis on anything before college. Even your college experience should be minimized as soon as you have real work experience to replace it. Your resume should be short (one to two pages) and easy to read.

A résumé should include:

> Name
> Education (college and summer festivals attended)
> Conducting Experience
> Related Work Experience (if applicable)
> Honors and Awards (1–5)
> References (3)

As you mature, less emphasis should be placed on education and more on your experience. A sample résumé is available in the Resource section.

Along with your résumé, you should also include a short biography of your work. This is usually one page or less in length. It should be centered on the page with your name in bold at the top. It is a prose version of the highlights of your résumé. I usually include this first in my press packet, after the photo.

Repertoire

Repertoire conducted should be listed on a separately attached repertoire sheet. This should be updated yearly as you progress in the field. It is not always to your advantage to list which orchestras performed each piece you have conducted. If the orchestras you have conducted are not larger, well-established orchestras, this will probably work against you, and it is better to leave them off, unless specifically requested.

Reviews

In addition to a photo, your résumé, and a repertoire list, a press packet should include one to three reviews, if you have them available. It is good to outline the parts of the review that deal directly with your conducting; this will enable the reader to find them quickly.

Conductor and guest artist dazzle audience

The Lumberton Symphony Orchestra opened its season with great excitement and panache on Saturday night. Performing a concert of great masterpieces, under the baton of Frederic Jones, the orchestra has never sounded better. The strings sound resonated with clarity and warmth, and the intonation in the woodwinds was exceptional.

The concert opened with a rousing performance of Mozart's Overture to the Magic Flute. This was followed by the second suite of Respighi's Ancient Airs and Dances, a piece that captures the essence of Renaissance dances in the colors of modern orchestration. The orchestra began the piece tentatively, but soon was playing with heart and soul.

Throughout the first half, Jones conducted confidently - showing a deep understanding of the work, and conveying his interpretation through clear baton technique and a fluid use of the left hand.

During the second half of the concert, the orchestra was joined by pianist, Mikhail Varinsky performing Brahms' Piano Concerto No. 2. Each note of the Brahms was a jewel. Varinsky offered us a performance that was dazzling and powerful, and yet also introspective and sincere. He was able to connect the entire audience to the music.

The orchestra's intimate response and interpretation of the Brahms was filled with strength that comes from a depth of musical understanding, communication, and inspiration. The audience showed their appreciation with a standing ovation. Varinsky obliged by performing an encore.

Under the musical leadership of maestro Jones the Lumberton Symphony is off to a fine start for the season!

By all means, never include a bad review! Do not include reviews that are hard to read. Often it is difficult to photocopy newspaper reviews adequately. If you are not able to create a "clean" copy, I would advise you to retype the article in a newspaper format. This will keep your press packet looking professional. Do not include reviews in other languages. This creates a pretentious element that will not work in your favor. If you absolutely want to include the review, include a translation. Do not include copies of programs or excessive materials. Symphony offices are drowning in paperwork—do not give them more.

References

You also may be asked to provide letters of reference. Usually three are required. It is good to have a generic letter from your most recent conducting teacher, a letter from a colleague or orchestra member, and a letter from someone on the staff or board of an orchestra you have worked with. Make sure these people know you well enough to write a good recommendation before you ask them. They should be personally familiar with your work. These letters are usually addressed "To whom it may concern," with no specific date. Once you have these letters, you will not have to bother your contacts every few weeks when you want to apply for yet another job. If the job is a very specialized position and you think that a personalized letter would be more effective, by all means ask for one and include it in the packet.

Some people only ask for the names and contact information of the three references, not letters. Make sure that, as you are listing people, you have contacted them to let them know you are using their name as a reference. No one likes to receive an unexpected phone call. You also should send them an updated resume so they have the most recent information to refer to if someone contacts them. Often, this type of referencing now takes place though e-mail. Make sure you have a current e-mail address for your references and permission to distribute it.

The names you use as references are very important. If someone on the committee knows one of your references personally, this will go far toward moving your resume to the "yes" pile. You will probably want to vary your reference names for each job to which you apply. This way you can identify people who you think might have a relationship with the organization. Try to utilize contacts who know your work but also are well-respected by the field at large. If you don't yet know people in the larger circles, then use people who have very persuading personalities and who totally believe in you. Good references are very important to getting the position. Also, recognize that the search committee will undoubtedly be contacting people who are not listed as references. This is why it is so important not to ever burn your bridges. The music world is a very small field; the blind reference is the one they will usually take more seriously.

Be very clear with the organization to which you are applying whether it is proper for them to contact anyone at your current orchestra. Often, you will not want to rock the boat with your present job, yet you still want to be looking for your next step up the ladder. Most search committees are sensitive to this and will not contact your current employer without notifying you, but you might want to double check. This is usually only done in the final round of a search.

Videotapes

More and more, videotapes are being required in the second and third rounds of applications, before people are actually invited to conduct. As much as we would prefer the search committee to come and observe us in person, realistically this is often not possible. Videotapes or DVDs give the committee an opportunity to see your work, so that they can narrow down their search to the people who will work best with their orchestra.

It is difficult as a conductor to make a good videotape. Conductors new to the field are greatly limited by the quality of their musicians and also by the quality of the sound produced from the built-in microphones of most low- to mid-range video cameras. It is good to invest early in a high-quality video camera. This will not only help you create a decent audition tape but also will enable you to use it as a learning tool your whole life. If you are a conductor who happens to be working with a union orchestra, it is important that you get authorization to video-tape at rehearsals and concerts, and that you have permission to use portions of this tape for auditions.

For your video, the camera should be focused on the conductor's upper torso (shot from within the orchestra), not too close, but not so far that they have difficulty seeing what you are doing. Be sure that you have adequate lighting and that all gestures are clearly within focus. It is also important to see a little of the relationship with the players, so make sure the camera is not focused too "tight."

Sound is always an issue with conducting videotapes, because the camera is often placed by the percussion or other loud instruments that totally distort the sound. If you are able to have a professional video produced, you can take the sound feed off the audio recording. This is the best solution, and well worth the cost. You also can look into purchasing a remote microphone system, where a mike can be placed in the hall that will react with a radio-controlled unit on your camera. This will produce a better musical impression for the search committee to evaluate your work.

The overall tape should be short (twelve to fifteen minutes) but no longer than twenty minutes (unless a different length has been specified by the search committee for the job to which you are applying). Everything should be clearly marked on both the tape and the box. The labels for your tapes and boxes should be prepared on your computer so they look as professional as possible. Make sure your name is on everything you submit, because it is easy to confuse video tapes and packets when the committee is looking through over a hundred. It is also good to include the name of the ensemble and a little background on the type of orchestra. A repertoire list of the contents of the tape is also important to include, along with the starting points (in minutes or tracking numbers) of each piece.

In selecting repertoire to put on your videotape, you can either submit an entire piece or often the committee likes to see short selections from two to three contrasting pieces. Try to demonstrate a variety of music style periods. If you do have access to both concert video footage and rehearsal footage, it is good to include both. In order to prepare short examples, you will need to purchase a video editing program for your computer. This is a useful tool because it allows you to insert titles and to add fades, up and down, of both the music and the picture. This will add to the professionalism of your presentation. If you do not have access to this type of video editing equipment and programs, try to locate a person in your community who films weddings. They will be very experienced in editing tapes and they will be more reasonably priced than a commercial editing studio.

There is a trend to shift from videotape to DVD technology. DVDs are actually easier to copy than VHS tapes. Search committees are now accepting DVD formats, so either is acceptable to send. If you are sending VHS, you need to be very careful when making copies of the tape. Often, two different VHS machines will vary in speed. This will actually distort your sound and image. Make sure you take the time to check each tape before it is sent. Sometimes a tape becomes distorted or the picture is not clear. Above all, you want to avoid sending an inferior-quality or defective videotape. It also is important to note that European and Asian VHS and DVD formats are different, and not compatible with what is used in the United States. Applicants should be aware of this when they are preparing their tapes, and they should make every effort to have the tape adapted to the proper format for the country to which they are applying.

Cover Letter

When you submit your materials, you often will be required to write a cover letter that expresses why you are interested in this position. With this letter, be positive and honest. Try to phrase things in terms of what strengths you would bring to the organization. Emphasize your work experience and accomplishments that parallel their job description. Try to let your personality come through, but don't ramble on and on. It is advisable to keep the letter short, no more than two pages. A three paragraph format is usually the best approach. During the first paragraph, tell them why you think you are a good match for this position. In the second paragraph, emphasize the two or three main examples of your experience that qualify you for this job. In the third paragraph, thank them and make sure they have your contact information. After you have finished the letter, always have someone else proof your resume and cover letter for typos and grammar before you send them. A good, concise cover letter is your best opportunity to make a unique impression.

Submitting the Press Packet

When you submit your cover letter and press packet, be sure to mail it weeks before the deadline. Sometimes organizations look at applications as they arrive. They might spend more time reviewing the ones that arrive early before the rush. Make sure that your name is on the front of your press packet. Once again, it is easy to confuse packets that are not well labeled. Before you mail your packet, double check to make sure it includes the following:

> Cover letter
> Bio and résumé
> Photo
> Repertoire list
> Two to three reviews (in English)
> Two to three letters of recommendation
> Copy of brochures or programming from current job (if available)
> Videotape or DVD (only if required)

Dealing with Rejection

There will be many times when you will send a press packet, but you will not hear anything for months. If you do not hear back from the committee within a month after the close of their deadline for applications, this usually means that they have selected other candidates for their second and third rounds. Often the entire search will take place before you are officially notified that you are no longer being considered. This constant waiting can be extremely stressful. The best strategy is to apply for many jobs, but do not get your hopes up for any of them. Conducting is an incredibly competitive occupation. You might get rejected for fifty positions before you get your first interview. Just because you are not selected for the finals round does not mean that you are not qualified to be a conductor. Each organization is looking for the right match for their position. They also want to make sure it is the right job for the candidate and that the person they select will be able to work within the artistic level of their orchestra and fit in the community.

There also are other elements that affect conductor searches. What type of image does the organization want to convey to the community? If an orchestra had an older conductor, they might want to hire someone young. If they had someone European as their previous music director, they might want to try an American. If the orchestra specializes in new music, or in chamber orchestra repertoire, or opera, these considerations will affect whom they promote to the next round of their search. Regardless of these factors, you cannot change who you are. You must always be true to your musical beliefs, standards, and creativity. Never try to add a foreign accent, change your name, or alter your true musical passions, just to get the job. Just believe that the right job is out there for you that is the perfect match for your skill set and for your current artistic level.

Conducting is not an occupation for the faint of heart. It can be very discouraging to get one rejection letter after another. Having the door constantly shut in your face can make you want to do something else with your life. Resist the temptation to just give up. If you really want to conduct for the right reasons, you will somehow find a way. Often, you will have to conduct for free to simply acquire the experience and résumé material to apply at the next level. The more you conduct, the better you will become. Look at every opportunity and try to build it into a stepping-stone to the next one. Concentrate on continually growing as a musician so that when the right opportunity drops in your lap, you are ready to shine. Keeping a positive attitude throughout your career is one of the most important factors in achieving success.

The Interview

Phone Interview

If you have made it through the first round and your reference checks have gone well, you might have the opportunity of a phone interview before you are invited in person to work with an orchestra. Interviewing is an art and not one in which most conductors have a lot of experience. Before this interview, do your research about the orchestra you are applying with. You should know about its past programming, the size of its budget, the number of concerts it performs, and the size of the board. Much of this research can now be done on the Web because almost every orchestra has a Web site. You also can use Guidestar.com to obtain information regarding an orchestra's IRS 990 tax filing or simply ask them for last year's audited financial records. This will give you a window into their financial position, and it will help you to evaluate where they spend their money. It also may help with assessing the salary level. Before the interview, write out a few (but not more than five) questions that you would like to ask. Usually, at the end of the conversation they will ask you if you have any questions. During a phone interview it is only appropriate to ask one or two, but a longer list helps to keep you focused during the rest of the conversation. One question I always ask is, "Where would you like this organization to be in five years?" Their answer to this question will tell me a little more about their vision of the future of the organization. From this answer, I can see if I would be a good "fit" to take them where they want to go. It is also important to spend time writing out, and answering, some of the main questions that you think may be asked. Some popular interview questions include:

1. Tell us a little about your background and why you think this position would be the right position for you.
2. What have you accomplished in your current job that you are proud of?
3. How would your current employer describe your strengths and weaknesses?
4. What do you consider the three most important responsibilities of a conductor?
5. Describe your programming style and how you select your music.
6. What are your feelings about new music?
7. Describe some ideas you have in the areas of education and outreach.
8. What is your opinion on a conductor's involvement in fund-raising?
9. How would you balance this job with your other current responsibilities?
10. Where would you like to be in five years?

As you go through the interview, answer each question in three to five minutes or less. Avoid talking too much, and make sure that you really answer the question they asked. Never go into long explanations about things they haven't asked you about. The interviewers are usually on a schedule, and a person who meanders in a phone conversation might also be "unfocused" on the job. Try to avoid asking or answering any questions about salary and benefits. A phone interview is too early in the process to talk about these details. Above all, make sure you convince them that you *really* want the job. No matter how good you look on paper, if they perceive that you are not really interested, they will move on to someone else. Everyone wants to feel that their job is the most important. Make sure that, even if you already have other conducting jobs, the search committee feels that the position with their orchestra is your ultimate goal. Take time to create a warm, open rapport with the search committee, but don't joke around during the interview. Above all, be honest. Remember that they are judging and weighing every word you say. They need to sense that you are a person whom they can trust.

Live Interview

If you are lucky enough to progress to the live interview round, it will probably be in the context of a guest conducting offer or an audition with an interview component. When you arrive, make sure that you are professionally dressed to assume the level of job for which you are applying. The same preparation and questions apply for this interview as the phone interview, only now they will have an opportunity to judge your personality and your presence. Find out as much as possible about the process and who will be involved in advance. Continue to do as much research as you can about the organization, and be prepared to answer questions about your future career goals and how this position would fit in.

If the interview is for an assistant conductor position with a large orchestra, you should be confident, but you should also appear moldable. No one wants a know-it-all as an assistant conductor. During this interview, you will probably be asked about programming educational concerts and pops concerts. You should have a couple of programming examples ready so that you can demonstrate your expertise in both of these areas. You also should bring a copy of the repertoire that you have studied and conducted so that they can see the depth of your experience. You also might be asked to present a short preconcert talk as part of the interview process, or to speak with the education committee about how you might be involved with the educational outreach of the organization.

If you are interviewing for a music director position, you will want to talk about your programming philosophy and artistic vision. The committee will often ask for examples of subscription concerts or seasons you have conducted in the past. In addition to this, you might be given an exercise to submit repertoire for the next two seasons of their orchestra. Do not be worried about giving up your "great" programming ideas. This type of request is part of the process to see if you are a good fit for the organization and most of the repertoire examples are only used during the interview process. After they have finished their list of questions, you will have an opportunity to find out more about their organization. Questions you might want to ask them could include:

1. What are some of the biggest challenges that this organization faces?
2. How are you dealing with these challenges?
3. Describe your ideal music director.
4. How many subscribers or regular audience members do you have currently? Is that number going up or down? To what do you attribute this trend?
5. Describe the backgrounds of some of the orchestra members and elaborate on the strengths and weaknesses of the overall ensemble.

6. Describe a concert experience that you really felt was exciting.

7. Where would you like this orchestra to be artistically in five years?

As with the phone interview, avoid talking about salary and benefits. When the subject does come up, try to avoid being the first one to state a number. If you have done your homework well, you should have a pretty accurate idea of what they should be offering. When they have decided that you, and only you, are the one they want, you will be in the best position to negotiate a good package.

The Audition

Short Auditions

A conducting audition can range in length from ten minutes to an entire week. For assistant conductor jobs, most large orchestras select a field of seven to ten candidates and run them through a very short audition process (sometimes only ten minutes each). Finalists may be invited back to conduct a longer rehearsal or to perform a children's concert. Usually the repertoire for these auditions is provided just a few weeks in advance, so you will not have a lot of time to prepare. Often they will specify sections of a larger work. Even if this is the case, in preparing for the audition, make sure you are familiar with the entire composition. This will bring further depth to your interpretation.

One of the biggest questions you might have during your audition is whether to rehearse or to just run through the pieces. It is usually best to ask the committee in advance what they would like, although often they are not clear in their expectation. Ultimately, you will have to rely upon your best judgment. Regardless, don't stop to rehearse anything until you have given the orchestra a few minutes to get used to your style of conducting. Every orchestra needs time to settle. If you are going to correct something, try to talk about the music and what you want regarding phrasing and articulation; do not single out individuals. Sometimes an orchestra will use an audition as an ear-training test. Be sure to listen for purposely played wrong notes. Often, if you do not correct these wrong notes, you will have failed the test, and they will move on to the next person.

When you first come onstage, be pleasant and shake the concertmaster's hand. Smiling at the orchestra will help you feel more relaxed, and it also helps them to feel more comfortable. Tell them where you want to start, and then begin. The time will usually go quickly. At the end of the audition, make sure that you thank the orchestra. It is also common to shake the concertmaster's hand before you leave.

Guest Conducting Auditions

For guest conducting auditions, you will probably be involved with the organization for four to five days. Remember that every minute of this time you are being judged and analyzed. Usually you will have four rehearsals to prepare a concert. Sometimes you will be involved in selecting the repertoire and sometimes it will be already chosen. Often, it is a combination of the two, where perhaps the guest artist's repertoire is decided beforehand, but you can submit ideas for the rest of the program. These suggestions are usually narrowed down through conversations with the executive director or the search committee, until you come up with a mutually satisfying program. If you really want the job, it is best to fill your short list of suggestions with pieces such as Tchaikovsky's Symphony No. 4, Respighi's *Pines of Rome*, or Mussorgsky's *Pictures at an Exhibition*, repertoire that has proven over and over to be "standing ovation" pieces. Your success as a guest conductor will be weighed not only on your response from the orchestra, but also by the response of the audience. Make sure that you put your best foot forward on both fronts. A piece with an exciting, dramatic ending will help seal the deal.

At least five weeks before the concert, make sure that you have sent all of the information that might be needed to make the concert a success. This would include special instructions for the crew, seating diagrams if you like the orchestra arranged a certain way, and specific notes for the staff or orchestra members. In doing this, you will demonstrate that you are an organized person who pays attention to details. Often you will be required to do a preconcert lecture as part of the audition process. Let the staff know what type of equipment you will need for the lecture and make sure you are fully prepared. If you are going to use musical examples during the talk, test all equipment with your recording samples ahead of time. Nothing is worse than a lecture with musical examples that play incorrectly.

As you work with the orchestra throughout the week, keep a chart of their names handy on your music stand. Try to call people by name as much as possible. Make sure that you have sent an accurate rehearsal schedule ahead of time, and stick with it. You will be judged on how well you use your time. During rehearsals, as in the shorter audition, try to focus on musical concepts. You want the musicians to know that you have something to say musically. Be relaxed and pleasant at all times, and no matter what happens, never appear frustrated, angry, or nervous. The ability to "keep one's cool" in stressful situations is the mark of a good leader. Sometimes, this skill alone will actually get you the job.

Usually, any of the five finalists for a position are all educationally prepared to do the job. At this level, it often comes down to chemistry. The job must feel right for the person auditioning, and the relationship must feel right for the orchestra members. The search committee and orchestra members must have confidence in this person's ability to take them to the next level, and the audience must connect with the energy that is coming from the stage. You could conduct a very presentable concert, but if the excitement is not there, you will probably not be offered the job. Like any type of competition, there must be winners and losers. Don't let it bother you. View the guest conducting as an opportunity to make new friends and to conduct great music. The rest will take care of itself.

Negotiating the Contract
Negotiating Different Types of Jobs

After the search committee has decided that you are the one they want for the job, it is time to negotiate a contract. A contract is really just an outline of basic responsibilities and a definition of the payment structure. A well-drafted contract is important, but even more important is a clear understanding from both parties of the mutual expectation. You need to clarify, understand, and fully accept your responsibilities. Your contract will usually be signed by the president of the board, or the chairman of the department if the job is at a university, and you will report to him directly. With smaller orchestras, this contract will be negotiated by the president of the board. With larger orchestras, it might be negotiated through the executive director. Regardless, you will work closely with the leadership of the organization and it is important that you retain a good relationship with them at all times. If you have professional management, the negotiations will be probably coordinated between the executive director and your manager. The board may be brought in only to approve the final contract.

Do not allow yourself to be talked into accepting a job without a written contract or at least a letter of agreement. Many conductors have experienced hardship because of items verbally promised, where they had no written confirmation or clarification. It is not only critical that your agreement is done in writing, but also that in multi-year contracts, both parties honor the dates for renegotiation. After you have been with an orchestra for a few years, it is easy to become relaxed about this issue. This is when it is most important for you to remind the board of their renewal commitments regarding your contract. Failure to do this might end in a surprising end of your tenure without proper notification.

You are in a strong negotiating position when you begin a job. Arts organizations, however, tend to be relatively set in their pay levels, and you may find that encouraging them to spend more money is not always possible. Sometimes it is better to negotiate flexibility of schedule, fewer concerts or classes to teach (if it is a university), or other benefits such as the use of a car or an apartment when you are in town (for a regional orchestra). Sometimes these additional perks can be donated to the organization so they do not add substantially to the budget. Look for creative solutions that add to your overall compensation package but that don't add additional stress to the organizational budget. The search committee will appreciate your efforts in this area.

The negotiation will be dramatically different depending on the type of orchestra. Assistant conductor jobs are usually fixed in salary and they often will not pay travel or extra expenses. Youth conductor jobs will usually require that you live within driving distance of the orchestra. They will also be fixed in salary with very little room for negotiating. University jobs have criteria of course loads and committee responsibilities that are defined by the university, but sometimes this can be negotiated. With a university, really push for the highest salary possible when you begin the job because after that, raises are often fixed across the board for the entire university. Benefits at a university also tend to be the same for everyone. Regional orchestras will be the most flexible in the negotiating process.

It is important to remember that the actual act of negotiating is not only acceptable, but it is expected by the other party. Do not be concerned that they will think less of you if you are specific in what your needs are; and do not be afraid that they will rescind their job offer if your stated needs are different than what they first offered. Do your homework ahead of time and know your full worth. It is also good to know what similar orchestras are paying across the country. You will actually gain respect if you can present your needs in a clear, professional manner. As you negotiate, try to help your new employer find creative ways to meet your needs.

Strategies of Negotiation

Success in negotiating is relative. It usually depends on knowing what you really want, and knowing what you will settle for. It is important to have your goals defined in your mind before you start. Usually, when you go into a negotiation, the higher your aspirations, the higher your rewards will be. Every person enters a negotiation with a preconceived idea of what they want. You will adjust this goal during the negotiating process in response to a positive reaction from the other party, or a negative. When you do this, recognize that you have more power than you think. If the orchestra has gone through a two-year search process to identify that you are the chosen one—they really want you. Using this power, however, entails risks. You do not want to alienate people before you even begin the job.

Prenegotiation Questions

Before you begin the negotiation, answer these questions:

> What compensation do you really want?
> In what ways can you be flexible?
> What areas do you both agree on already?
> How can you help them see your needs more clearly?
> What are your unique strengths that merit higher compensation?
> How can you turn your weaknesses into strengths during the
>   negotiation process?
> What are the financial limitations of the orchestra association
>   or university?
> What is their deadline for completing the contract?

When communicating about issues, it is more effective to present both sides of an issue and to discuss the pros and cons involved. This enables you to let the other side know that you fully understand their concerns. As you do this, you will have a better relationship during the negotiation if importance is placed on similar issues and positions rather than differences. Often, agreement over controversial issues is greatly improved if these items can be related to issues on which agreement can easily be reached. Repeating items that are important to you will help these concepts to be accepted more readily. Repetition is a very useful negotiating tool. When you are discussing pros and cons, it is best to present your favored viewpoint last. Somehow, listeners always remember the last thing that was presented. In addition to remembering the ending statements, you will note that people remember the beginning of a conversation more than they remember the middle. Keep this in mind as you organize the presentation of your wants and needs.

Community Orchestra and Youth Orchestra Contracts

Community orchestra or youth orchestra positions will probably involve weekly rehearsals and between three to five concerts per year. During the contract negotiations, you should clarify what your specific duties are, both on and off the podium. Some of the basic categories that should be included on your contract are:

> Terms of agreement and terms of renewal
> Number of years
> Renewal notification dates and process
> Services and duties
> Number of concerts

> Basic schedule of rehearsals
> Procedures and responsibilities for:
>> Selection of music
>> Auditioning and terminating players
>> Selection of guest artists
> Other responsibilities
> Compensation

Because community and youth orchestras often do not have paid staffs, you may find yourself assuming the roles of librarian, stage manager, personnel manager, and conductor. It is important that these separate duties, along with the compensation, are clearly stated in the contract. As the organization grows, you may be able to delegate some of these responsibilities to members of the orchestra. Make sure that the contract also clarifies your role in selecting the music, arranging for soloists, and working with the board and the community. You should ask for a multi-year contract so that you are able to plan for the long-term artistic development of the orchestra and it is always advisable for the written contract to state the terms for renewal. At least six months' notification by either party is standard if the contract is not going to be renewed.

Regional Orchestra Contracts

Regional orchestra positions are the jobs that will give you the most flexibility in your contract. There are a variety of variables that will need to be settled before you can come to a mutually beneficial agreement. Most conductors with regional orchestras will schedule their time by the week. Often, they might have more than one orchestra. It is very important to be clear regarding how much of a conductor's time will be available to the organization according to the current contract. These types of contracts will also specify how many concerts will be performed, and what other duties the conductor will be responsible for. Sometimes, the fees in the contract will be separated into two areas or even two separate contracts. One would apply specifically to your duties as a music director; the others would clarify your fees and responsibilities as a conductor, including the number of concerts and the additional fees to add or subtract if this number changes over the years. This type of contract allows for more flexibility for the organization during times of growth. Most orchestras will offer a new music director a three-year contract that includes terms for renewal. If you are successful in your first three years, you might be offered a five-year contract. It is rare to see a contract longer than five years, as most contracts are negotiated far in advance.

In every contract you will see the same basic categories. Each of these categories must be discussed and negotiated, but the most important sections are those dealing with duties and compensation. A generic regional orchestra contract is available in the Resource section.

Contract Categories

Definition of terms (not always necessary):
>Board, Concert Week, Executive Director, Orchestra,
>Musical Event, Subscription Series,
>Week, Year

Engagement

Term of agreement and terms of renewal
>Number of years
>Renewal notification dates and process

Services and duty of a conductor
>Audition and recommend engagement and termination of orchestral musicians
>Recommend engagement of guest artists
>Plan repertoire
>Rehearse and conduct concerts
>Provide overall musical direction and guidance
>Involvement in the community

Presence and Availability
>Percentage of time, number of trips, or specific number of days

Compensation
>Salary
>Benefits (if applicable)
>Who pays for travel and housing (if applicable)
>Independent contract or employee (who pays taxes)
>Extra concert fees

Disability, Death, and Force Majeure

Miscellaneous

Exhibit A: Job description
>Artistic responsibilities
>Operations and community responsibilities
>Board interface

Exhibit B: List of specific concerts and dates covered under this contract

Compensation

When discussing compensation, you need to keep in mind the overall budget level of the orchestra. Music directors of regional orchestras are known for being paid anywhere between 5 to 10 percent of the overall budget. Additional perks, such as housing and travel expenses, can often be more beneficial than a higher salary. Contracts can be written either as an employee contract or an independent contractor contract. The independent contractor contract is only helpful if it allows you to avoid paying extra state tax. Either way, if you agree to an independent contractor contract, make sure that you are making enough extra money so that you can pay the federal (FICA) taxes that the employer usually pays. It is also good to negotiate preset fees for additional concerts. These fees should be lower than your standard guest-conducting rate. This allows the organization to consider expansion without any unknown variables. With your negotiations, try to make sure that if the orchestra is large enough, you are covered on its medical benefits plan. Also, you should try to negotiate into your contract the option for personal development. See if they will agree to pay your expenses to attend the ASOL conference, the Conductors Guild conference, or a special conducting seminar. An extra $1,500 per year for personal development will keep you fresh and help you to stay on the cutting edge of the field. The knowledge you bring back from these conferences and seminars should be very beneficial for the orchestra in the long run. Often there are special grants that the organization can apply for to cover these additional costs. Below is a more concise list of some of the negotiable points in a music director's contract:

- Salary
- Number of days in contract
- Number of concerts, types of concerts
- Fees for additional concerts
- Fees for additional meeting days or weeks
- Benefits (health, disability, workers' comp)
- Retirement contributions, 403(b)/401(k), or pension plan
- Housing provided/housing stipend
- Meals or entertaining expense reimbursement
- Travel paid for or a partial reimbursement
- Personal development monies for attending conferences
- Use of a car
- Score purchase stipend
- Phone stipend

With a music director's contract, the phrases "part-time" and "full-time" are not really applicable. When you sign a contract, you are responsible for the duties promised and the basic time it takes to accomplish them. Because you do not have to be at the office every day, your job can be perceived as part-time. As a music director, though, you are also responsible for the overall artistic direction of the organization. This is seen by many to be a full-time responsibility. Whether you are full-time or part-time is not really relevant as long as you are performing all aspects of the job. Sometimes, this distinction has more to do with your qualification for medical benefits than anything else. Also, the higher the salary, the more likely you are to be listed as full-time. Being full-time with one orchestra should not exclude you from working full-time for another.

Single-concert Contracts

As you go through your career, you will have a need for contracts that cover a single concert. This type of contract can also be used for guest conducting jobs that double as interviews. Often a job interview guest conducting will pay a fee much lower than a normal guest conducting fee. To avoid confusion later on, make sure that the fee is discussed before you agree to be put into the finals. If you have a manager, make sure that you have told the search committee that they should speak to your manager regarding the schedule and the guest conducting fees. If you are interested in the job, it is not advisable to argue too much over the fee. That will only create conflict, which will follow you through the search process.

A single-concert contract will cover many of the same basic parameters as a regular contract, but it will be shorter and more specific. (A sample of a single-concert contract is available in the Resource section.) These contracts should include the exact dates of the rehearsal and concerts. They should specify who is paying for the airfare or travel reimbursement and whether hotel or other appropriate accommodations are included. (Meals are usually the individual's responsibility.) They also should clarify any other expectations, such as a preconcert talk or a reception after the concert. If the concert is also a job interview, the administration should include a separate schedule of interview activities that will take place during the week.

A single-concert contract will include all of the following:
>   Rehearsal and concert dates
>   Fee
>   Repertoire

Travel and hotel

Other expectations

Payment of Fees

Usually the check for a guest conducting performance is given to the conductor before the last concert of the set. If you have a manager, it will be mailed to them right after the concert. Your manager will take their percentage and mail you a check for the remainder.

Getting a Manager

As you move forward in your career, at some point you are going to think about getting a manager. There are a few different ways you can go about this. The first question to ask yourself is whether you *really need* management. A manager will usually take 20 percent of your fee for each guest conducting engagement. They will also take 15 percent of your salary the first year of a new job and 10 percent for each consecutive year after that. Some smaller management companies also charge retainer fees that amount to between $200 and $500 per month. In addition to this, you are also responsible for paying for all of the phone calls, mailing expenses, and publicity done on your behalf.

Even though having a manager will give you a position of perceived success, you must evaluate whether you really have enough work to merit it. One of the good things about management is that it is easy for people to find you nationally. Most managers advertise in *Musical America*, a national directory source that everyone in the industry uses to keep track of guest artists and performing groups. It often has been said that if you are not listed in *Musical America*, you do not exist. It is advisable to figure out a way to have your name in this directory, even if you have to take out your own ad. You want to make sure that you are always easy to find.

As the Internet has developed into an industry tool, most musicians are establishing their own Web sites. Check early in your career to see if you can buy the domain name of your own name. This will be very useful later on to help people find your Web site. This way, no matter how many times you change addresses, everyone will still be able to track you down.

If you are working toward a career as a conductor of a regional orchestra, it is advisable to take some time, if you are near the New York City area, to meet with some of the artist managers. If you stay in the field you will be hiring guest artists from them, and these relationships will become stronger over the years. Try to meet at least one person from each of the major management companies (contact information is available in the Resource section). See if they are open to looking at your press materials and giving you career advice. Make sure you are not pushy, and understand that, just because they are willing to meet with you does not mean that they are in any way interested in adding you to their list of artists. Young conducting talent is a very hard sell, and they will be cautious about adding names to their roster that will not bring in enough work.

First Year—Do's and Don'ts

Now that you have accepted the job and signed the contract, you are ready to begin your new position. What you do in your first year on the job is critical to your ongoing success with the organization. Every conductor has a preconceived idea of how things should be done and what constitutes a standard of high quality of music. I encourage you to put most of your thoughts and ideas on hold for the first year. The most important thing to do during this time is to develop trusting relationships and to learn more about the current vision and goals that have already been established by the organization.

Building Relationships

Board

Many orchestras are governed by a board of directors. During your first year, systematically try to meet as many individual members of the board as possible. They will be flattered that you made the effort to know them better. Ask each of them why they are involved and what goals they hope the organization will accomplish in the next five years. You will probably discover that the answers will be very personal and will vary tremendously. Keep notes regarding what you have learned. During these conversations, you may "test" a few new ideas, but spend most of the time just listening. If you don't have a board of directors, apply the same techniques to the parents' organization, if it is a youth orchestra, or to the other faculty members if you are working at a university.

Orchestra

Next, meet with as many of the principal players in the orchestra as possible. If time allows, try to do this separate from the orchestra's regular rehearsals. This can be done individually or in small groups of similar instruments. Your goal is to learn more about each person's personal expectations and their history with the orchestra. If appropriate, have them assess the strengths and weaknesses of their section. Also, ask *them* where they would like the orchestra to be in four to five years. Make sure that you really listen to the answers. Don't spend time telling them about the wonderful things you have done with other orchestras; they are only concerned with *their* orchestra. If you are working in a university setting your role will be more of a teacher/student relationship than a colleague relationship but it is still important to develop a good rapport with your musicians and to discover ways to motivate them to perform at their highest level.

Staff

Spend time talking with the staff to see what types of things have been tried in the past: what has worked, what has failed, and why. This might be a paid staff, a volunteer staff, or student helpers. It is especially important that you work closely with the people performing the duties of librarian, stage manager, and personnel manager. In some situations, you will be directly supervising these people. Assess their capacity to take on new projects and assess their tolerance for change. Having a good relationship with the staff is important because they will be the people who will eventually implement change throughout the organization. A solid relationship with the people who work behind the scenes will facilitate everything you do.

Community

If you are conducting a youth orchestra, community orchestra, or regional orchestra, it is very important in your first year that you get to know the community that surrounds your orchestra. You should work with the executive director, the president of the board, or the head of the parents association to develop a list of people to meet. This list should cover four categories: community leaders, music educators, current top-level donors for the symphony, and other possible new donors. If you are with a youth or community orchestra, you will probably set up the meetings and make the introductions yourself. If you are music director of a regional orchestra, the introductions should be set up through members of the board and through the office. It is important to establish these relationships in the community early during your tenure. You should make it a goal to have met everyone on the list by the end of the first year.

All of this will take time. As a conductor, you are probably not used to spending time in this manner. I cannot stress enough how important it is to spend the time learning about the organization and building a trusting relationship with everyone involved. It is the foundation upon which everything will be built. Ultimately, if you want to be successful as an artistic leader, you simply cannot afford not to do this.

Process of Change

Begin the process of change *slowly.* Once you have begun to see an intersection of goals and ideas, you can begin to formulate and prioritize the artistic vision for the orchestra. You will want to spend a lot of time with the executive director as you further define the areas to move forward in. It is most effective if you can present ideas together to the board where you have anticipated every concern. You will need the executive director's full support for any projects or programming challenges that you wish to undertake. Everything you propose should be in alignment with what you have learned about the board, the orchestra, and the staff. Make sure that you also spend time analyzing past concert programs and outreach activities. This will give you a better idea of where your audience is, and what type of expectations they have for the organization.

Unless the organization is in complete disarray, you should not implement major organizational changes or new initiatives in the first six months or so. Allow yourself time to learn about the organization so that you can be sure that you are moving in the right direction. The only time I would change this philosophy is if you have accepted a job with an orchestra that is disorganized, with rapidly falling subscription sales and in immediate need of a major transfusion of funds. These types of situations call for immediate creative programming and new outreach programs that will stimulate community interest and increase fund-raising capacity.

First Season

Assess Your Audience

With most orchestras, you will inherit either a completely planned season or a partially planned one. It is frustrating when you are starting a new job to not be able to demonstrate your programming creativity right from the start. Work closely with the executive director and the board chair, or the department chair of the university, to evaluate if any personalization of the concert programs is possible. You want to make sure that you are able to meet the expectations of your long-term audience members, and not come across to the community as if you are changing things at the last minute. If the programming is already planned, it is best to leave it and to get through the year as best as you can. If only the soloists are confirmed and you are in a position to select the remainder of the repertoire, make sure that you have studied the past programming philosophy so that you are in alignment with most of your audience's listening level and expectations. To perform a large work beyond their current expectation or comfort level is not a good thing to do in your first season. You will only alienate people before you start. It is best to create interesting and exciting programs exactly at their expectation level during your first season. This will allow you to develop trust. Later on, you can put in place the plan to expand the audience's listening skills and to take them where you want to go.

Do Not Reaudition the Orchestra

Some conductors are asked by the board or by the executive director if they would like to re-audition the orchestra when they begin the job. To do this is the "kiss of death." When you announce that you want to reaudition the orchestra, you will erect instant walls of distrust and fear between you and the current members of the orchestra. And what would you really accomplish if you did require everyone to audition? You certainly are not going to terminate a large portion of your orchestra. The fact is, you will accomplish very little. It is best to work with the orchestra for the first year and to spend that time assessing the strengths and weaknesses of each player. You will be able to tell as you conduct who is not playing up to your standard. It is best not to put any players on probation during your first year as a conductor of a new orchestra. They are still trying to get accustomed to you, your conducting technique, and your artistic standards. Besides this, you will need a year or so to assess the level of players available in your community and the surrounding areas. Every orchestra is limited by its pay scale, but often, no matter how much you pay, if you are a long way from a major city, your pool of excellent players will be limited. At the end of your first year or into your second year, you can begin to have individual meetings with specific players to see if they can improve. Because everyone's situation will be different, it is best to deal individually with each person rather than requiring a mass audition. Remember to keep good notes of issues and to create an environment where people are treated fairly and given every opportunity to achieve.

Prioritizing Your Time

Many conductors fail during their first year because they are suddenly faced not only with the task of preparing a lot of music for concerts but also with large administrative responsibilities. There will be many demands on your time during your first season. You will be called on to attend more meetings than normal and extra time will be spent with marketing and publicity opportunities. It is important that you make this time available to the organization, but you also have to know when to say no. You always must reserve enough time for yourself so you have time to properly prepare for the concerts. It is important for you to make this priority clear to the board and the staff. Never lose sight of the fact that the music is the major focus of your job. Everything else is important, but not critical. Sometimes just asking them to move a meeting to a time after the concert will release the pressure and provide the extra time you need for your preparation. Also, discourage the organization from scheduling your meetings right before rehearsals. You need time to regroup and focus so that your thoughts can be centered totally on the music.

Your Leadership Role on the Team

Make sure that you spend your first year in the job bonding with the executive director and the president of the board or the chairman of your department. It is very important that you are all on the same page. Some of this time should be during formal meetings but also take the time to meet informally over dinner or at social events. Strive to know the people behind the job titles. This is a relationship that is critical, not only for your personal success but also for the success of the entire organization.

GETTING ORGANIZED
Time Management

If you become a conductor, there will always be many demands on your time. First and foremost, it is important that you have enough time to study your scores. In order to do this, you must be very good at controlling the use of your time. In anyone's life, there are important issues, as opposed to issues that are urgent. You must be able to assess the difference quickly so that you can identify the best use of your time to accomplish your goals.

Urgent versus Important

If you haven't yet developed a really clear view of who you are and where you want to go, it is easy to get distracted into dealing with the supposedly urgent, but unimportant matters. Often, these issues are important to others, so there is a lot of pressure for you to deal with them. We are lured into spending our precious time solving little situations and problems that have no real lasting impact on our long-term goals. Train yourself to deal only with important issues. If something is important, it moves you toward your goals and ties in with your mission. Deal first with issues that are both urgent and important. Then concentrate the majority of your time and energy on items that are important but not urgent. Time spent in this fashion will develop your perspective for your long-term musical vision and move you toward your long-term musical goals. Often we put off what is truly important because it is not urgent. We run around seeming to look very busy, but at the end of the day, what have we really accomplished?

Relationships and Results

In dealing with time management, the other area to concentrate on is your relationships with other people. So often we are taught to use our time efficiently and told not to waste it socializing. But as conductors, all of our music-making is created and heard through other people. It is critical that you allow time to develop and nurture your personal relationships with the musicians, the staff, and your colleagues. Preserving and enhancing these relationships will allow you to be more successful in the end. This will have a larger impact on your overall success than that immaculately clean office desk, or the fact that you finished everything on your to-do list.

Proper Tools and Work Space

As you begin your career as a conductor, you will need specific tools to do your job. Set up an office area that is conducive to creative study. The type of space you work in is important to the quality of work that you produce. It should afford a lot of light and be a room that you like to spend time in, and be both comfortable and productive. Your office should have a ready supply of various types of paper, stationery, and mailing supplies. This will save you from having to make a trip to the store every time you need single items. You also will need many bookcases and file cabinets for your score collection, your research books, and reference CDs and recordings. The paper work you accumulate as a music director is tremendous. It is helpful to develop a filing system early on that enable you to deal with the massive amounts of paper, press packets, and new scores that will arrive on your desk.

Time-Saving Procedures

Everyone is given the same twenty-four hours in a day, and yet some people achieve so much more than others. Why is this true? In reality, what is important is not the amount of time that you spend working each day, but how much you actually accomplish. To ensure that you make the *best* use of your time, here are a few timesaving tips:

E-Mail

Be clear with the office regarding the types of issues on which you need to be copied

Organize your e-mail into folders

Work folder—everyday important items

Industry e-mails—all trade e-mails, or e-mail lists, or newsletters

Personal e-mails

Limit the time you allow yourself to be on the Internet to one hour per day

Tell the musicians, the staff, and your colleagues that you check your e-mail once a day at a specified time. If they need to reach you about important items at other times, they should phone

Paperwork

Concentrate on accomplishing major goals, not on finishing paperwork

Keep only one project on your desk at a time

Only handle each piece of paper once—throw it out, or file it

Avoid all unnecessary paper

Master dictating and pay someone to type your letters

Use the phone and learn to keep your conversations short

Never spend time doing something you can have someone else do—delegate!

Phone

Return phone calls in a timely manner

Leave detailed messages so that a response is not always necessary

Time your conversations so you can see how you utilize your time

Keep the conversation related to the specific topic you called about

When possible, return your phone calls personally—this will strengthen your network

Delegating

Delegating is part of being a leader. No one can possibly do everything themselves. A good leader knows how to delegate effectively. When you are delegating a project—like the researching of a community-wide Beethoven Festival, the forming of a new civic chorus, or perhaps just requesting that the librarian research the cost and availability of the repertoire for the following season—be sure that you first clarify and prioritize exactly what you want to have done. This will help the person you have assigned to do the task know what you expect. It is important that you assign the "right" person to the job so that the required skill set matches the strengths of the person involved. If you assign the wrong person, not only will the job not get done, but you will also have a demoralized person whose attitude will affect others. Once you have selected the person and they have agreed to the task, they will need you to explain the "big picture" before they begin. This will enable them to keep focused on what is truly important to you and to the organization. Allow them time to ask you questions about the project before they start so you are sure they understand exactly what you want them to accomplish. As you are clarifying the issues, you can also help define the timeline and the deadlines that you expect to be met. After the job has been explained, it is important that you give them the full authority and responsibility for getting the project completed, and that they verbally accept this responsibility.

Timely follow-up is a key to successful delegation. After you have assigned a project, don't just forget about it and move on to other things. You will need to check back with the person or group of people periodically to make sure they are moving forward on the goals and to see if they need any additional help. As projects are completed, you will want to review the results with them, both positive and negative. It is important to be generous with your rewards and to publicly compliment people for a job well done.

Take time to develop a system for delegating. If you can afford it, it is good to hire a personal secretary to do your weekly paperwork so you can spend your time on more important things like score study. Remember, if someone else can do it, have them complete the task. As you are working with the orchestra staff or the board, if someone throws a problem at you, develop the ability to toss it right back with a few suggestions on how they can solve it themselves. This deflection skill is dependent upon your knowing what your *own* job is. This way you won't waste time on details that belong to others. Try to minimize interruptions and focus your concentration on your primary responsibilities. This is the only way that you will be able to stay on top of the administrative as well as the musical responsibilities of being a music director.

Scheduling Your Day

Score Study

Reserve a block of at least two to three hours daily for score study. Just as an instrumentalist practices daily, so you must study. This should be at a time when you are fresh. (I prefer the morning hours.) During that time, do not answer the telephone or allow yourself to be distracted with other paperwork. Tell everyone that you will not be available during these specific hours each day. Block your study time into sections of one hour or less; changing the piece you are studying each hour or so will help to keep your mind fresh. You might be familiar with the score study outline that is used by the Brussels Conservatory and also the Paris Conservatory. This entails going through a composition multiple times in order to master it. Each time you work through the score you focus on a different area:

1. Instrumentation and transpositions
2. Tempos and tempo relationships
3. Form analysis of the composition
4. Harmonic structural analysis
5. Melodic line analysis
6. Study of the phrasing and inner relationships
7. Dynamics, phrase climaxes, and specific articulations
8. Identification of special effects and possible problem spots

As you can tell, this process is quite time-consuming. You will want to make notes of major melodies and themes, harmonic charts, and structural graphs for each piece. A thorough knowledge of the score is the only way that you will be successful as a conductor. Make sure that you reserve the time in your schedule to properly prepare for your concerts.

Planning Time

You should spend a little time each evening reviewing what you accomplished that day and preparing your list for the following day and the rest of the week. By doing this in the evening, you start the next day with your goals clearly set in your mind. During your planning time, prioritize your activities so that you are concentrating on the most important tasks. Develop a chart of your concert dates and which pieces have to be prepared for each rehearsal. Your planning should reflect gradual progress on many pieces at the same time. This keeps you focused during your study time and allows for better absorption of the material.

Organizational Time

I prefer to do my paperwork and phone calling in the early afternoon, when my concentration level is lowest. Most paperwork is "process" work and does not require a lot of creativity. Put a limit on the amount of time you are going to spend on paperwork each day, or it will expand to fit the time that you have available (like all afternoon). Group "like" tasks so that they can be done even more quickly. For example, I always listen and respond to sample CDs and résumés from potential guest artists and new composers about once a month. Until then, I keep everything in a box so that it does not clutter my work space. After listening to each CD, I dictate a response letter, and then I throw out everything, unless it is an artist with whom I want to work in the next year or two. I collect these press packets in a special "guest artist" file.

Meetings

As a conductor, you will be asked to attend many meetings and fund-raising events. Depending on the size of your organization, this might become overwhelming. Avoid agreeing to be present at every meeting you are asked to attend; assess whether your attendance at the meeting is necessary. Do you have information that needs to be conveyed? Is this the only way this information can be communicated? Is this the best way to get this information out to other people? Do others attending the meeting have information that you need to know? Are there other ways to get this information? Does the meeting relate directly to how you perform your job? If you are not at the meeting, will it be interpreted that you don't care, or that you don't want to be involved? Are there ways of changing this perception?

Work closely with your board chairperson, executive director, and volunteer committee members so that everyone understands what types of meetings are the most efficient use of your time. Make sure you express your willingness to do whatever is necessary for the organization, but that your major focus must remain on the artistic product.

Recreation

As a conductor, you often will work on evenings and weekends. Even though you are busy, block out some time every week just for you. It may seem that you can't spare this time, but it is essential to creating a balanced life and to allowing yourself moments to reflect. Without this, your interpretation of the music could become stilted and mechanical. After taking time off, you will find that you return to your daily tasks with a renewed vigor and commitment.

Chapter 4

Artistic Leadership

Understanding Leadership
Leadership Styles

Leadership requires two things: someone to lead and someone to follow. Just because you want to be a leader and think that you have good ideas does not mean that anyone will automatically follow you. The art of leadership is an art of persuasion. All great leaders know where they are going and they are able to persuade others to follow them. They can do this through two different types of leadership power: the power of position, or the power of trust.

Power of Position

The power of position is one of the most basic types of leadership. It is used by leaders who take control because they have the positional authority to command, reprimand, or fire if things are not done to their satisfaction. This is the manner in which many of the great maestros of the past functioned. Because they were the "music directors," their commands were unquestionable by the orchestra members. Some even resorted to intimidation and fear as their means of accomplishing their goals. People followed, not always because they wanted to, but because they *had* to. They did not trust the leader, nor did the leader trust the followers.

Unfortunately, examples of this type of leadership are still present in our field, and some conductors are taught early on that this is the means to their greatness. Although this type of leadership has worked in the past, due to the restructuring of unions and the structure of most orchestras' administrative staffs, this is no longer a viable way to move one's career, or an organization, forward.

Power of Trust

To be great leaders today, we must select and master the more difficult but more effective type of leadership power, the power of "respect and trust" that comes from the coworkers themselves and is entrusted to the leader. This type of leadership is based upon inspiring people to work for you when they are not obligated. Everyone wants to be led by leaders who have knowledge and expertise, but they also need to be led by people they can trust. They will follow you because of what you have done for them personally, they will follow you because of what you are doing or have done for the organization, and, finally, they will follow you because of who you are and the values that you represent. Leaders empower people. You cannot accomplish great goals for an organization without many people working together towards those goals; you cannot make great music without inspiring 100 percent from your orchestra; and you cannot lead people without loving them.

Some conductors are afraid of their orchestras—afraid they will be questioned; afraid that they might be wrong; afraid that the musicians will not want to cooperate; afraid that their imperfections will be exposed. To hide their fears, they flaunt overconfidence and sometimes put others down in order to make themselves look good. A leader cannot lead if they are afraid. The leader has to be vulnerable, willing to fail and able to admit their mistakes. A leader must lead through trust, not intimidation. Inclusive leadership forgoes superficiality. It is based upon a relationship that allows people to be involved and fully accountable. Some of the traits of a good leader include the following:

- Excellent leaders lead by example—they are energetic, enthusiastic, and confident. They are able to use persuasion to help people see what is in it for them.
- All leaders are totally committed to the organization and the overall vision. They are able to stay focused on the major goals.
- Leaders inspire others and they care about the people they work with. They are able to delegate to people and they are consistent with their follow-up.
- Leaders consider the "right" people in each position their most valuable asset. They show appreciation and respect.
- Leaders embrace change and see it as a great opportunity.

I read a very important quote early on in my career—and it has stuck with me. "People don't care how much you know until they know how much you care" (*Reflections for Managers* by Bruce Hyland and Merle Yost, p. 2). Remember, as a conductor, you do not personally create any sound; you rely fully on your orchestra to produce what you hear in your head. Keep this in mind the next time you are about to berate a player in front of other members of the orchestra.

Steps to Becoming a Successful Leader
Meeting Individual Needs

Effective leadership is based on relationships. A successful leader needs only two things: (1) knowledge of what followers want or need, and (2) a spirit of excitement and commitment that energizes people. To be successful as a leader, you need to make those who work with you more successful. You need to identify—what is in it for them? People are concerned first and foremost with themselves. They often can't concentrate on the good of the whole unless their own needs are being met. Some of these individual needs might include:

> The need for security
> The need to be appreciated, thanked, and rewarded
> The need to be able to control their future
> The need to be held accountable for their actions
> The need to be part of something larger than themselves

As you work with your orchestra, you must ask yourself: How can I incorporate activities for the musicians that might meet some of these needs? How can I change the way I deal with individual musicians to reflect these issues? Often, the repertoire and the organizational goals are just fleetingly presented to the orchestra members. Playing music is their future, yet often they are the last to be involved in organizational changes. As you develop your skills as a music director, I encourage you to explore avenues for further involvement of your orchestra members. Try experimenting with surveys regarding what repertoire they would like to perform and involve the players in long-range planning for the organization.

Strive to get to know your players personally. Take time to learn all their names. Try to find out about their families, how many children they have, and what the names of their spouses or significant others are. Honor your orchestra members by knowing their personal likes and dislikes. Remember, if problems occur in the workplace, it might not be about work at all, but rather be reflective of other larger (and perhaps more critical) problems in an individual's personal life. People deal with death, pain, illness, and other challenges every day. Take the time to listen, and try to see the world first from their eyes.

Players usually want to do their best, but as standards rise in an organization, there may be a variety of artistic levels that people feel are acceptable. Periodically, have little prodding conversations with players to encourage excellence in a supportive way and to develop systems of accountability. Try to do this before problems become larger. Good leadership requires asking the right questions, setting the right standard, and giving the right assistance. It is your job to help everyone be successful.

It is the leader's job not only to set the standard but also to make it easy for your orchestra members to do their work at the highest possible level. Ask them what they really need to be successful in their jobs. Do they need the music earlier? Do they need more places to warm up before rehearsals? Do they need sample recordings of unfamiliar works to help them prepare better? Do they need more light on stage? Do they need better instruments? Do they need a new shell on the stage? Do they need more risers? Fewer risers? More restrooms? Remember, they might not all agree, but just going through this process with the musicians will go far toward building a better relationship. Work with them in trying to prioritize these needs into categories such as: "essential," "important," "would be great if . . . ," or "could probably survive without . . . " In all of these discussions, the major focus should be on how you and the administration can give the musicians the tools to promote a higher caliber of musical performance. As a music director, you must be totally committed to this goal. It is only after you have given the orchestra all of the tools they need that you can hold them accountable for producing at the highest level.

Unifying Principles and Goals

Once you have identified individual needs within an organization and found ways of incorporating these into the overall goals, you then need to identify unifying principles and goals. These are items that transcend personal interests and that would universally be considered a high priority item by all the members of your organization. Perhaps you want to instill the goal of being the best orchestra in the region, or you want to do a European tour the following season. Are there items you could incorporate that would create a symbol of a united vision? Something as simple as providing the orchestra members with shirts showcasing the symphony's name with the byline "music for the region," goes a long way in developing pride in the organization. Or perhaps you could organize a fundraising concert to help raise the money for the European tour. Personal involvement is the key to personal buy-in with an organization. Find ways of sending the message, not only to the orchestra but to the entire community.

Energize, Inspire, and Empower

Creating positive energy and momentum in an organization is necessary for success. It is the leader's job to set the positive "can-do" attitude and to lead by example. It is easy for a music director to become burdened with too much work and too much pressure. Keep your own motivation and energy level high by taking time out for yourself. This will allow you to return to the project with renewed vigor. Encourage your players to do the same and you will avoid "burnout" within the organization.

When working with musicians, be sure to praise even the slightest improvements. Praise and recognition is one of the most powerful motivators. These actions will inspire others to keep striving toward excellence. Everyone loves to feel as though they are making progress, and they enjoy being rewarded and appreciated in front of others. We all work for money, but most will go the extra mile for recognition and praise. Take the time to celebrate the little triumphs, and inspire and empower the musicians to set and achieve their own artistic goals.

Institutional Values and Universal Purpose

Discovering Your Values

Institutional values are the fundamental qualities that define the way an institution does business and the way it wants to be perceived by the community. These values create hierarchies that influence priorities in terms of the allocation of the resources of time and money. They are a definitive statement about what is vitally important to the organization. An organization's values are universal and will not change over time. Usually an organization will have fewer than five main values. If, in trying to come to consensus on your value structure, you identify more than five items, chances are you are confusing values with goals. Some sample values for orchestras in the United States, as defined by those organizations are:

Cleveland Orchestra

> Individual and collective excellence
> Artistic integrity
> Always striving
> Tradition of continuity and stability
> A symbol of community pride

Saint Paul Chamber Orchestra

EXCELLENCE: Striving for peak performance individually and collectively throughout the organization

INTIMACY: Striving to create powerful, deep connections through music between and among performers and audiences; fostering close collaboration and respect among all internal constituencies

INNOVATION: Aspiring toward versatility and the ability to invent and do whatever is needed; being willing to risk failure

CONTINUITY: Aspiring intentionally to stay the course in pursuit of long-term goals, through thick and thin

Other values that you might commonly see associated with a not-for-profit organization are:

Common Nonprofit Values

> We make a contribution to society
> We are dedicated to quality
> We make life easier . . . better . . . more enjoyable . . .
> We value quality service
> Honesty and integrity

After you have identified your orchestra's main values, refine the list by asking the following questions: if financial circumstances changed, would this value still be important to the organization? If our current leadership changed—would it still be important? If we had to pick only one thing to stand for, would this be it? Is this particular value important to everyone in the organization? Would we ever want to produce concerts without this value?

From this process of elimination, you should be able to identify your three most important values. Once you have done this, you will need to revisit your purpose, or your primary reason for existence. Often this is done in organizations in terms of their mission statement. Be careful, however, because mission statements tend to be packed with "something for everybody." They may avoid centering on one true purpose. Of all the areas mentioned in your mission statement, what is the one item that your community would really miss if your orchestra did not exist? Use this to help you identify the most important thing that you do.

As a leader, you need to understand the values and the mission of the organization you work for. It is only through a complete understanding of these that you can eventually formulate a plan to move the organization forward. As you clarify these in your mind, be sure that the board, the orchestra, and the staff are coming to the same conclusions; then work to establish a group culture that constantly displays, reinforces, and encourages these values. Soon everyone will understand that "This is the way we do things around here." When everyone is on the same page, it is easier to strive toward and achieve common goals.

Conflicts of Values

Leaders are accountable for expressing the values of the organization and these values should be compatible with your own personal set of values. If you find that you are personally at odds with the organizational values of an institution or if the orchestra association is in any way corrupt, look to change jobs. Trying to work within a structure that is contrary to your personal values will damage you. This will affect your performance both as a musician and an employee, and it will be difficult for you to be a positive leader.

Developing Artistic Vision

The artistic vision for an organization incorporates why you exist, identifies where you currently are, and then focuses on where you want to be in the envisioned future. Your vision should be based upon goals that are not currently within your grasp. These should be concepts that the entire organization can support and rally around. Eventually, you must translate the vision from words on a page to a living description of how you will achieve these goals. But how do you come up with a unified vision of where the organization should be in ten to twenty years? Most orchestras start by converting the mission statement into specifics and by trying to improve upon what they are already doing. Others evaluate the needs of the community and assess where they can really make a difference. Still others might identify what they do the best and try to focus upon similar types of activities. As you work toward envisioning your future, it helps to first develop an artistic profile: What type of music do you play? Where do you perform? And what would you like to improve on? This profile will keep you centered as you discuss realistic plans for the future and develop your long-range plan.

Ideally, the focus and direction of your long-range plan for the organization will be the measuring stick from which everything is judged. It will dictate and clarify artistic programming decisions; it will control the expansion activities of the organization; and it will help you decide where to spend your time and your money in order to move you closer to your goals. The important thing in remaining focused as an organization is to pursue only what is essential to the "big picture."

Setting up the Vision

As you begin to develop your institutional vision, you need to identify who should be involved in the process. Often, it is good to start with some general brainstorming sessions. You might want to involve members from the orchestra, board of directors or faculty, office staff, volunteers, donors, and ticket purchasers. Start with a specific assessment of your current artistic profile, and then allow people to dream a little about the possibilities of the future. At this point, do not allow anyone to limit their thinking due to lack of organizational resources, space, or time. It is only after all ideas are expressed that you should prioritize and select the best ideas for the envisioned future.

To discern the detailed components of the organizational plan, however, you will need a much smaller group. Make sure that you get the "right" people involved who can really help to move the institution forward, both artistically and organizationally. It is the collective vision of the three centers of leadership (orchestra/music director; staff/executive director; and community/board chair) that must balance and ultimately determine the future direction of the orchestra.

Once the direction has been set by this committee, it is critical that the vision concepts be translated into a vividly exciting expression of what the organization will become. This written document should be continually revisited as goals are achieved along the way. At this point, you must strive to develop "ownership" and build bridges between steps on the overall plan of the organization and each individual's goals. "What is in it for them?" Remember, people are concerned first and foremost about themselves, and secondly about the good of a cause greater than themselves. You will need to draw upon the commonality of a shared set of values. To be ultimately successful you should paint them a beautiful picture of what could be. Let them see it, understand it, appreciate it, and ultimately "own" it.

Setting Goals

As you define the specific goals for the organization, test them against your values and purpose. Are they in alignment? It is also important to make sure that your goals are achievable and that your time line is realistic. In goal-setting, two different models are often followed. The first takes one step forward at a time. This type of planning will move you forward, but depending on *where* you choose to step each time, you may end in a different place than where you wanted to be.

The other, more effective, way of outlining your goals is deciding where you are, outlining where you want to be, and then working backward to create a plan of manageable steps to achieve your ultimate goal.

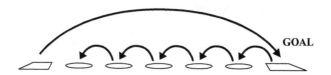

Goals should be large and just outside of reach—a great "stretch" for the organization. Things such as expanding to double concerts, commissioning a new composition, or adding a resident string quartet can be very exciting goals for an orchestra. Beware, however, if a goal is too large or overwhelming; instead of creating excitement and energy, it might actually create dissension and discouragement. Therefore, it is important to break your larger goals down into achievable activities. It is the leader's job to always maintain forward motion by defining intermediary goals that are enticing, but just barely out of reach. Perhaps your string quartet is only in residence for a month the first year, and then two months the second year, and so forth. As you succeed with your intermediary goal, you will build more support for the final goal of having the quartet in residence permanently.

Dealing with Change and Assessing Risk

Change

As with any process, achieving a new vision will involve both change and risk. This will cause fear, reluctance, and concerns within your organization. Artistic leadership is about change. It is about improving and moving the organization forward. In working with your orchestra, you must remember that most people view change as a threat and that resistance to change is normal. Any type of change, both positive and negative, is personally stressful. Because of this, people tend to encourage and support sameness and predictability within an organization.

Your orchestra, staff, and board members will resist change for a variety of reasons. It is important for you to identify the center of their resistance so that you know best how to move them past this level. The first, instinctive reaction to something new is always the fear of the unknown. To combat this, try to provide as much information as possible about the effects of the change proposed, both on the individuals involved and the group as a whole. If the person's individual routine is going to be disrupted because you are changing the entire rehearsal and concert schedule and they were not given a say in the process, they will undoubtedly resist. If you want to move the concerts from Thursday night (which has been Symphony night for the last twenty years) to Saturday night in order to attract new subscribers, you had better involve your audience and orchestra members early in the process if you want them to support it. Often, people will not understand why a change is necessary, or why they need to deviate from "how we have always done it." Tradition is a formidable obstacle to change. You will have to explain how the new concert schedule will position the orchestra for potential larger audiences in the future, which will create more fund-raising possibilities, which will support the programming of larger works and wage increases for the musicians, which will then help you to attract and retain a higher caliber of player.

Other reasons for resisting change may center on an individual's fear of failing; the fear of personal loss of position or money; or the inability of the musician to make the effort required. This problem often occurs when a new music director sets an artistic standard that is substantially higher than what was acceptable in the past. Often, you will have to move forward with very small steps so that this fear factor is reduced and you don't totally destroy your rapport with the orchestra as you strive to improve the quality level. Change and new levels of expectation require a solid base of respect and trust between the people involved. Make sure that you have worked with your orchestra long enough to earn that trust before you start moving musicians around and proposing new ideas.

As you are asking members of the organization to take ownership of new concepts, activities, or actions, you must assess what is holding them back. Are their concerns financial? Or are they worried about the manpower required to achieve the goal? Perhaps there are historical concerns that you are not aware of. It is important that you understand the history of the organization, past successes and failures, and that you do not deviate from its core mission. In order to be effective you must create a climate that is open and supportive and encourages dialogue about the new ideas. As the members begin to understand the reason for the proposed actions and as they see their input incorporated, they will begin to support the new directions. Small accomplishments go a long way in confirming that the changes you proposed were justified. Make sure that the first few things you suggest are guaranteed successes and avoid changing too many things at one time.

Once people are no longer afraid to change, you will notice that a general process occurs. Over time, they will move forward through each of these phases into finally accepting and embracing organizational change.

Phases of Change

Conflict	Individuals within the organization cannot see the reasons or benefits for changing.
Awareness	People begin to understand the benefits involved.
Acceptance	You experience buy-in and the input of ideas regarding the change.
Commitment	Staff, board, or musicians make the commitment to change themselves.
Impact	All the individual changes begin to have effect throughout the organization.
Reassessment	Time must be spent analyzing what is working and what is not.
Success	You see the results of the change and the organization's goals are achieved.

Assessing Goals

As you develop artistic goals and objectives for your orchestra, encourage discussions regarding how best to meet these goals and how to assess new ideas. As a music director, you will be constantly approached with concert ideas, collaborations, and growth opportunities for the organization. In the process of analyzing new ideas, before you make a decision, you might ask the following questions:

> What are the positive and negative aspects of this idea?
> How does this idea move us forward toward our long-range goals?
> Does this idea fit with our values and with what is important to us?
> Are the possible advantages so great that it must be considered further?
> Are the negative issues so great that we should not go further?
> Is this an opportunity or a hindrance?

Assessing Risk

Every new idea or project involves a certain amount of risk, and each person in your organization has a certain tolerance for risk. In order to move the organization forward, you will have to identify a median level of risk that most members of your orchestra or board will accept. As you are assessing the risk level for an important decision, ask yourself: Is this a risk that we can afford to take? Do we have the money, the manpower, and the artistic credibility to be successful? If the answer is "no," then you should move on. There are, however, situations in which the risk level is great but the envisioned future of the organization is dependent on this change. Sometimes, in order to be successful, you have to dramatically alter the way you do things. This might require more resources than you have available at the time. Not to move forward, however, would be the wrong decision. In these cases, you have to step forward boldly and trust that the organization will make it happen. If, however, everyone agrees too quickly on an issue that is large and risky, *do not* make an immediate decision. Adjourn the meeting and give people more time to think. If there is not some discussion of contention when large organizational changes are proposed, then people are not taking the decision seriously. Important decisions *should* be somewhat controversial and it is important for everyone to know what they are committing themselves to accomplish.

Implementation

It is important to discuss the implementation of any project before the final decision is made to move forward. You will need to identify how things will be accomplished and by whom. If you decide that you want the orchestra to spearhead a community Beethoven Festival, be sure to select someone to be accountable for the project and help them to organize a work plan, goals, and specific deadlines. It is important that everyone fully understands what is being asked of them. If possible, "test" the idea with other community members before you make your full commitment to move ahead. Along with the testing stage, establish an emergency plan. Some projects fail to come together, no matter how hard you try. Think through fall-back alternatives ahead of time and be ready to implement them if the original idea does not work out.

As the years pass and the organization moves forward, continue to analyze your past activities and programs. Do these programs still serve a need? Are these the right activities to continue to spend time and money on? Are you still producing outstanding results and impacting people's lives? It is important to always evaluate and fine-tune the future direction of your organization. Once you've joined an organization, made your changes, and established your style of doing things, you too can get stuck in that rut of "we've always done it this way."

Negative Change

Sometimes the organization will change in directions that you do not support such as moving to a pops concert format, or changing from a full symphony into a chamber orchestra. When this happens, you first need to refer back to the values and vision of the organization. Are these new ideas in alignment with the organization's core values? Who is pushing for the change, and why? Is it financially driven? How strong is your own support base within the organization? Is this a battle worth fighting, or are there better uses of your time? Any time you go against organizational change, you use up tremendous amounts of energy. If the issue at hand is small and inconsequential, learn to be flexible and learn to change for the good of the whole, even if you do not personally believe in this change. It is best to pick your fights carefully and to not risk winning the battle, but losing the war. If, however, the change in the organization's direction is in direct conflict with your personal core values, or in direct conflict with the current artistic goals, you have a larger problem. First, you must rally your followers to see if you have the support system to go against the current trend. Patience and perseverance are necessary, and, obviously, good diplomatic skills. Work with those closest to you to persuade them to your way of thinking. If your thoughts resonate with the values and mission of the orchestra, this should be easy. Let them move through the organization and gather followers who can help refocus the mission. If your ideas are in alignment with the vision and you can accurately express your concerns over the current direction and define why it is not in alignment, then you will have a good chance of succeeding. If, however, you do not have good relationships within the organization, or if the organization is split in its understanding of the future direction, you might want to look for another position.

In order to lead, you must have followers, and people must want to follow you in the direction you are leading. You can easily destroy an organization by encouraging feuding within its various constituents. Then all attention and energy is used up for the fight and there is nothing left for moving the organization forward. Be careful never to turn the board members against each other or actively help to create dissension within an organization, no matter how strongly you feel about an issue. This will only weaken the organization and create instability for the future.

The Leadership Team

As a music director, you are directly accountable for the artistic vision of an organization, but you will work closely with the executive director and the board chair regarding the overall institutional vision. It is important that this leadership team be cohesive and aligned. Together, you will be able to move the organization to new heights. Make the time to meet regularly to assess how the organization is doing on its institutional goals. This will also allow for feedback from all parties regarding where resources are being allocated and how this is helpful or detrimental in the pursuit of approved goals. As you work as a team to move the organization forward, there is a progression of strategies and actions that will make the transition happen more smoothly. Here are some steps that a leadership team should keep in mind as they develop a united vision for the organization:

Step 1

>   Identify and survey stakeholders
>   S.W.O.T—Analyze strengths, weaknesses, opportunities, and threats
>   Identify unifying themes
>   Define everyone's self-interests

Step 2

>   Identify values and overall vision
>   Communicate this vision to all of the stakeholders

Step 3

>   Define and allocate resources (prioritize)
>   Research and seek out best practices
>   Identify one or two unifying projects to build followers
>   Create an action plan

Step 4

> Implement the plan
> Assess results
> Reward people

Remember, the sum of the parts is always more powerful than the whole. If you can empower those in your circle to share values, share a vision, and to work toward common goals, you will truly be able to make a difference as a leader. By being an effective artistic leader, you will experience more success in achieving your musical goals and you will be able to have a lasting impact on the people that you work with. To be a music director, you must fully understand, support, and bring to fruition the artistic vision of the orchestra that you conduct. It is only then that music can truly make a difference in a community.

THOUGHTS ABOUT ARTISTIC VISION

Interview: Leonard Slatkin, Saint Louis Symphony/National Symphony

"Everyone working together to make the
vision a reality"—*Leonard Slatkin*

Creating Vision

Vision is a perfect word. If you are hired to be the head of an organization, hopefully, it's not just because of your skills as a conductor but because of what you envision for the organization. In your new position, you have to explain your vision to the administration and the board. You need to tell them "This is what I have in mind. This is why you hired me." If eventually your own vision and your own goals are not the same as theirs, then you have to face the fact that perhaps you shouldn't be there any longer, or you shouldn't be there at all. Unless everyone gets on the same page and sees what those goals are, then you are not going to accomplish much.

A lot of orchestras today do not have a clear idea of where they want to be five to ten years from now. They are worried about whether they are going to have an audience next week, or how they will raise the money for payroll. These are important things to worry about, but the bigger issue is, where do they want to be in the future and how are they going to get there? What are the objective and goals?

I went back to Saint Louis after my time in New Orleans, and the reason it worked was not just because I had this idea for the orchestra about where I thought it should be going, but because the executive director and the artistic administrator also saw it the same way. Frequently we were at odds with each other, but at the core, we all had the same end goals. We wanted the orchestra to have exposure in specific new repertoire nationally and internationally; at home we wanted to have a broad-based repertoire that would serve the Saint Louis area; and I wanted to grow the orchestra in terms of having an individual and unique sound. The three of us worked very hard for many, many years to try to achieve these goals. Most people will say that we did. We put ourselves on the map because we had a focus. We knew what we wanted to accomplish.

I don't take credit for that alone. I worked closely with the executive director and the artistic administrator. It was done as a group with everyone working together to make the vision a reality. One person cannot make an orchestra successful. You have to be a team player in the sense that you work with the people in management, and together, you bring your board along. The three, together pushing for the same goals, are the ones that drive the board. The board often doesn't realize that you are leading them. This is what we call leadership. Leadership of the orchestra, leadership of the board, and leadership of the community is essential to the vision.

Artistic Programming

With both the Saint Louis Symphony and the National Symphony, trying to expand the American repertoire became important as part of the core vision. Championing new composers, many who have gone on to be quite successful, has been very satisfying for me. Understanding the importance of the creative process in this country as well as in Europe was also something I emphasized. With the orchestra here in Washington, D.C., the nation's capital, we have a mandate to play music of our own country as well as presenting as many American solo artists as we can. I keep this in mind as I plan each season.

Identifying Strengths and Weaknesses

As you work to establish the objectives and goals to make your vision a reality, you need to make a list. Write down your strengths and your weakness, and then write down your *real* weaknesses. After that, identify what you want to achieve. How do assign your strengths to achieve your goals? How do you shore up the weaknesses that you need to achieve your goals? And what weaknesses do you have that you don't think you can ever change? Everyone needs to do this. Everyone needs to assess not only the organization they work for, but themselves. I do a self-evaluation all the time. You have to be honest with yourself: What can you do? What can't you do? Not just as a musician, but as a person. Your life is not just about the music, although sometimes we wish it was. You don't want to be a different person on the podium and off the podium. Part of your strengths in any organizational situation is assessing your own personal strengths and weakness as well as your musical ones.

Interview: Robert Spano, Atlanta Symphony

"I don't think vision is something one
creates in a vacuum"—*Robert Spano*

Creating Vision

I feel that my role as a music director is to create artistic vision for an institution, but not unilaterally. In Atlanta, we have these fantastic meetings where we have a lot of the staff present when we do our planning. We call it the "War Room," which we started saying because in the film *Dr. Strangelove*, there is that wonderful line, "Gentlemen, you can't fight in here, this is the war room." In this room we have the executive director, the general manager, the marketing director, the education director, the artistic administrator, the vice president of development, and my assistant.

During the discussion, we all bring what we know from members of the orchestra, members of the chorus, members of the board, of the volunteers, and we talk about their interests, concerns, and desires. Together, we bring a lot of perspective to the table. I think, for a music director, it is incumbent upon us to know our constituency. Who are the parties involved? And what do we all want? After that, we have to bring it into focus and give it shape.

There is a great line in John Cage's "Lecture On Nothing": "Form without life is dead, but life without form is unseen." It is up to us to understand all of the messages that we are getting from all of these parties, and to sift through them to come up with something that is real. What I have found very valuable in working in this committee way is that we have a shared vision at the end of this process. We all came to these things together and it gives a kind of an institutional unity about what is going on and why that is commonly understood by all of us. I find that very powerful because I don't think vision is something that one creates in a vacuum.

I feel incredibly lucky because both in Brooklyn and now in Atlanta, I've had really great partners on the staff. I know that this is not always the case. I couldn't do it without them. Our executive director here brings such a wealth of experience and perspective and understanding to all of the aspects of what we are doing that I am least equipped to deal with—matters of money and ticket sales. We talk all the time and we have very common causes and we play our respective roles to achieve those goals. It is a critical relationship. That is why we have so many different skill sets to run an orchestra. We need the input of all these people to make the whole thing work. It is important for me to know what is going on so that I can do my part of the process.

The other aspect you need for the artistic vision of an organization is community buy-in. In Atlanta, I get involved in the program copy for the season brochure and the concert press releases because I enjoy it, and I want the message to truly reflect the music. Another thing important to developing community buy-in is the public speaking. I go to colleges and high schools, and other groups throughout the area. I think that that is incredibly valuable.

Artistic Programming

The biggest issue for me then ends up being our programming, and trying to develop an institutional identity. What does the Atlanta Symphony Orchestra need to be, in the City of Atlanta, for the City of Atlanta, and for the cause of great music and great art? During our war room discussions, we write a lot of ideas down and we test our decisions against certain things we want to be satisfying. Every year, I will look at the season, from a number of angles. How much of the traditional repertoire is being sustained and presented? How much American music are we performing? How much diverse world music is programmed? How is the balance of the new and the old? The Atlanta Symphony is a flagship institution. We are very different then the Brooklyn Philharmonic, where the focus was upon trying to create a "niche" identity in a very competitive market.

As I am looking at the overall programming, there are things that I don't feel particularly interested in conducting that I know should be done. I know that I am not a Bruckner person, but other guest conductors can satisfy musical agendas that aren't suited to me. On the other hand, I am pretty eclectic and a lot of music does interest me. So, because of my voracious musical appetite, it is easy for me to satisfy my interests and still be doing a wide range of repertoire. I find that this way of looking at programming opens up things for me. For example, I don't generally do all-Beethoven concerts, but I do them here and I love doing them. For the Atlanta Symphony, an all-Beethoven concert is very appropriate in the larger diet of what we are doing.

Interview: JoAnn Falletta, Buffalo Philharmonic

"You create vision through enthusiasm and
passion about music"—*JoAnn Falletta*

Creating Vision

I believe that the music director is the person responsible for the spark of vision and mission that can galvanize an institution. You can accomplish this through your enthusiasm and your passion about music. People look to the music director to provide a special energy. You work with gifted people who create wonderful ideas, solutions and possibilities, inspired by the fact that *you* believe it can be done.

As you strive to create a unified artistic vision, you must always put the organization first—this is critical. The vision that we have must serve the orchestra to make it stronger, to make it more relevant to the community, and to make it a shining presence in a city or a region. If the music director is enthused, committed, and dedicated to the orchestra and to the possibilities for the orchestra, people will come on board. In this process, the executive director can be your strongest ally and you will work closely with him or her, but your enthusiasm needs to embrace the entire team. Whether the person is the finance director, or the intern who meets and greets artists, or the principal oboist, or a member of the violin section, you must help them know that they are important to creating success. Share the challenges and share the triumphs, too, because that spirit of cooperation will make a difference.

Artistic vision develops slowly. When you take over an orchestra as music director, you should delve into the history of the organization. You must understand the community. What have they enjoyed? What has been problematic? How do they feel about themselves? What is the self-image of the community as a whole? And what is the self-image of the orchestra? All of this is very important.

I have become more and more an advocate of slow careful building, rather than radical change. I think the changes that really matter take time. When you come into a new situation, you need to meet with as many of the constituents as possible. You need to talk to the board member who doesn't want to hear any music written after Brahms. You must meet with the mayor, who is not really sure that the community can support this orchestra. You should talk to every single "share-holder," sharing your vision.

Not everyone will agree, and you will hear many different ideas about what the orchestra should do. Should it be bigger, should it be smaller, should it do more education concerts, should it go to Carnegie Hall, should it start to record? In the long run, you have to make those decisions. But I think that if you have shared your ideas with the community, people can come to understand why you want to do something and may be willing to give it a chance. If you don't spend the time to get to know the background of the community, I don't think you have a chance of real success. Some music directors may know what they want to play, and know what they want to accomplish in each concert, but they don't see the value, or even the beauty, of getting to know the community. Every community is different and each community should treasure the orchestra because it is theirs. But you have to help them to understand the artistic, educational and economic value of their orchestra. There is no shortcut to building a shared artistic vision. It takes a great deal of time, energy, commitment, and passion.

Artistic Programming

The repertoire you choose should reflect your enthusiasm for the artistic mission. You may choose some new pieces that you are excited about introducing to the community, or you may choose some repertoire that is good for the orchestra's development. Perhaps they haven't done much of the French repertoire, or maybe they haven't mastered complicated rhythms, so you might start to include those challenges. If the community hasn't heard any American music from the 20th century, you should start to slowly incorporate some important works. If you decide to do a piece that you feel strongly about or commission a new work, everyone in the organization must feel your passion and your commitment to that project. I have had my share of letters from irate subscribers and board members who ask "Why are we doing this?" You have to take risks. Maybe everyone is not going to like all your choices. Maybe the commissioned work doesn't turn out exactly as you hoped, but you are taking chances and the orchestra is growing. All of the enthusiasm and love you have for music has to be present in everything you do.

Part of building vision is building quality into everything that happens. Quality must be reflected, not only in the performances, but in everything you do as an organization. It should influence the pieces you choose, the auditions you hold, the pre-concert talks, the appearances in the community. Everything that happens around the orchestra has to be at the highest level of excellence that is possible. This doesn't mean that we are all going to try to be the New York Philharmonic. What really matters is that your orchestra is playing at *its* highest possible level. The people who live and work in your community simply want their orchestra to be the best it can be. They want to see the passion in the music making and to enjoy a positive relationship between the music director and the musicians as they make music together.

It is important to have strategic plans for the next five years or so and we are encouraged to plan our programs far in advance, but I think the best planning always allows for flexibility. Occasionally a piece, a theme, or an idea is unexpectedly intriguing to the audience or to the orchestra. All of a sudden this might create a different direction with your programming. The same thing might apply to building the supporting elements of an orchestra. Let the organization be flexible so that you can react to what is happening around you. Don't be afraid to make changes in response to new information. Sometimes the largest organizations have the most difficulty being flexible because they have so much structure at the core. Often the smaller orchestras can be extremely creative, risk-taking, and experimental.

Financial Challenges

Certainly, all of us deal with the reality of the financial situations in our communities and sometimes this can be very frustrating. You know that you desperately need to have more violins in the orchestra, or that you really need to have a new concert hall, but it is not a possibility at this time. This can be very disappointing, but we can build creative steps to work around our challenges and to lay the groundwork for future growth. As artistic leaders, we need to create positive change where we can, but we also need to be able to make the best of the artistic tools we have at the moment.

Chapter 5

ARTISTIC PROGRAMMING

SUBSCRIPTION CONCERT PROGRAMMING

Once the institutional vision has been set, all of the artistic programming must align with this vision. If the goal is to become the largest orchestra in the area, you will want to work toward building your audience and performing more concerts. If the goal is to become the best orchestra, you might need to increase your pay scale, set higher artistic standards, and find ways of motivating players to improve performance. If your goal is to be the most "well-known" orchestra in your area, you might want to concentrate on doing more recordings and putting more money into your marketing efforts. The institutional vision should define the course of action for the organization.

After you have identified the larger goals, it is the music director's job to establish a set of smaller initiatives that will move the organization forward. In essence, you will need to develop very specific artistic goals. Many of these will be linked in some way to programming.

Excellent programming is the result of tremendous effort, thought, and careful planning. Sometimes the programming is done by the music director alone; other times it is chosen in consultation with the executive director or an artistic committee. In larger orchestras, programming may be selected by a team consisting of the music director, an artistic administrator, and the executive director. Whether it is completed by an individual or a group, the important thing is to take into account all of the major variables and parameters.

Philosophy of Programming and Growth

Within most organizations, there is a general philosophy of programming. This is either evident in the history of the organization or it is cultivated by the current music director. Often, in doing a search for a new music director, organizations look for conductors who share a similar philosophy of programming.

Basic programming philosophies can be divided into large groupings. Some orchestras specialize in chamber orchestra repertoire, whereas others put the emphasis on full-orchestral works. Some specialize in new music; others center on a specific time period of music. There are even orchestras known for their creative style of presenting concerts. Within an organization, each conductor brings their own approach to programming and their own set of likes and dislikes. When you begin a new job, it is important to spend time discussing your personal approach to music making and to clarify the things that you feel are important with the executive director and the board. Your beliefs should be in alignment with the overall vision of the organization. This way they will become a means to achieve the end—not the end itself.

Programming with Passion

When beginning the programming process, you must look to your passions. Obviously, you went into the field of music because you love it. You probably have an intimate relationship with certain types of music and a flair for certain types of concerts. This personal stamp is what makes each music director unique. When selecting music to perform, you must consider your personal strengths as a conductor. What music do you have experience conducting? What repertoire would you like to conduct? It is essential that you love the pieces you select to conduct and that you are committed to them artistically. You want to focus upon the types of music that you relate to emotionally and you want to share that emotional relationship with your audience. Your musical passions should drive all of the major repertoire decisions, yet you will need to carefully temper this according to the limitations of your organization.

Assessing Limitations

When programming for an entire organization, there are a variety of parameters and issues to evaluate as you select the music for each concert season. What are your programming constraints? Have you analyzed the strengths and weaknesses of the individual sections of your orchestra? Through your choice of repertoire, can you emphasize the strengths and minimize the weaknesses? Your goal should be to improve the quality of your orchestra over time by a careful selection of pieces that gradually challenge the orchestra to perform at a higher level. This will help to establish a level of trust between yourself and the orchestra members. Attention should be paid to intertwining various styles of musical playing so that the orchestra can grow both stylistically as well as technically. Analyze what moves the organization forward artistically and incorporate these ideas into your programming. Find out how you can be different, better, and more exciting than any other orchestra in your area.

The pieces you select to perform must be directly related to the amount of rehearsal time you have available. Do you have enough time to properly rehearse the works you have chosen? Will the budget allow for extra rehearsals if necessary? Or can you help financially by selecting a quality program that can be done with fewer rehearsals? Sometime you can program a concert that uses music that is in the public domain. This can create tremendous savings in your music rental costs. All of these are factors to consider in your programming process. Most orchestras allow for three to four rehearsals for a standard subscription concert, and one to two rehearsals for pops or light classics. Youth concerts are almost always performed with just one rehearsal. Make sure that you use your rehearsals wisely and efficiently during the season. The budget will also determine the approximate size of your orchestra. Look for clever ways to shift pieces around to create more flexibility in this area. By programming an all-Mozart program for one of your concerts, you might be able to afford the extra personnel for a Mahler symphony later on.

When a concert occurs in the season must also be considered in planning the programming. Is there a specific occasion linked with the concert date? If you have a concert that is taking place on or near Valentine's Day, you might want to include programming that addresses that theme. Other popular dates are New Year's Eve, Black History Month, Music in Schools Week, St. Patrick's Day, and so on. Thematic programming is covered more in depth later in this section.

There are additional financial considerations that affect programming. Because concert sponsorship is critical to an orchestra's survival, you will want to develop concerts that help to increase this funding stream. Your concerts should be easy to market to both your subscribers and to the single-ticket audience members. If overall ticket sales in an organization are going downward, you will need to program much differently than if they were increasing steadily. If you need more audience members, program a "warhorse" piece, but try to tie it to something else that is new and fresh. The secret is to never allow your programming to become status quo or predictable. Always give your audience a little more than they expect.

Through your programming you are trying to build institutional ownership of the product—the concerts. What builds ownership? Ownership is built by participation. Have you asked the orchestra recently what repertoire they would like to play? What they think they play well? Have you surveyed your audience to find out which pieces they are excited about hearing performed? It is amazing how the suggestions from the audience will vary. The concept of "something for everyone" has to be incorporated into your overall philosophy for programming for the season. In selecting the music, you will need to consider what the audience is used to hearing. How ingrained is this expectation? Have they been exposed to a variety of new music or controversial pieces in the past? You must carefully anticipate your audience's tolerance for change. Much of this will be based on their trust level with you as the music director for the organization. If you select music that they perceive to be bad, that trust level will quickly become eroded and you will have dissension within the organization.

As you select your repertoire, it may be your personal goal to "grow" the organization. This is always a fun and challenging proposition. Before you start creating new programs and concerts, however, make sure that you have worked closely with the executive director and the board chair to identify priorities. You need to understand the hierarchy of the allocation of resources in relationship to the overall institutional goals fully. Too many conductors have regarded an orchestra as *their* orchestra, and failed to take into account that the orchestra was there before they were hired and will probably be there long after they are gone. Being a music director for an orchestra is like being entrusted with the care of a child. You can guide and encourage it; train it and move it forward on its growth path; but ultimately it will, and should, have a life of its own. It is not yours. The decisions you make must be in its best interest, not just your own. When the music you love matches up with all the parameters set forth here, then you are on the right track in your programming for an organization.

The more experience you have as a conductor, the more you will gravitate toward that which resonates with you personally. Notice, however, that "what will look good on your résumé, what will increase your career opportunities, or what you just conducted last week with another orchestra" are not mentioned at all. Many young conductors are too interested in increasing their list of works conducted or in making their life easier than in selecting the most suitable pieces for the orchestra they are working with. Remember, becoming a great conductor is not about you: It is about the music. If the music sounds bad because it was too hard for the group, there was not enough rehearsal time, or you did not have the right-size orchestra to play the piece because of budget restrictions—then you are personally at fault. If any of these occur, the performance of the music will suffer. No one wants to hear great music played poorly.

The Audience

Music is made to be shared, to be heard, to be interactive. Therefore, we cannot talk further about programming unless we first talk about the receiving side of the equation: the audience. As you plan for the future, take time to ask yourself some basic questions about your audience.

Where is your audience regarding their listening skills?

Have you taken the time to get to know your audience?

How has this been done? Conversation? Surveys? Focus groups?

What music are they excited about currently?

What type of listeners would you like them to be in five years?

How much trust do they have in you as a music director?

Would they come to a concert of "unfamiliar" music because they trust your ability to judge quality?

How much change can they tolerate? (You must be careful not to change too fast.)

Meet your audience where they are with your programming, and then work to take them where you want them to go. A high level of trust is essential if you are dramatically changing the artistic direction for an organization or varying substantially from its programming history. I knew a conductor once who took over the reigns of a small regional orchestra and didn't do his homework. During his very first season, he chose to program works that were far beyond the listening capacity of his audience and the playing ability of his orchestra. Attendance immediately dropped off, as did contributed income. It was only by re-adjusting the programming in future seasons that they were able to recover and rebalance the organization.

To get to know your audience better, first you might want to analyze some of the reasons why they go to concerts. The reasons are many and diverse. People go to concerts because:

- They want to be inspired
- It is the social thing to do
- They know and like the pieces being performed
- They use the time to rest, unwind, or escape
- They want to expand their knowledge and learn more
- They feel it is their civic duty
- They want to connect with other people
- They are looking to be entertained
- They like the sensual character of sound
- They want to hear a famous or talented guest artist
- They truly love music and connect to it personally
- Music takes them into a different world—it is a transformation
- Attending concerts makes them feel successful

(*This list was derived from a seminar offered by the American Symphony Orchestra League's Orchestra Leadership Academy.*)

As you can see, the motivating factors vary tremendously. Many audience members are there for the music and how the music affects them. Others attend for the experience and for all of the aspects surrounding the experience. Some people go to concerts because of social pressure from a spouse or their job, when they really would prefer to be elsewhere. How can you create a stimulating concert experience that reaches out to all of these people?

From the people who regularly attend concerts, the audience can be further broken down into subcategories.

LONG-TIME SUBSCRIBERS. Usually enjoy the music but they might be entrenched in defined expectations of concert formats and repertoire. They often will renew their subscription regardless of programming and soloists because they value their seats. These people usually believe in the organization as a whole.

NEW SUBSCRIBERS. These people might not have as much experience with the art form, or they might be avid music lovers who are new to the area. They often are testing the quality of the organization overall. Usually they are interested in programming that they feel is familiar, unusual, or directly relevant to them. They tend to be curious about the organization as a whole but not necessarily committed.

SINGLE TICKETS. Single-ticket buyers are interested in a specific program. This can be because of familiarity with the music or theme, or they might be attracted by the star quality of the guest artist. Price is usually not an obstacle; they value their flexibility more. These people usually do not develop a long-term commitment to the overall organization.

The audience divides further along the lines of the types of concerts they attend.

CLASSICAL. Usually people who grew up playing an instrument, or who were exposed to classical music early in their lives. The music is important to them. The social structure of a concert is important to them. They like to hear music they are familiar with, but they are also there to learn, to grow, to be engaged, and to be inspired. Many of these subscribers like to be seen at a concert. They also like to talk about the music with friends who are attending.

POPS. Pops audiences are looking for entertainment. They might like the "sound" of the symphony orchestra, but they want to hear music that is easy to listen to and fun. They often want to sing along quietly, or tap their feet. They prefer to be familiar with the music that the guest artist is performing.

FAMILY. Parents or grandparents bring children and grandchildren to family concerts in order to teach them about classical music and to help make them "better-educated" individuals. This audience can be very dedicated and will subscribe to a series year after year. They are usually looking for a combination of education and entertainment.

EDUCATIONAL. These concerts are usually presented for schoolchildren who are bused to the concert hall. The educational component of these concerts must be very high. They are usually accompanied by study tapes and educational lesson plans. Teachers often have the students participate in preconcert and postconcert tests. It is best if you can relate the concepts being explored in the concert to the educational standards of the school district.

Even though these audience members may differ greatly in the number of times they attend a concert or in the types of concerts they choose to attend, you will find that their ideas about what makes a great concert are quite similar. Remember, a concert is an art form that occurs during a specified moment of time, never to be repeated exactly the same way again. During this time period, magical things should happen. It is your job as a music director to make every concert a great one. A great concert must involve the following aspects:

- Active involvement of audience and performers
- Continuity and variety; accessibility and the unexpected
- Discovery
- Passion
- Sense of occasion
- Overall atmosphere
- The personal conviction of the performance
- Great music performed well
- The irreplaceable moment when something incredible happens

- Energy and electricity
- Risk-taking—by the conductor, the performers, or through the repertoire

(*This list was derived from a seminar offered by the American Symphony Orchestra League's Orchestra Leadership Academy.*)

Concert Nonattenders

Often we will encounter people who say they do not like classical music, or who have never been in a concert hall. One of the challenges we face as music directors is how to reach this potential audience. Even the best-planned and performed concert will be a failure if no one attends the performance. How do you convince a nonattender that this music is relevant to their life?

One of the first steps is to develop a personal relationship with new potential audience members. This can be done by the music director through community talks or through musicians reaching out into the community. If people feel they know someone involved in the concert, they are much more likely to attend. Some people are afraid to come to concerts because they have never been in the concert hall. You might want to encourage the organization to set up tours of the facility or to have special daytime events that allow people to wander through the hall and become more comfortable with the surroundings without the added element of the concert performance.

Others might not be aware of how to get tickets to symphony events. Make sure that your orchestra has the capacity to sell tickets online and that your seating chart is easy to read. This will appeal to many new audience members, because searching and purchasing items and services on the Web is something they know and understand. More and more, orchestras are reaching out to new audiences through e-mail marketing and items posted on their Web sites. As you review your pricing structure, make sure that you have tickets that are affordable for all levels of income or interest. A current nonattender might be willing to try out the symphony if they could get a ticket for $10 instead of $25, or if they could purchase a family pack that would allow their entire family to attend.

As you select your programming for each season, be conscious of including familiar repertoire that might encourage a nonattender to come. True masterpieces of music communicate to all, and audience members like to hear pieces that they are familiar with. You also might want to search for connections outside of the realm of music that would appeal to someone interested in that specific field. For example, you could program a concert of music inspired by Shakespeare's plays, which might bring a theatrical audience into the concert hall; or you could incorporate elements of art, or dance. Additional ideas might include making a concert less formal in structure with some dialogue from the podium, or changing the time or day of the concert to cater to a different audience. This has been very successfully done with "Rush Hour" concerts and Sunday afternoon "Family Concerts."

Finally, if you are still having trouble attracting new concert listeners, if your budget will allow, try bringing in a big-name soloist. The name recognition of the artist will help get people into the hall, and if your orchestral concert is exciting, sincere, and relevant, these audience members will come back.

Increasing Listening Ability

Once you have figured out how to get your audience into the hall and you have programmed exciting concerts full of personal conviction and risk taking, then you have to work continually with your audience to increase their ability for active listening. It is only through this type of listening that a concert can be fully enjoyed. In order to move your audience forward and to prepare them for even more complex repertoire, you must identify access points into the music. Access points are created by taking the time to explain what to listen for. This can be done through:

1. A preconcert talk
2. Postconcert conversations
3. Innovative approaches to program notes
4. Newsletter articles to your subscribers
5. Actual dialogue during the concert

Talking to the audience at concerts has sometimes been a controversial subject. Some subscribers love it, others find it objectionable. My general rule of thumb is to talk only when I have something meaningful to say. Many conductors talk simply to help create a rapport with the audience. This is an acceptable approach if it works for your organization. Sometimes we are even seeing this bond-building role taken by the orchestra members who speak from the stage and welcome the audience. For pops and family concerts, it is very common for the music director to act as a "host" for the occasion and introduce each piece. Classical audiences tend to shy away from this type of concert format but they still love to hear the conductor talk sincerely about what a piece means to them. When you speak, try to focus on a few specific points that the audience can listen for in a composition. This can be a wonderful mechanism for connecting your audience to the concert experience. It is especially effective if you are playing a piece that might be less well known, or that might be difficult for your audience to appreciate. By giving them access points to listen for throughout the performance, you will greatly increase their appreciation and involvement with the music.

Beginning the Programming Process

Now that you have identified and defined the areas of consideration for your programming decisions and you have analyzed the audience that you will be performing for, you can begin to put your programs together. Programming is indeed an art, not a science. I like to compare the balance of programming to a good meal. All musical pieces have weights and textures; they have tastes and distinct flavors. Select your programs like you would choose courses for a fine dinner. You want to experience a progression: an appetizer, a first course, a second course, a heavy main dish, the possibility of sherbet in between, and the intrigue of dessert. Of course, not all of these levels are necessary for all concerts. In fact, you would probably never have all of these on the same concert, and sometimes there may be concerts that comprise only one of these categories—just a main dish, or perhaps even a complete concert of desserts! The only thing I would really caution about is too many "main dishes" on the same concert. A Mahler symphony and a Bruckner symphony on the same program is not digestible by anyone I know.

Categorize the Music

As you think of some of the pieces you might want to program, try to group them in overall categories that assess their texture (instrumentation, timbre), weight (length and concentration level required), and flavor (composer's musical language, national characteristics, and style period). Beyond this, each piece also has a basic form and individual characteristics that create an emotional level of communication. Some examples might be:

Dense Works

> Varèse—*Ionization*
> Rouse—*The Infernal Machine*

Intense Works

> Sheng—*H'un (Lacerations) In memoriam 1966–1976*
> Barber—*Adagio*
> Penderecki—*Threnody to the Victims of Hiroshima*

Calm Works

> Mendelssohn—*Hebrides Overture*
> Beethoven—Symphony No. 6

Fluid Works

> Debussy—*Afternoon of a Faun*
> Ravel—*Pavane for a Dead Princess*

Heavy Works

> Shostakovich—Symphony No. 5
> Mahler—Symphony No. 8

Triumphant Works

> Beethoven—Symphony No. 9
> Liszt—*Les Preludes*
> Tchaikovsky—Symphony No. 4

Angular Works

> Honegger—*Pacific 231*
> Ruggles—*Sun Treader*

Soothing Works

> Delius—*Two Pieces for Small Orchestra*
> Mascagni—*Cavalleria Rusticana: Intermezzo*
> Pachelbel—*Canon*

Lush Romantic Works

> Strauss—*Rosenkavalier Suite*
> Hanson—Symphony No. 2
> Ravel—*Daphnis et Chloé*

Theatrical Works

> Kodaly—*Hary Janos Suite*
> Prokofiev—*Peter and the Wolf*

Popular Works

> Tchaikovsky—*1812 Overture*
> Smetana—*The Moldau*

Well-known Compositions

> Beethoven—Symphonies and Concerti

Masterpieces

> Mozart—Symphonies
> Brahms—Symphonies

Pieces with National Flavor

> Khachaturian—*Sabre Dance*
> Rimsky Korsakov—*Capriccio Espagnol*
> Walton—*Crown Imperial Coronation March*
> Copland—*Four Dances from Rodeo*
> De Falla—*The Three-Cornered Hat*

Pieces of music are similar to pieces of a puzzle waiting to be placed in the right spot on the right program. Don't try to cram a piece where it doesn't fit (an angular piece next to another angular piece). It is better to start over with the programming of a concert than to have a musical disconnect between pieces.

Research Program History

To begin programming, first look at the pieces that the orchestra has done in the last seven years: these are in the recent memory of the community, so you should not perform them again. Next, look for "holes" in the past seven years of programming; these would be popular pieces that have not been performed but the audience would probably like to hear. After this step, identify masterpieces that have not been played recently that would help improve and develop the sound of the orchestra. Finally, compile a list of pieces that would showcase your orchestra's strengths. You should also consider once-popular pieces that have fallen from favor, or lesser-known pieces by popular composers. Write all of the possibilities down on a list. You may not program all of these into the current season, but you can gradually work your way through the list during the next five seasons or so.

Survey the Orchestra and the Audience

Now look at the list that you have developed from surveying your orchestra members. Is there any duplication of pieces? Move these pieces to a higher-priority list. Look at the musician's list again and see if there are other pieces that you haven't thought of that would work well for the orchestra—add these to your higher list. Now do the same with your audience survey. If there are pieces that the audience would like to hear that have not been done in the past seven years, move them to your high-priority list.

Investigate Soloists

Next, you need to make a detailed list of soloists who are within your orchestra's budget range that you would like to work with during the next three years or so. You also should consider using principal members of your orchestra as soloists, or performing artists who happen to live in your community. Once this list is completed, you should gather information regarding each guest artist's "short" list for performance. Remember that the repertoire list most managers send out is not the performer's short list. The short list is usually the three to four specific pieces that they are playing the following season. (Sometimes they are only playing one piece!) Now go back and look at the list of concertos that your orchestra has performed recently. Cross off all of these pieces. Then look at the concertos that have not been performed, but are audience favorites, or works you would like to perform. Is there an intersection? Place these pieces on a short list. After that, assess what other solo instruments you might want to feature to round out the season.

Identify Important Events

Event programming can be very successful. An event does not have to be something as obvious as Christmas or Halloween, although these are often used as themes for programming. Often it can be as simple as an important anniversary of a composer or the celebration of a nation's anniversary. Events create opportunities for doing special programming that otherwise might not be accepted. As you look at your concert dates, see if any of them fall on well-known holidays. These are excellent concerts to consider for thematic programming.

New Music

Each season should include new music compositions that people will be excited about hearing or pieces that will create a dialogue throughout the community. You can create extra interest by having the composer attend the concert (if they are still living). Composer availability might be a consideration in your programming or date selection. You also have the options of commissioning a composition, or providing second or third performances of newer works. In making your decision regarding what to put on your list, keep in mind your constraints of rehearsal time, size of orchestra, difficulty of piece, and the listening level of your audience.

Personal Preferences

You also need to make a list of music that you feel connected to that you really want to conduct with this orchestra. Each conductor has their own strengths and weaknesses. You want to emphasize your strengths and center upon the repertoire that you are comfortable communicating. As you select pieces for performance, don't program pieces that you do not like. Sometimes, this is impossible when it comes to a world premiere, or when you are an assistant at a major orchestra and your job is to conduct whatever you are assigned. But remember, it is very difficult to inspire people when you are not inspired yourself. Try to focus on music with which you have a personal relationship.

Cornerstone Approach to Programming

Once you have developed your lists, it is time to move on to the actual programming. For my own classical programming, I use the "cornerstone" approach. Sometimes, my cornerstone is a big work—a "main-course" symphony, or large composition. Other times, my cornerstone is a soloist and a concerto that might be the only choice of repertoire available if we are to engage a specific soloist whom I think would be tremendously successful with the organization. Finally, the cornerstone might be a theme or concept. Perhaps the concert is on Halloween and we want to emphasize spooky pieces. Your goal should be to present a variety of cornerstone pieces or concepts during your season.

As you begin your programming, draw out a chart for each of your concerts. For exercise purposes, we will say that you are programming a season of six classical concerts. Perhaps three of these concerts have a major work as their cornerstone; two are defined by the repertoire of the soloist you want to work with, and one is centered around a theme because of a collaborative project you are doing with a local theater group. Your chart might look something like this:

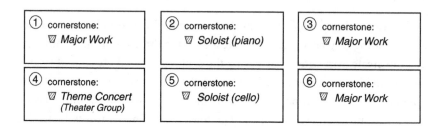

After you have established your cornerstones, you need to decide what other solo instruments you want to feature during the year. Let's say that you chose to feature violin and flute, in addition to the piano and cello on which you have already decided. In addition, an important board member has suggested that you should collaborate with the local chorus for one of the concerts.

Now, your chart might look like the one below. Adding the chorus might require you to rethink one of your cornerstone pieces. Perhaps you can find a large piece for chorus that would be a better selection for the program.

① cornerstone:	② cornerstone:	③ cornerstone:
☑ *Major Work* *(Symphony 45')* • *Violin Concerto*	☑ *Soloist (piano)* *(Piano Concerto 35')* • *Suite*	☑ *Major Work* *(Symphony 37')* • *Flute Concerto*
④ cornerstone:	⑤ cornerstone:	⑥ cornerstone:
☑ *Theme Concert* *(Theater Group)* • *Shakespeare*	☑ *Soloist (cello)* *(Cello Concerto 40')* • *Symphony*	☑ *Major Work* *(Choral Piece)* • *Overture*

Now you must identify the best position on each concert for your large works and your concertos—first half, second half, and so on. This decision is based on the timing of the piece, the overall flavor of the composition, and the beginning and ending of the piece, particularly the ending. The concert order is often dependent on which piece is more popular and has the better ending and if the soloist is well-known or not. Timing also might be a factor. People often like concerts in which the second half is shorter than the first half, but if you are doing a very weighty symphony, even though it is longer, it must be on the second half. Hopefully it will have a great ending. Whenever possible, it is best to let your audience go out on an "up" note.

Timing, Shape, and Trajectory of a Concert

All concerts have a basic shape and trajectory that enhances or diminishes the energy. Each piece of music has a real time and a perceived time, depending on the texture and weight of the piece. Some pieces seem much longer than they really are, whereas others are over before you know it. Keep this in mind as you create your combinations of pieces. After you have established the placement of your cornerstone piece on the program, you will want to begin to establish the timing and the trajectory for the overall concert. Most classical concerts range in length from seventy minutes to ninety minutes. I like to keep my concerts around seventy-five minutes, unless I am doing a really massive work such as a Mahler Symphony.

Some sample shapes of concerts are:

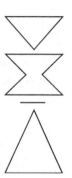

Opening piece starts big, ends soft

Second piece starts big, gets soft in middle, ends big

Intermission

Final piece starts soft, has changes within, but ultimately
  ends big

Other examples of shapes might look like these below. Any shape can be created during a concert, and each shape has it advantages and disadvantages. In creating concert trajectories, we are combining the basic "shapes" of the pieces with the number and types of pieces.

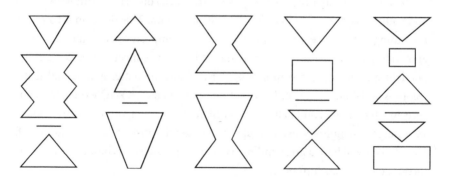

Programming Combinations

Three-Piece and Two-Piece Concerts

	Length	Mood
Standard Three Pieces		
Overture or new work	10–15 mins	Angular
Concerto	20–25 mins	Showcase piece
———		
Cornerstone: Major work	40–50 mins	Serious and contemplative
Encore	3–4 mins	Light and fun

	Length	*Mood*
Alternative Three Pieces		
Overture or new work	7–12 mins	Flashy
Short Symphony or Suite	25–30 mins	Calm
———		
Cornerstone: Large concerto	40–50 mins	Dramatic and powerful
Big name soloist		
Two-Piece Concerts		
Symphony or other large work	45–50 mins	Well-known masterpiece
———		
Cornerstone: Concerto	40–45 mins	Soloist showcase
OR		
Concerto	30–35 mins	Lyrical concerto
———		
Cornerstone: Symphony	50–60 mins	Triumphant symphony

Four-Piece Concerts

This type of concert still needs a cornerstone piece, or it might come across as being disconnected. One piece of the four must be more weighted than the others. The four-piece program is very successful when you are dealing with short symphonies or short concertos. This is especially true when you are featuring instruments such as flute, clarinet, guitar, horn, trumpet, and so on. For all of these instruments, the concertos available tend to be on the short side.

	Length	*Mood*
Four-Piece Concerts		
Overture, Suite, or Tone poem	15–20 mins	Popular piece
Concerto	20–25 mins	New composition
———		
Lighter work	7–12 mins	Soothing piece
Symphony or Tone poem	20–25 mins	Heavy or Dense piece

Five-Pieces or More Concerts

These are not seen as often in classical concerts because they sometimes can be difficult to hold together. You will tend to have more pieces on opera concerts where you might have a section of short opera arias. The multiple pieces concert is most effective, pacing wise, when pieces are grouped together. For example, you might want to perform a collection of love songs instead of a concerto, but they fill the "concerto" slot of twenty-five to thirty minutes on the concert. This type of programming is also popular if you have a concert centered on a guest artist. The guest artist might want to perform shorter works in both the first and the second half of the concert. Also, if you perform a lot of baroque music, the pieces in general are much shorter. Therefore, you might have three or four pieces on the first half and the same on the second. In programming concerts with many compositions, you must pay special attention to the overall shape of the concert to make sure there is a good build-up of tension and release.

New and Old Trends

If you look back at the programming of the major orchestras in the United States in the nineteenth or early twentieth centuries, you might be quite surprised. Our staid format of "overture, concerto, symphony," was not the prevalent style of programming at that time. Instead, programs were composed of quite a variety of popular tunes and arias, newly composed symphonies, single movements of symphonies, light overtures, and concertos. Sometimes there were two intermissions, and people were not required to stay for all three sections. The overall presentation of the concert was much more informal. Here are some examples of the New York Philharmonic programming in the 1840s to 1860s:

New York Philharmonic
November 1845

Part I

Symphony No. 3, Op. 56 (first time in America) . . . . F. MENDELSSOHN

Part II

Overture to Anacreon . . . . L. CHERUBINI

Aria "Se M'Abbandoni" . . . . S. MERCADANTE
               Mrs. Mott

Solo Harp
               Madame Jenny Lazare

Aria "Fac ut Portem" (Stabat Mater) . . . . G. ROSSINI
               Mrs. Mott

Fantasia on Themes from the Opera of Charles .... S. Heller
VI.   Halevy (Piano Forte)
Mr. Hermann Wollenhauft

Overture "De La chasse du Jeune Henri" .... E. N. Méhul

New York Philharmonic
December 1848

Part I

Grand Symphony (1st time in this country) .... N. W. Gade
(dedicated to Mendelssohn)

Adagio and Rondo.—from the last concerto .... H. Vieuxtemps
Violin, Master Luigi Elena

Part II

Concert Overture—The Wood Nymph (First time) .... S. Bennett

Concert Stucke (Piano Forte with Orchestral Accomp) ...... C. M. Von Weber
Piano, Mr. Richard Hoffman

Overture Triomphale .... F. Ries

New York Philharmonic
January 1854

Part I

Second Symphony, in C, Op. 61 (first time) .... R. Schumann

Song "Ave Maria" .... F. Schubert
Miss M. S. Brainerd

Adagio et Rondo, in F (Bassoon) .... C. M. Von Weber
Bassoon, Mr. Eltz

Part II

Second Symphony in D, Op 36 . . . . L. Van Beethoven

Aria from *the Messiah* "Rejoice greatly" . . . . G. F. Handel
Miss M. S. Brainerd

Overture in D, Op. 27 . . . . F. Mendelssohn
(Calm Sea and Happy Voyage)

New York Philharmonic
November 1864

Part I

Symphony No. 3, Op. 55 in E Flat . . . . L. van Beethoven

Part II

Polonaise Brillante, Op. 72 (1st time) . . . . C. M. von Weber
Arr. Liszt

Mr. S. B. Mills

Concerto for Violin, Op. 64, in E . . . . F. Mendelssohn
Mr. Theodore Thomas

Overture to "Oberon" in D . . . . C. M. von Weber

Part III

Les Preludes "Poeme Symphonique" . . . . F. Liszt

Notice that many of these programs had multiple guest artists, overtures were performed as the conclusion of concerts, and almost every program seemed to include a newer work or a first performance. With these diverse examples in mind, you are challenged to not be afraid to break the mold and to create interesting new formats for balancing programs and for presenting these programs to your audience. The standard three-piece format is accepted, but certainly not the only way to program. Be creative and don't be afraid to try something new.

Last Steps in the Process of Programming

Review Your Constraints

Every concert is hampered by programming restrictions. Perhaps the perfect piece for the slot you have open was already performed last year, so you have to identify another piece. Once the cornerstone piece is defined, you have a basic instrumentation to work within. This is not to say that you can't perform pieces that call for larger or smaller forces, but you must try to use the resources available to you wisely. Staying within a basic instrumentation framework for the entire concert seems to make sense for both the musicians and for the use of the rehearsal time. The rental fees of the music you program might also be an issue within the organization. Take time to research the rental fees to help keep a handle on the artistic costs. Sometimes a less expensive piece might be just as effective. As you are finalizing your choices for a specific program, remember that every piece must fit regarding timing, instrumentation, flavor or texture, difficulty level (both playing and listening), and tonality. Every aspect and angle must be considered thoroughly and incorporated ahead of time to ensure the most balanced programming for your organization.

Balance across the Season

As you are finalizing the repertoire, you must keep in mind that not only must each individual concert be balanced but also that all the concerts over the course of the season must balance as a whole. As you select your other pieces for each program, use your instinct regarding style, timing, accessibility, and contrast, to take pieces from your priority lists and to gradually slot them into spaces within your concert programming grid. Sometimes it is useful to draft two or more seasons at once, because you can begin to develop larger trends and cycles. By working further in advance, more pieces that you really want to do can eventually be worked in. Do not try to make a piece fit just because you want to conduct it during the present season. Remember, you must program what is best for the organization, not just what is best for you.

Sometimes you will run into a problem where you know what flavor of piece you want, and yet you can't find the right piece to put into the slot. When trying to solve this type of problem, David Daniels's book *Orchestral Music—A Handbook* can be an invaluable tool. Through using the reference pages in the back, you can sort by instrumentation, solo instruments or voices, timings, nationality of composer, or major anniversaries. Just taking the time to browse through these pages often sparks an idea about a piece that you might not have thought of otherwise. This is especially helpful if you have instrumentation or timing restrictions to work within.

You will need to have a good sense of each composer's style in order to program well. Placing a piece of music on a concert is like hanging a great piece of art. It needs the proper surroundings to bring out its full beauty. Don't crowd a piece that needs time to breathe. Don't put violently contrasting pieces next to each other if either will detract from the other. Make sure that your concert presentations are smooth, and never bump—don't serve jalapenos on your ice cream.

Analyze Your Programming

After you have finished your programming chart and you are satisfied with the basic balance of the programs, put it aside for a few days. Let it simmer in your head. Then, when you look at it again, try to see it with fresh eyes. With the eyes of an audience member, react instinctually to your own programming. Would you want to attend this concert? Is it new and interesting, or boring? Take the time to ask yourself the following questions to help fine tune your programming.

Programming Questions

Do the pieces within the season compare and contrast well with each other? If not, what can you do to change this?

Is there something on this concert season for everyone? Do you feature representation of a variety of composers, and not too many pieces by the same composer?

Is there a balance of musical styles? Do you showcase pieces from different style periods?

Does the pacing of each concert make sense? What is the overall length of the concert? What is the timing relationship of the individual pieces? Do you have too many "long" pieces in a row?

Is there a balance of harmonic tension and release on each concert? Make sure that you avoid programming pieces that are all in the same key, or that represent the same emotion.

If the concert is celebrating a special event, have you captured the spirit of that event? Are the selected pieces quality music? There is so much great music out there, why consider doing anything else? Your concert programming should always center around quality music.

Is there balance between the programming of this concert season and the seasons before it? Try to establish cycles and trends to which your audience can follow and look forward.

Do you present a good balance between new, familiar, and tried and true? It is helpful to actually count the season's well-known pieces and the probable unknown pieces. Make sure there is a balance.

Do you display a balance of featured solo instruments? Even though piano sells, look beyond bringing in too many piano soloists. Your audience is attracted to variety.

Do the compositions you have selected enhance each other? The right combination of pieces is critical for the success of the concert.

Will the pacing of the concert keep the attention of your audience? Real and perceived time must be evaluated for each piece. Does the shape of the overall program work? Is it a snooze or a roller-coaster ride?

Are there any pieces that really do not fit? If something doesn't fit—find another piece. There are incredible resources to draw on.

Once you have satisfied all of these questions in your own mind, you are ready to present the program to the executive director and the board of directors. In situations in which you are working on programming with the executive director or the artistic director as a team, they would have already been involved in all of these previous steps. Even if you are doing the programming alone, it is advisable to inform the executive director and board chair about trends and cornerstone pieces in advance, especially if these might require additional resources in time or money.

THEMATIC PROGRAMMING

Programming Theme Concerts

Thematic programming tends to be easy to market and easy for the audience to connect to. For this reason, there is a trend across the United States toward more and more thematic programming. You will find that even if your concert program is not based upon a theme, the marketing department, committee, or staff person will try to assign it one. Ideas for themes are everywhere, and you are only limited by your own creativity. Make sure you select themes that will resonate with your community and that provide a wide enough platform for selecting quality repertoire. You always will want to be able to program exciting, high-quality music. Make sure you never include a bad piece just because the title fits your theme; this is the error that many inexperienced conductors make. Programmatic music lends itself easily to thematic programming. As a result, you may find yourself gravitating toward selecting only "program" music for your thematic concert. With this, you run the risk of the concert having no "main course," or appearing "too light." Work hard to find clever and creative ways to incorporate non-programmatic pieces into your thematic programming.

Sources for Ideas

When you are faced with selecting pieces for a thematic program, you must first brainstorm and research all of the repertoire that might fit this theme. *The Book of Classical Music Lists* by Herbert Kupferberg can help. If you are looking for pieces about fish or operas that have the character "Don" in them, this book is invaluable. It includes lists of pieces inspired by Shakespeare, lists of bachelor composers, lists of musical geography and of musical astronomy, Faust in music, music and art, sports in music, World War II in music, and more! There is even a section that includes a list of all the national anthems sorted by country. It is a treasure chest of unusual ideas and information.

Other sources for thematic programming ideas can be obtained from rental music publishers. They all have web sites, and many publish booklets that list pieces according to the occasion on which they might be performed. A note of caution—sometimes the connections made by the music publisher are quite broad and might not be relevant to the normal audience member. *Orchestral Music—A Handbook*, mentioned earlier, is a good source for research on composers from specific countries. Make sure that you also look for repertoire about a country written by someone from another country.

Lists and Examples of Themes

The following table (5.1) shows some of the most common topics of thematic programming. A more in-depth list, with samples of repertoire, is included in the Resource section. I encourage you to develop your own lists of repertoire and to update them throughout your career. Again and again, you will be asked to create thematic programs.

Most thematic programs will follow a classical concert structure, although special-event Holiday themed concerts fit more within the pops structure. (These will be discussed later under Pops Programming.) Either way, thematic concerts can be more open to featuring multiple pieces and to altering the balance between the pieces. Within this structure, be sure that you still have some "meat" in your program and that the theme does not make everything feel like "fluff." Remember, people still want to hear good, exciting music.

Table 5.1 Common Topics of Thematic Programming

International themes	Programming themes	
Russia	Animals	Night
France	Art (music inspired by)	Patriotism
Germany/Austria	Birds	Planets
Italy	Circus	Romance/Love
England	Fairy Tales/Stories	Royalty
Ireland	Fire	Seasons
Scotland	Flowers	Shakespeare
Spanish/Latin America	Halloween	Storms
African-American	Holidays/Carnivals	Water
American	Machines	War
	Magic	Wedding
	Nature	

Pops Programming

The purpose of pops concerts is mainly to entertain, and, of course, to make money for the organization. Most conductors will be required to conduct pops concerts at some point in their careers. Assistant conductors with mid-size to major orchestras may have to conduct *lots* of pops concerts. One of the challenges with pops concerts is to keep them artistically viable. Pops programming should not just be an "extra" in your overall programming or merely something you are required to do. Rather, you need to find ways to incorporate an artistic philosophy of pops programming that is equally as strong as your approach to classical concert programming. It has been proven over time that very few pops audience members will gravitate over to your traditional classical concerts. Despite this fact, pops audiences still make up a large percentage of your overall audience. They deserve artistically well-planned and exciting concerts. The musical standards of your orchestra need to be upheld in all of the different types of concerts you present and perform.

As you program your pops concerts, you will have some of the same concerns that were discussed with the classical programs. Below are questions you will have to evaluate as you make your decisions about programming:

Artistic

Is your emphasis on the guest artist or the orchestra and conductor?
Do you want to try to move your audience over to classical concerts, or do you view them as an entirely different audience group?

Financial

> How much money is available for guest artists?
> What size orchestra can be hired for these concerts?
> How many rehearsals are budgeted?
> How much will the music cost?

Programming

> Is it a pre-planned show complete with music? or
> Is it half of a concert and you plan the rest of the program, or
>   are you building a show from scratch?
> Are there copyright issues involved? (This is especially important with
>   film projects and special pops arrangements.)

Extras

> Will this show require extra sound, lighting, or visuals?
> Do you need to hire experts to run this equipment?

Audience

> What is the age of the anticipated audience?
> Are they your regular pops audience, or mostly single-ticket buyers?

Clarifying these parameters will help you to focus your pops programming and to develop pops concerts that are artistically sound and effective.

Pops Programs and Formats

Guest-Artist Driven

Most pops programs are either theme driven or guest-artist driven. Guest-artist driven concerts are pops programs where you bring in a big name guest artist who has orchestral charts. The guest artist will often only play on the second half of the concert. Your job is to find some standard orchestral music to put on the first half that won't turn people off. Most of the audience members attending this type of concert are pops subscribers and single ticket buyers. They are usually there to hear the guest artist, and so the orchestra comes as icing on the cake.

ADVANTAGES. Big-name pops artists usually sell really well. They come with a set of arrangements that are marked and ready for the librarian to hand out. Usually the music is pretty easy. Often, they send their own conductor who already knows the show, so that the organization does not have to worry about having the music director or a staff conductor learn the music.

Disadvantages. These shows are very expensive and they have little, if anything, to do with your overall mission. The music usually arrives very late, so there is little time for orchestra members to prepare. Guest artists sometimes do not even show up for the rehearsal, which the orchestra members may find insulting. It is very hard to select a first half of music that works. This often results in an uncomfortable juxtaposition of musical styles, and no one is happy in the end.

Prepackaged Shows

These programs also tend to be expensive, but there also are affordable ones. More and more artists are creating entire shows for which the conductor does not do any programming, or for which you might just select an orchestral piece to open the first or second halves of the concert. These shows usually do not involve household pop stars. Instead, they feature well-respected artists who have worked on Broadway or in clubs across the United States. Often, these programs will also involve film or dance. These extras might increase your technical expenses. Keep this in mind as you are creating your budgets.

Advantages.   Shows like this are much more affordable. Guest artists are willing to work with the conductor on programming. They will usually provide most, if not all, of the music. These artists enjoy doing these types of programs and are fun to work with. The quality can be very good.

Disadvantages.   Sometimes these shows are a "hard sell" because your audience is unfamiliar with the group or the soloist. Marketing might need to be increased and should be based more upon the style of music they play, or who they sound like. The quality of the charts tends to vary. Sometimes, these groups are not as organized with the music because they lack appropriate staff to follow through quickly. Often the show features a group of musicians. This will increase your expenses in airfare and hotel charges, even though the general fee might still be very reasonable.

Conductor-Based Programs

The Boston Pops Orchestra has made a fine art out of creating a pops series centered on their conductors. Each of their conductors has achieved almost legendary status, both locally and nationally. The concert experience is based on the relationship between the audience and the conductor. No matter what is on the stage, the audience will return again and again because a level of trust has been developed with the conductor. This is one of the best models for pops programming, and it will help move your organization forward artistically. It avoids the fickleness of programs based on an ever-changing list of guest artists, and it allows the conductor to keep the focus on the orchestra. Many orchestras are now hiring resident pops conductors who provide this continuity of artistic quality and relationship throughout the entire pops series.

Theme-Based Pops Programs

All orchestras will perform some theme-based pops programs. Some of these will be prepackaged shows; some of these you will be asked to build from scratch. If you look at brochures from across the country, everyone seems to focus on the same basic themes for pops programming. You will find the following themes evident in both prepackaged and organizationally created programs:

General Pops Themes

>Broadway (Gershwin, Porter, Kern, Hammerstein, etc.)
>Jazz, Swing or Big Band
>Tribute to a Country (Italian night, Spanish night, Celtic night)
>Patriotic America
>Salute to the Movies (TV or film composers)
>Country Western Night
>A Night of Adventure
>Romance
>Opera Night

Unusual Combinations

>Magic
>Ice Skating
>Juggling/Acrobatics
>Dance
>Film

Light Classics Pops

>All Tchaikovsky Night
>All Marches
>All Waltzes
>Opera or Operetta

Special Event Pops

>Christmas or Holiday Concerts

New Year's Eve Concerts
Independence Day, Veterans Day, Memorial Day Concerts
Martin Luther King Concerts
Halloween Concerts
Local Celebrations or Events

Creating Your Own Shows

In programming pops, you will mostly be concerned with creating your own shows from scratch. Most of the other shows will already come complete, or partially complete. Sometimes the theme will be decided for you by the guest artist you have chosen to work with; other times, you will select the theme.

Guest Artists

When selecting guest artists for a show that you are building from scratch, you need to evaluate whether you want a "name artist" or whether the theme will sell the show. If you decide to go with a name, you must find out if they have charts (arrangements) for the orchestra, or if you will have to pay someone to arrange the music. An orchestra I worked with in Texas decided they wanted to put together a country-western pops show with a local singer who was making it big. He was willing to come back and perform in his hometown for a reasonable fee, but he did not have any music arranged for symphony orchestra. In order to make the concert happen, the orchestra association had to be willing to spend time and money to have some of his repertoire arranged for orchestra. The same might be true of a rising jazz or rock star. These individuals or groups often only have small combo arrangements. Although it is nice to intersperse a section in the program that involves a small combo, this will not work for the whole concert. You will need arrangements that use the full orchestra. Because of this, it is essential for an orchestra to have connections to good and reasonably priced pops arrangers.

Guest artists can be locally based, regional talent, or well-known on a national level. The type of guest artists you use will be dictated by the budget for the concert. The budget will be defined according to how the organization feels pops programming fits in within the overall artistic goals. *Musical America* is a good place to gather general information on nationally known guest artists and prepackaged shows. There is also a pretty good grapevine within the orchestral world regarding which packaged shows have been successful.

Selecting the Music

Identifying Repertoire

Perhaps you have decided that you are going to do a Broadway-themed pops concert. You can either fly in singers from New York, or select local singers to work with you in creating the program. As you begin to shape the show, the first thing you must do is to have your guest artist(s) identify all of the repertoire they are comfortable performing for which the music is already available. You want them to send you a list of at least twenty pieces. If you are not familiar with these pieces, you need to go to a library and listen to them or purchase CDs. It is vitally important that you become personally familiar with this repertoire. Most Broadway songs and jazz standards are easily available. Even though the arrangements will vary, you will begin to develop a feel for the style.

Once you feel that you understand the "flavor" of the pieces they have suggested, you need to scour your mind and musical sources to identify five to seven orchestral pieces that fit within this style and flavor. This is the hardest part of your task. The Overture to *Candide* can not be done on every pops program. You will need to develop a solid list of pieces that are effective. In the industry, there are publishers that specialize in pops repertoire (see Resource section: "Pops Publishers"). It is good to carefully go through their websites and catalogues as you are selecting pieces. Often these publishers will not send perusal scores. This means you will not be able to judge the quality of a piece until you have already ordered it. Try to get feedback from colleagues who have done the piece before you order it. This is now very easy to do with *OrchestraList* and *ConductorList* (see the resource section "Internet Resources and Forums"). After a while, you will become familiar with the arranger's name and you will know who writes quality orchestral charts. Avoid trying to squeeze classical pieces onto pops concerts simply because the orchestra has already rehearsed them for another concert. This is setting the concert up for failure. The audience has bought a ticket to a pops concert. Don't bait and switch.

Defining Your Program

So now you have a working list of about twenty-five to thirty pieces. You are not going to perform all of these, but you want a variety to select from. Most pops concerts last about 90 to 110 minutes. If possible, you want to integrate your guest artist(s) into both halves of the concert so you have the feel of a complete show. Most of the pieces you perform for a pops concert will be about three to seven minutes long. Occasionally, you might have a medley that would be ten to fifteen minutes long. Be careful not to put too many medleys on the concert, and certainly avoid performing two medleys right after each other. The following is a sample of the basic pacing for a pops concert involving singers or a combo group:

1. Orchestra only—fast opening number   3–7 mins
      Dialogue—conductor introduces theme and guest artist
2. Guest artist performs an upbeat number   3–6 mins
      Dialogue—guest artist talks and develops a rapport
         with the audience
3. Guest artist—medium tempo piece   3–6 mins
4. Guest artist—slower tempo piece   3–7 mins
      Dialogue—guest artist or conductor
5. Orchestra only medley is possible here   10–15 mins
      Dialogue—conductor
6. Guest artist up-tempo piece   3–4 mins
7. Guest artist up-tempo piece   3–4 mins
      Dialogue—guest artist or conductor
8. Orchestra only or guest artist—upbeat ender   3–5 mins
   Intermission   **First half should be 45–50 minutes**
9. Orchestra only—upbeat opener   5–7 mins
      Dialogue—conductor or guest artist
10. Guest artist medley or group of songs on similar
       themes, or combo section   10–15 mins
       Dialogue—conductor or guest artist
11. Orchestra piece only   5–7 mins
       Dialogue—conductor or guest artist
12. Guest artist—medium paced piece   3–5 mins
13. Guest artist—upbeat piece   3–5 mins
       (might involve audience interaction)
14. Guest artist—another upbeat piece   4–6 mins
       Dialogue—guest artist, announce ending of show
15. Guest artist—great ending piece   4–5 mins
    Second half of show should be 45–50 minutes
16. Encore   2 min

As you may have noticed, it is important in developing the flow of the concert to have some dialogue, but you do not want talking between every piece. Let the pieces fall into natural groupings and introduce a few at once so the program is not too choppy. When you have a lot of three minute tunes, it is hard to build continuity.

Try to keep a basic shape for your pops programs. I usually keep the first half pretty fast-paced. After intermission, I open the second half big, but then immediately take it down to a more intimate section, with maybe some combo playing or a group of ballads. About halfway through the second half, I begin to work the energy back up to provide a good ending for the show. Make sure you have at least two or three upbeat pieces at the end of the second half to really send the audience out on a high note. Encores are a must for pops concerts. The guest artist should be involved with the encore. Keep all encores short and upbeat.

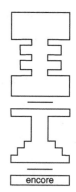

Music Sources

Your pops arrangements often will come from a different network of publishers than the standard classical music. It is very difficult to track down good charts because of copyright issues. Often you can get permission to arrange a piece for a pops concert, but you are not allowed to rent that music to anyone. If you do arrange a piece, the number of times you are allowed to perform it might be limited.

Pops arrangements are usually done by arrangers who have their own publishing company. Once you are working in the field, leaflets will cross your desk about different arrangements. It is best to file these away for the time when you might be looking for a specific piece. A few major sources for pops music are listed below and a more complete list including contact information is included in the Resources part of the book.

Carmen Dragon Library	Paramount Theater Music Library
Disney Library	Rogers and Hammerstein Library
Jazz Artists International	G. Schirmer Rental Library
Music Theater International	Themes and Variations (Movie music)
Musician's Publications	Warner Brothers Music

Luck's Music Library also has a good selection of basic pops arrangements in their catalogue. Many are composed for school orchestras. Some of these can be adapted and spiced up for professional orchestras by adding drum-set and by re-orchestrating specific sections. I have used these when a guest artist didn't have an orchestral arrangement of a piece, but where we wanted orchestral involvement. The orchestra might start by playing half of the arrangement, and then we would open the middle of the piece and insert a section using the guest artist with a small combo. Most of this section would be improvised. After a few minutes, we could then segue back to the orchestra for the ending of the piece. Luck's Music Library is one of the few pops publishers that will send you a perusal score. This is a wonderful thing to take advantage of so you can familiarize yourself with what is available.

Other Considerations

Orchestra Involvement

As you are selecting pieces for your pops concert, always take into consideration the orchestra. Playing a pops concert can either be a fun or terrible experience for the orchestra. This is dependent on the quality of the music. There are many inferior pops arrangements out there. When possible, try to select music that is challenging and exciting for the orchestra to play. If they enjoy playing the concert, this energy will transmit to the audience. If they feel the music is bad, or boring (or both), their lack of involvement will be interpreted by the audience that they don't care. This reflects poorly on the entire organization. Encourage the orchestra to be professional at all times, even if pops concerts are not their favorite concerts to play. Try to work in orchestral pieces that are fun and that feature orchestra members in the same style as the guest artists. This helps create balance for the show and allows the orchestra to remain equally in the spotlight.

Special Requirements

Pops concerts require special musical skills from the orchestra members that are outside their normal expertise. Many shows will call for a lead trumpet player who has a great high register and truly understands jazz improvisation. If this is not the strength of your principal trumpet player, you will want to talk with them in advance to see if they are open to your bringing in another lead player for the concert. The same is sometimes true in the trombone section, but usually the trombone part is not quite as exposed. You also will need an experienced set drummer. Finding a player who has orchestral experience, but also understands pops, jazz, and rock styles is very difficult. You will often have to pay this person extra because they will be turning down more lucrative club dates. A good drummer is worth every penny. They can save your show. The other instrument that is usually required is jazz bass. Sometimes there is a qualified player in your orchestra, but if not, you will have to hire from outside. A good jazz bass player can improvise and will be able to ad lib from a regular bass part or a piano chord sheet. Finally, it is best to hire a *jazz* pianist for your pops shows. You need someone who is well trained and can read music fluently, but who can also play chord charts and improvise. This will allow you to create combo sections on the spot or to have musical ad lib sections underneath a spoken introduction of a piece. This helps bring fluidness and continuity to the show. Speak with your regular players in *advance* if they don't possess the skills to do this type of playing.

Concert Attire

Sometimes it is appropriate to change the dress of the orchestra to fit the theme of the concert or to help promote a much more relaxed atmosphere. I encourage these types of ideas: bandanas for western concerts; splashes of red for Valentine's Day concerts; colorful shirts for outdoor concerts; all add a wonderful atmosphere. Pops concerts tend to focus on the visual. Let the orchestra be involved in helping to enhance the overall mood.

Considerations for Singers

Pops concerts often feature singers. Make sure when you are working with vocalists that you do not have them sing too many pieces in a row. This is important, both in the concert programming and during rehearsals. It is easier if they are a pop singer with a microphone, but if they are an opera singer, you want to help them save their voice. Before ordering your music for pieces involving singers, be sure you check the keys of the arrangements with your soloists in advance. If you can't find the arrangement in the key the singer is comfortable singing, you might have to change the piece. The right key is critical to success. Also, once you have copies of the arrangement, send your soloist a copy to confirm that all the introductions, verses, and bridge sections, are as they would like. You do not want to discover discrepancies at the first and only rehearsal. If you are doing a pops concert of opera arias, you should know that many of the "arrangements" available, are not arrangements at all, but instead are excerpted directly from the opera. Therefore, they might not have the proper introduction or ending that would be expected at a pops concert. Check these details well in advance. Once again, you may either need to locate a more complete arrangement or hire someone to write an introduction and ending.

Finishing Touches—Scripting and Lighting

All of your pops concerts must be scripted. Even if your guest artist would rather ad lib, you must get them to agree to the basic outline of what introductions should be covered, who is doing them, and when spoken dialogue should occur in the show. If you are working with a group, have them assign one person as the spokesperson. This person will handle most of the dialogue. If the others wish to speak, make sure that you inform the stage crew so they will know whose microphone to turn on. After you have finished the script, take the time to meet with your stage crew to add components of lighting. You may have to decide whether you want to use stand lights or not. Using stand lights creates many more possibilities for changing the overall lighting on the stage. In general, I would recommend stand lights to enable you to achieve the maximum lighting effect of the stage. If the show involves visual effects and film, then stand lights are a necessity. You may want to consult a lighting expert as you look for ways to make your pops show more exciting to the eye.

As you are finishing your pops programs, you should keep the following concepts and goals in mind:

> Strive for overall unity of artistic concept
> Select good arrangements
> Concentrate on the importance of pacing, timing, and emotional flow of the show
> Script everything—include timings throughout
> If possible, review your script with a professional theater and/or lighting person

EDUCATIONAL AND FAMILY PROGRAMS

Identifying the Parameters

Programming good educational and family concerts is an art form unto itself. It is a necessary skill for conductors, and well worth acquiring. When planning concerts of this type, you will be faced with some limiting parameters and questions to assess.

What is the budget and what size orchestra will be allowed? Often, you will be requested to squeeze your programming ideas into very small instrumentations requirements. It is common to rewrite or drop out lesser important parts in order to stay within the instrumentation required by the organization for educational concerts.

Do you have extra money for guest artist or props? Unfortunately, educational concerts are usually planned and programmed last, so there is rarely any extra money for guest artists. Another issue is that these concerts also involve multiple performances and so guest artist availability is sometimes a problem.

Take advantage of the fact that these types of concerts can be a wonderful opportunity to showcase members of the orchestra, concerto competition winners, or local talent of all ages and work closely with the executive director or the education committee as you are planning your concerts so that you can request the funds you need to do the job right.

How much rehearsal time will you have? Educational concerts are usually done on just one rehearsal. Sometimes, if you are very lucky you might have two, but this is unusual. Make sure that the music you select to perform can be adequately prepared in one rehearsal. You will have to use your time wisely to ensure that everyone understands all the components of the show.

Can you use rental music? Music directors and staff conductors are always encouraged to use nonrental music for their educational concerts. This is because multiple performances of rental music significantly increase the budget. Most publishers charge by the number of performances you are doing. Keep this in mind as you program but also emphasize the importance of introducing the young people to a variety of composers and musical styles. Many of the publishers will work with you in adjusting the rental price for a piece if the performances are for educational purposes. Try to always use the best composition to communicate your educational ideas and concepts.

Can you incorporate technical effects? Some educational concerts are more theatrical in nature. If you have an inclination toward this type of programming, make sure you assess whether all the performances are in one venue, or if the concerts will take place in a variety of locations. If you are traveling, keep it simple. If the performances are in a place in which you perform regularly, don't be afraid to add special lighting and effects. Students are very visual in the way they learn.

The Audience

Most educational audiences will break down into specific categories, according to the type of concerts they attend.

Kinder-concerts	Students up to about 6 years old
Family concerts	Children with their parents—3 years old to about 12
School concerts	Students in the third to sixth grades
School concerts	On site for Junior High or High School students
Side-by-Side concerts	Families, or Junior High and High School students

If you are involved in school concerts, *do not* simply perform the same program that you prepared for the younger students for students at high school or junior high level; take the time to work with the school to prepare a program that is effective for their school environment. If possible, try to involve music students from the school directly in the performance.

Writing Children's Concerts

Selecting an Educational Concept or Theme

All educational concerts need to communicate and center on a single educational concept. When you are designing programming of this type, you need to first decide on your theme. Some sample themes include:

> Theme and Variations
> Musical Form and Patterns
> Introduction of the Instruments (individually)
> Introduction of the Families of Instruments
> Musical History
> Music as it Relates to Dance
> Music and the Emotions it Conveys
> Stories and Music
> *(Note: these are not titles for the concerts, just a working educational theme.)*

Once you have your theme, you will need to brainstorm to identify pieces that are appropriate. They must meet your instrumentation limitations; they must be able to be practically sight-read by the orchestra; and they must be short! Pieces for this type of concert should never exceed seven minutes, and should probably average about four minutes each. Clever cuts to reduce the length of pieces for educational programs are accepted throughout the industry.

Good programming requires a thorough knowledge of the repertoire. Often the inner movements of suites and larger works provide the core material for good children's concerts. Make sure that the piece really fits the theme and that there is nothing confusing about it. Look for very clear examples. Otherwise, you run the risk of alienating your listeners.

Each piece should involve something special that can be pointed out to the audience. This is the only way we can help teach active listening. Students should be given access points to listen for, and they should be asked about these details afterwards to make sure they listened carefully. For example, if I were to do a program on musical form, I could perform *The Little Fugue in G minor* by J.S. Bach (arr. by Caillet). Before we played this piece, I might have the clarinet player demonstrate the melody or fugue theme. Then, during the performance, I would have the students count the number of times they heard that melody. The piece is only three minutes long. During the concert, you will have your audience actively listening to every note because they want to have the right answer. Afterward, I ask them how many times they heard the melody, and they have the opportunity to be congratulated for their great listening skill.

I also encourage you to bring some of the students on to the stage area. You can teach the entire audience how to conduct a basic two-beat pattern, and then invite a student to conduct the orchestra during the concert. Another idea is to invite students to participate playing percussion instruments, or home-made instruments, as you talk about the specific qualities of the different families of instruments. You can do this during the concert, or you can add a component before the concert like a "Musical Petting Zoo" where the student are allowed to try out all of the instruments of the orchestra in a separate room before the concert begins. Any personal involvement will increase the enjoyment of the concert experience. We want the students to feel that music making can be a part of their lives.

Use of Demos

During the program, it is fun to have members of the orchestra demonstrate certain melodies or motifs that you want the students to listen for. Sometimes, you just want them to be able to identify the sound of the individual instruments. In order to have your demos run smoothly, you will need a detailed cue sheet of instructions for the members of the orchestra. Be clear with your orchestra musicians regarding which demos are fixed—must always be what you specified—and which they can have some fun with, and vary from concert to concert. Most players will enjoy bringing in new "demos," and the orchestra will enjoy listening to see how the demos change from performance to performance.

Timing and Pacing

The timing of an education concert is very important. Often you are dealing with school schedules and orchestra union policies. You need to make sure that your concerts fit within the time frame permitted. Usually, this is forty-five minutes per show (two concerts in a two-and-a-half-hour period). Sometimes you are allowed the extra five minutes grace time (fifty minutes total concert time) but not always. After years of doing these types of programs, I have developed a timing of pieces and a pacing relationship that seems to work.

Normally I will have seven or eight pieces on a forty-five minute children's concert. Of this total time, only twenty-eight to thirty minutes will be music. Therefore, my pieces average about four minutes each.

Opening Piece   Three Minutes—Upbeat in Character

I always start with a good upbeat opener. This is usually preceded by a backstage announcement to grab the attention of the audience (who often has been sitting there for half an hour already) and to let them know that the show is about to start. There have been times when I have talked first, but I still think playing the music itself is the best way to begin a concert. I usually keep this opening piece under three minutes in length.

Dialogue

After the opening piece, I welcome the audience and I begin to tell them what we are going to discover together. I always try to include unusual things that they are not expecting to happen and I always incorporate audience participation.

Main Repertoire   Five or Six Pieces—Two to Seven Minutes Each
                                              (Longer Pieces First)

We now perform five or six pieces that fit the theme. Each piece should move us further towards understanding and being curious about music. Between each piece there is dialogue (and applause) that ranges from thirty seconds to two minutes. *Never* talk more than two minutes between pieces on an educational concert. I always try to keep the longer pieces near the top of the show when a student's attention span is fresher, and no "length expectations" have been set. If you organize it the other way and have two or three short pieces early on, the students will be preprogrammed to stop listening to a longer piece about halfway through. Make sure that each piece has a special activity or something fun for the students to hear or see.

Finale Piece   Three Minutes

Before the final piece on an educational concert, I always tell the audience that this is going to be the last piece. I use phrases such as: "To close the program today . . . " This is important because the students usually do not have printed programs, and they are unaware of where they are in the performance. This helps to keep their expectations clear and gives a finite ending to the concert. I also like to keep this piece short, less than three minutes if possible.

Afterward, make sure you thank the students for being a great audience and encourage them to come to other concerts; give special thanks to all of the members of the orchestra, and recognize any guest artists who might have participated. Young audience members are very appreciative of the orchestra, and they will show this through their applause. It is important to remind them who really performs the music—the musicians.

Scripting

Each concert will need a good script that brings out the points of emphasis in the concert. My scripts are usually four pages or less, single-spaced, with paragraph breaks for each piece. Write the script as if you are having a conversation with someone you respect and imagine that you are telling them about something you are really excited about. Keep it conversational in tone. Never lecture or talk down. The students can meet you on your level. After you write your script, double check that (1) your dialogue sections are not too long (less than two minutes) and (2) that the pacing of the total show works.

The figure below shows a diagram for the basic timing of a youth concert's repertoire and dialogue.

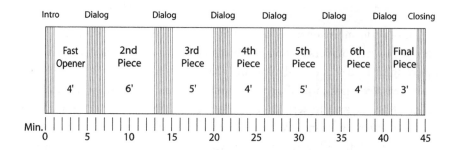

THE OVERALL CONCERT EXPERIENCE
Use of Extras to Enhance the Concert

Creative programming takes creative thinking. Accept the challenge to push the parameters and to change the standard concert format. With all of your concerts, you will face production issues—how do you get the piano on stage without stopping the concert cold as all the violinists get up to create more space? How does the orchestra tune when you want to start the children's concert with everyone offstage? How do you convince your orchestra members to play on tuned bottles to make a musical point? Make sure you think carefully through these issues in advance and give the orchestra members and the stage crew detailed instruction.

I also encourage you to use "extras" for all your concerts such as unusual lighting, interesting props, incorporating actors or dancers, featuring unusual soloists, making use of unexpected entrances of player or guest artists through the hall, using video, slides, or other multimedia components. Each concert should have a feeling of discovery and engagement. These types of extras help move us in that direction. Remember, though, everything you do should be done to *enhance* the music. The focus must remain on the music, and the enhancements must make the musical experience even more meaningful and inspiring.

Total Quality Experience

Programming is the key to the success of a musical arts organization, but even good programming can be undermined if the presentation has flaws. When people attend a concert, they are there for the total experience. If they just want to listen to a specific piece of music, they can do that in their living room. Instead, they want to see the musicians, they want to feel the energy in the hall, and they want to mingle with people during intermission. They do not want to wait in lines, sit in uncomfortable seats, look at people dressed sloppily on stage, or listen to a lackluster performance. Everything matters. As the music director, you are held responsible for everything that happens on stage, regardless of whether it is your job or not. Therefore, take regular assessment of the overall concert experience.

How does the orchestra look? Personal grooming, dress, shoes? It is amazing how much time the audience spends discussing this during intermission. Are there extra bags or purses on stage? Are shoes polished? Is someone's attire inappropriate? Do the musicians turn out and smile when they accept the applause? Work with your personnel manager to convey the importance of the total look on stage.

How does the orchestra sound? Sound is everything. Do you need to make an adjustment in the risers to improve the balance? Do you need a new shell? Does the hall help the sound resonate? Are there things you can do to improve the sound? It is your job as a music director to bring attention to anything that might improve the overall sound of the orchestra.

What is the quality of the performance? Did you have enough rehearsal time for the concert? How did you utilize this time? Was it well spent? Do people need to prepare better before the first rehearsal? Was each composition performed a quality piece? If the concert was not a musical success in your mind, what can you do to change that for the future?

How was the lighting for the concert? Were the soloist's eyes in shadows? Did the violins have enough light to see their music? Did the wind players' instruments go out of tune because of the excessive heat of the lights? Can you decrease the heat onstage and still have good lighting for the concert? Work with the stage crew and the orchestra committee to find solutions.

How smooth were the changes between pieces? Was there a big gap in the concert to create a new setup for a new music piece? Did the moving of the piano create a disturbance to the flow of the performance? How can you keep continuity of the concert and yet provide the staging changes necessary for the musicians? Careful planning in advance will help to alleviate some of these issues.

How was the musical pacing of the concert and the combination of pieces? Was the audience excited about the repertoire? Were people totally engaged, or was there widespread coughing and movement during the concert? Did the orchestra enjoy playing the repertoire? You want to program musical combinations that work and engage both the audience and the musicians.

How was the quality of the soloist? Did you share a mutual interpretation with this artist, or was it like a tug-of-war? Did the audience respond to this artist? Why or why not? Should you invite them again? The chemistry between the guest artist and the conductor is critical to a successful musical interpretation of the piece.

How was your relationship with the orchestra and the audience? Were you able to create a sense of magical communication, or did you feel like a traffic cop? Did you get a warm, embracing feeling from the audience, or were they like a brick wall? What can you change to better the overall relationship? How was the energy in the hall? Was it an electrifying, once-in-a-lifetime concert? Or was it status quo? How can you bring fresh energy to every concert?

Take responsibility and accountability for the entire concert experience. You are the music director, and you have the ability to inspire change and improvement on all levels of the organization. Even though some areas of the concert experience fall outside your direct chain of command, they still reflect upon the total experience. Work closely with the executive director to make sure that the total experience is a quality experience.

The Big Picture

We have spent a lot of time talking about the specifics of programming and the overall concert experience. Successful programming reflects the values of the organization and helps to move the organization toward its goals. Don't fall into the trap of just "playing it safe." Remember, if you are not going up, you are going down. Programming should keep the organization on the cutting edge of the field and in the spotlight of its community. As a music director, it is your job to be leading the organization toward the goals that everyone involved helped to set. Remind them how those goals are reflected in the programming so the proper resources are allocated to enable you to do your job. Always remember—it is about the *music*!

Chapter 6

THE PEOPLE FACTOR

WORKING WITH PEOPLE
Communication Skills

As a conductor, the only way you can really accomplish your goals is through other people. You can understand and communicate the music, but communication is a two-way street. Ultimately, someone in the orchestra will actually be producing the sound. The way to inspire your orchestra to its best effort is through good lines of communication, both on and off the podium. Communication takes time. It involves delving beneath the surface causes and words to find out the root of any problem. It involves being willing to empathize and make people feel heard. Good communication is the key to your success.

Accessibility

As a leader, you need to make it easy for people to come to you. Spend time backstage with the players or come early to rehearsals, and be available in your dressing room. It is best not to be onstage before rehearsals when the orchestra is warming up. Respect their right to some privacy during this time. (Your presence might make them nervous.) You also can stay after rehearsals and concerts and be available to speak with orchestra members as they come off the stage. Try to give the orchestra priority, even over the audience members who may come back stage after a concert. Before and after rehearsals are the only times you have off the podium outside of formal meetings; use this time to strengthen your relationship with the members of the orchestra.

Another technique that can help with building this relationship is to learn everyone's name and to make each of them feel important. Really listen to what the orchestra members have to say, and once they risk telling you what they think, do not punish them for their openness. Never do anything that would discourage them from talking with you about their concerns.

Body Language

As you listen to people, you will be judged immediately on whether you are really listening by your body posture. Learn to look directly into a person's eyes when they are talking to you and try to avoid looking around the room at other distractions. Sit or stand with your arms open and try to have important conversations in nondistracting, quiet environments. As you are listening to someone, your attention should also take note of their body language. Make note of their facial expressions and observe vocal cues such as the rate of conversation, pitch, and tonal inflection. You also should notice their general appearance, posture, and gestures. Clothing and grooming can be a clue to what else is going on in their life at that moment. Remember, a member of your orchestra can be totally blind to their own emotions. It is your job to identify these emotions, however they appear, and to bring them to the surface.

Things Not to Do

As you are listening, don't pretend that you understand something you don't. Stop the speaker and ask for further clarification. When a player, board member, or staff member comes to you with a new idea, avoid responding quickly with reasons why something will not work. Instead, help them come to their own conclusions by asking questions that clarify the issues, both for you and for them. Also, even if you know a person is completely wrong, refrain from arguing. There is no glory in making someone look bad or feel inferior. Allow them to save face gracefully. And above all, as you are speaking with someone about a serious situation that they are experiencing, don't tell them that you "know how they feel." This just diminishes the power of their feelings and makes them feel like you really don't understand at all.

Remember, your job as their leader is to find out what people want and need in order to do their jobs, and to help them get it. You should be supportive and work to get rid of as much red tape as possible for this process. Make sure that you avoid excessive questioning, advising, and moralizing in conversations with members of the orchestra and staff. These reactions do not help to make a person feel heard and understood.

Master Reflective Listening

The actual process of listening goes through many levels: what you actually said—what the other person thinks they heard. Then it is bounced back—what the other person said, and—what you *think* the other person said. It is important during your conversation to get to the center of what is being communicated. You must find a way to clarify the entire message and to confirm that you are hearing correctly. This is often done through reflective listening.

Reflective listening not only enables you to communicate better but also increases the level of trust between the two people involved. As you are listening, do not immediately question what they have said or answer their questions. Instead, paraphrase what they have just told you to make sure you are hearing them correctly. The person with the problem needs a reflective listening response until they can move beyond the presented problem to identify whatever is the more basic problem. As they realize that there is a deeper issue at hand, you must help them once again through paraphrasing to come to terms with their feelings around this issue. As they are talking, continually reflect their feelings regarding what you think they are saying back to them. Continually summarize what you think they have told you. Once you are clear about the basic problem and the emotional feelings involved, you might want to ask some open-ended questions to establish the boundaries of the problem and to begin to work toward solutions.

Open-Ended Questions

Open-ended questions are questions that encourage an in-depth response. These types of questions cannot be answered "yes" or "no." Here are some examples of useful open-ended questions that can help stimulate a conversation.

> How do you feel about this situation?
> What is most important to you about this issue?
> What don't you like about _____?
> What can I do to help you?
> Can you explain further or give me more examples?
> Does anything else bother you or is there anything else I should know?

Through listening reflectively to the answers to these types of questions, you can help to create a stronger shared sense of purpose. Make sure that you put yourself in their shoes and, if possible, show them how they can get what they want or need.

Problem Solving and Decision Making

When faced with a problem, you must first remember that problems give meaning to life. It is through tension and release, the yin and yang of life, that progress is made. Problems that are *your* problems are things that you can do something about. All other problems are simple facts of life and you should not spend your time and energy worrying about them.

Attitude

To deal with solving problems effectively, you must be careful not to take the problem personally or to become too emotionally involved. Excessive emotional involvement will always decrease your effectiveness in looking at all sides of the issue. Individually, we are totally responsible for our feelings and how we handle our feelings toward a problem that must be solved. The attitude of the leader helps to determine the attitudes of the followers. It is important that you set the right attitude for the organization.

Identify, Define, and Prioritize the Problem

You will need to spend some time figuring out who is directly involved with each problem. Is someone upset about how the auditions were handled or disappointed regarding what part they were assigned? Or perhaps they are frustrated by the new rehearsal schedule or the lack of correct bowings in the parts. Ask yourself who is directly affected by the problem at hand. Is it only the person who has brought it to your attention, or are others involved? Once the individuals are identified, you will need to ask them questions. Make sure that you talk to the right people and that you do not make assumptions about who is involved. It is very important to get all the facts. As you are clarifying the problem, be sure that you ask those involved the hard question of "How have I as a leader, music director, or conductor contributed to the problem or situation?" Don't be afraid to open the door for criticism. This will keep the lines of communication open and hopefully lead to a stronger overall level of trust.

Collecting Solutions and Making Decisions

In dealing with the process of making decisions, there are a few things to remember. Not making a decision is actually deciding to do nothing. This can be a course of action, but it often creates larger problems in the long run. It also creates a lack of trust in those you work with unless you can explain why you are hesitant to move forward and take responsibility. Ultimately, it is usually better to make a wrong decision once in a while, than to appear indecisive. Remember that there are no foolproof decisions. An amount of uncertainty for everyone involved is always present, and all decisions and solutions have an element of risk.

Luckily, few decisions are engraved in stone, and therefore, most can be modified later when new information is available. Regardless, it is important to learn from your mistakes, admit them, and move forward quickly.

Never allow others to think that you always have the best answers to a problem. This will serve to make them dependent and wary of you as a leader. When you solve a problem, try to solve it at the lowest possible level with the people who are immediately involved. Have these people help to develop a list of possible solutions. Make sure that you integrate your own ideas into this list. Try to encourage win–win solutions. Encourage creative and unusual thinking. Musicians are better at this than most people. By involving musicians and staff in the solution process, you are giving them ownership and responsibility for the solution.

Implement the Best Solution

Work with the people involved with the situation to identify a solution to each problem. If someone is upset about how the seating has been done, you might want to survey the section for other suggestions regarding the seating procedure. If they are unhappy about the repertoire, ask for their input and try to incorporate some of their suggestions in the following season. Analyze the situation at hand and try to accommodate all parties so that there will be "buy-in" and ownership of the solution. Sometimes, you will not be able to meet their needs, but by having the discussion about the issue, you might at least clear the air and gain some good will. If you come to a solution, be sure to check back after some time has passed to make sure that it is still working. It is also good to clarify policies within the organization so that similar problems will not recur.

Motivating the Orchestra

The more you work with people, the more you should realize that most people want to do a good job. Everyone wants to succeed, and receive recognition for their accomplishments. Motivation is the energy that moves someone toward accomplishing a goal. Sometimes motivation involves an outside motivator who sets expectations, creates a positive environment for achieving the goal, and provides rewards for success. Great conductors understand human behavior. They compliment often and reward their players with great repertoire to perform. Conductors often fail if they have not mastered the art of inspiring and motivating others.

Setting Up the Expectation

When working with people, you need to first examine their individual artistic needs, and then set goals for both the individual needs and for the entire group. Motivation cannot be forced; people have to want to change and improve. Sometimes musicians are simply not performing the way they should. When this happens, it is usually because: (1) they are not clear about the musical standard expected; (2) they do not know how to do it correctly or currently lack the ability to do it correctly; or (3) there are obstacles beyond their control that are making it hard for them to do their job.

Setting Musical Standards

Attention to high musical standards must be established by the music director early in his or her tenure. Toleration of substandard playing or sloppy preparation of the music sends a signal to the rest of the players that quality is not important. All musical organizations are in transition and hopefully always improving in quality. Over the years, the quality level in the industry has risen dramatically. Graduating music students are being better trained in technique and intonation than ever before. In order to keep up, all members of the orchestra need to be continually upgrading their knowledge and exposure to new performance standards. Your goal as a music director is to establish a standard for preparation, intonation, orchestra tone color, and stylistic interpretation. This standard must be emphasized throughout all of your rehearsals. You need to know where you are going artistically and what you are trying to accomplish musically with the orchestra.

When the standard is clear in your mind and clearly presented to the orchestra, you need to assess where the individual musicians are artistically and who might need to be motivated to improve. Once you have identified specific problems, speak privately with the individuals to see if they are aware of them. Often when a player has been performing the same way for a long time, they can no longer see the strengths and weaknesses in their own playing, or they are up against a current standard of technique that surpasses what was required in the past. Give each musician time to talk through their perception of their playing as you tell them yours. End the conversation by setting defined expectations in a positive way. Let them know that you believe in their ability to meet these new challenges. Capitalize on gifts and strengths, not weaknesses.

Additional Training or Tools

Sometimes a player will need extra help to get to the next artistic level. I always provide sample tapes or CDs to orchestra members for concerts that might have unusual or difficult to locate repertoire. I also prepare a tempo sheet for each piece so all the difficult sections can be prepared up to tempo before the first rehearsal. Sometimes I encourage a player to take coaching sessions from a respected colleague in a larger orchestra. This is a great way for them to keep their music-making fresh.

If the musician is a section player, I will often work with the principal of the section to find ways to help them improve. Sometimes I meet privately with the principals to set goals on how they can help their entire section play at its highest level. I encourage them to hold sectionals or to take extra time before and after rehearsals to talk about section blend, tone quality, and tuning. I recognize that I cannot require them to spend this extra time, but often they are happy to be held responsible for helping to improve the overall quality of the orchestra.

It also is useful to organize all of your musicians into ensembles. Having them play together where they are completely responsible for the quality of the music making brings a personal attention to detail back into the routine. It also helps to stabilize the blend of sound and the intonation throughout the orchestra. Sometimes, if the orchestra only performs a small number of concerts, the musicians simply do not play together enough. Solve this problem by creating a chamber music series featuring your musicians.

Removing Barriers

Musicians often have unusual barriers that get in the way of doing their job. An example could be a conflict with their stand partner or a member of their section, or it could be the fact that they don't have an adequate place to practice at home. Perhaps they didn't get the music in a timely fashion, or they were hired late for the job so they had to sight-read the part at the first rehearsal. Whatever the excuse, make sure that everything possible on the administrative side of the organization is being done to make it easy for the musicians to perform. This goes from making sure the music goes out with the correct bowings at least three weeks in advance, to making sure the temperature in the hall is stable and that the lighting is good. Do not be afraid to change the seating in order to resolve a personality conflict, or to adjust sound baffles or risers so people can hear each other better.

If you are willing to make these small types of adjustments, the environment will be more conducive for great music-making. As a leader, you must work to create an environment where people can feel good about themselves and each other. You want to allow them to meet their own needs while at the same time contributing to the group as a whole.

Expect the Best

Once you have removed all barriers, you really can expect the best from your orchestra. You should be enthusiastic, lead the way, and trust them to do a great job. Always give credit for work well done, and if there are any problems, give immediate, specific, and accurate feedback. It is also important to create an environment where failure is not fatal. Each of us makes mistakes. Allow musicians and staff members the opportunity to fix mistakes and problems without blame or criticism. This is a very important step in both the learning process and the process of building trust. To really build a strong, independent team, everyone must be allowed to fail.

You also need to build in an allowance for nonconfrontational conflict. Everyone will not always agree on specific issues. This is fine, and often forces us to really analyze what we are doing as an organization. Encourage discussions on subjects where people are not in agreement. As you accept conflict, you must also encourage *open* communication. Continually remind people that you expect their best behavior as well as their best performance level.

Rewards

Most people who work for nonprofit organizations do not do it for the money. Musicians want to be well paid for their jobs, because that is how they measure their talent level and worth, but ultimately, this is usually not the most important thing to them. Instead, musicians really want to make music, and they want to have a say in the music they are making. They also want to create this music at the highest possible level. It is important in the process to recognize them for their hard work and talent. Too often they feel almost anonymous. Musicians need positive reinforcement as individuals as well as from being part of the group.

In an orchestral setting, this is sometimes difficult to do. Often, everyone is playing at the same time and the opportunities for singling people out in a positive way are limited. Because of this, a solo bow at a concert can be a very important thing for a musician. Make sure you notate on the last page of your score all of the players who are featured during the piece. This way, as you are giving your solo bows and acknowledgements, you won't accidentally skip someone. You also can encourage everyone in the orchestra to turn out and face the audience during the applause. This way, everyone will feel more recognized and the audience will feel they care. European orchestras even have the musicians shake hands with their colleagues before they leave the stage. It is a chance for them to recognize each other and their individual contributions to the performance.

Sometimes, rewards can be in the form of being featured as a soloist or being selected for a special chamber music performance. Even a call to play in a reduced orchestra concert can sometimes be interpreted as a reward for hard work when people really want to play. Systems of rotating the seating in the string sections can also provide people with more attention and exposure as they move to the front of the section. It is also possible to reward musicians with leadership roles outside the regular playing experience. Encourage members of the orchestra to be active on education, artistic, marketing, and fund-raising committees. In these areas, they can participate as volunteers, and they can use talents completely separate from their playing skill. A violin section member could be a great chairperson for the education committee, or they might be a wonderful fund-raiser.

Sample Reward Categories

    Money or financial perks
    Recognition and respect (individual and group)
    More responsibility
    Advancement in the section or solo opportunities
    More challenging repertoire

It is important that the rewards be properly aligned with the actual activity so that the players are motivated to work for them. Be specific in your praise as goals are reached. Make sure you recognize and applaud achievement on *all* levels.

Motivating the Board

Motivating the board is different from motivating the orchestra, but the basic principles apply. Your board will be composed of business leaders, and music lovers. A board has the constant pressure of being responsible for raising the money to keep the organization in business. When times are economically difficult, it is important for the music director to help keep the attitude positive and the direction forward. You will need to make it a priority to attend as many board meetings as possible; this emphasizes to the board your desire to be involved and your commitment to the organization as a whole.

Take time early on in your job to develop a strong relationship with each board member. This will be critical for your success with the board when there are problems to resolve. Become familiar with the special interests of each of the board members so that as the organization is moving in similar directions, these individuals can be encouraged to become more involved. It is very important for the music director, in collaboration with the executive director, to open the eyes of the board to the potential of the organization. You need to be on top of national standards, trends, and issues, so that you can keep the board up to date. You must continually educate the board regarding the orchestra members' needs, and you must constantly remind the board that no matter how many little details and issues need to be discussed and solved, the music and the quality of the performance must always remain the major focus. Because music making is often the thing they understand the least, this continuous reminder is very useful in keeping the organization on track. As with the musicians, you should always be a positive spirit at the board meetings. Reward and praise the board for their accomplishments, large and small, and be available to help them in any way you can.

Confrontation and Resolving Conflict

A problem every music director will eventually face is the tendency of people to rebel against authority. People desire a dynamic leader to inspire them, yet they can be openly hostile toward anyone who has real or perceived power over their destiny. Don't let this bother you. It is more important to have the players' confidence than their affection. There are times when you will not be popular—this is just part of the job. If you want to be liked by all people at all times, then the position of music director of an orchestra is *not* for you.

Difficult People

Throughout your career, you will deal with people who are simply difficult. Being able to deal with difficult people is a career asset. Difficult people are usually frightened; they can be very controlling, or terrified of losing control. They also can be very insecure. Overly critical people are often very critical of themselves and they constantly fight within themselves for an unachievable standard. The key to working with this type of person is to understand what they believe in and what they are afraid of. Try to discover how you can achieve your goals in spite of, or even by means of, the difficult person by being proactive with the situation, not reactive. Give them special attention and recognition and try to involve them in the inner workings of the organization. Often, their outspokenness is a direct result of their desire to be noticed and involved. Difficult people are often diffi-cult because they care. See if they can channel this caring into a useful activity for the good of the orchestra.

When dealing with the concerns of a difficult person, always assume that their motivation is positive, but disguised. Perhaps they are actively involved with the orchestra committee in a confrontational way because they are pushing for a pay increase for the musicians; or maybe they give the guest conductors a hard time for not fixing musical problems within the ensemble because they know when the orchestra is not playing at its top level. Difficult people usually want what is best for the orchestra; they take pride in their own expertise and want to be recognized for it; they want to help keep the organization from making costly mistakes; and they want to help us do things better. If you understand this positive motivation as a background, your relationship with the difficult person will improve.

Personality has a lot to do with difficult people and relationships. Know your own personality traits and be familiar with what irritates you personally in oth-ers. Do not allow people to push your buttons. Try to treat the difficult person with patience and humor. It helps if you can see the issue first from their per-spective. In dealing with difficult people, never assume that what is important to you is important to them. As you work with them, communicate how you feel about the effects of the other person's behavior—how it is affecting you and oth-ers in the organization. It is useful to note the information in table 6.1 to help you stay on track during the conversation.

Table 6.1 Concerns for Dealing with Difficult People

Behavior	*Feelings*	*Impact*
When you . . .	I feel . . .	Because . . .
When you . . .	Others feel . . . or think . . .	Which causes . . .

If you are dealing with a specific behavior problem, like late attendance to a rehearsal or disruptive behavior, try to suggest alternate behavior in a non-con-frontational manner. Be sure to deal with one behavior issue at a time. Break everything down into smaller components and start with problems that you think can be resolved easily. This creates a small level of trust which will be help-ful in resolving future issues.

During your interaction with this person, allow their emotions, which may be running quite high, to be expressed. Sometimes people just need to be able to vent a little. Do not judge these emotions; judging will not help you to resolve the con-flict. And, most important, never lose control of your own emotions. Expressing anger only adds fuel to the fire and lowers your ability to be effective as a leader.

Confrontation

When faced with confrontational situations, do not ignore the conflict hoping it will just go away. Problems with an orchestra that go on for a long time are only harder to resolve later on. Make sure that you address the issue, but do not jump in too quickly to deal with a confrontation when your emotional level is too high. Take some time to evaluate the situation from a distance to clarify your goals and outcomes. Never take confrontational situations personally; this will only get in the way of solving the problem and might create an additional layer of problems in the future. Study all complaints seriously. If a situation is bad enough for someone to bring it to your attention, it is important enough for you to deal with it.

When dealing with a personal confrontation, remember that all confrontations should be handled privately and the details should not be discussed with others. Confidentiality is critical for establishing trust. A meeting should be scheduled as soon as possible after the problem has occurred to discuss the issue and to arrive at solutions. In setting up this meeting, be direct and specific about the purpose of the meeting. The musician will probably already have an idea regarding what you want to talk about. If your orchestra is a union orchestra, they may wish to have a union representative at the meeting. When you are in the meeting, try to focus on only one issue at a time. In describing this issue, do not use words like always or never; these absolutes just tend to add flame to the fire. It is important once your point has been made, that you do not keep repeating it. They heard you the first time; additional statements just add salt to the wound. After you have stated your concerns, listen reflectively to their side of the story. Make sure you repeat back to them what you are hearing, and that you take time to clarify any statements that might be confusing. Once they are finished, instead of criticizing, try to present suggestions or ask questions that help them understand the deeper issues at hand. In closing, explain what you want to happen next or identify possible solutions and have them commit to one. After the meeting, it is important for you to document the conversation for your files. You also may choose to send them a copy. Make sure you list all people who were present and include the date the dialogue occurred.

When confronting a person, it is helpful to make use of open-ended questions. Here are some that might be useful in a confrontational situation:

> What solutions do you see for this situation?
> How do you feel about this?
> What is most important to you?
> How do you think your actions affect others in the orchestra?

What can I do to help?

What can we change to make this work better?

Termination

If you are continually having problems with a musician because of artistic quality problems or because of disruptive behavior, before you move to steps of termination make sure that you have asked yourself these questions:

> Have you been clear about your expectations—both verbally and
> in writing?
> Have you removed all obstacles for them to achieve the goal?
> Is the musician capable of making the changes necessary to achieve
> this goal?
> Have you set an official probationary period and given ongoing feedback?
> Have you followed the documenting procedure according to the
> orchestra agreement?

Tolerance of really poor performance can hurt morale and impact your overall quality. If you do have to terminate someone, encourage them to step down on their own. If this does not work, then move through the process quickly. Make sure you have documented all conversations and musical issues and that all policies have been followed. In preparing this paperwork, be sure to specify behavior and performance level, not attitude (except in a disruptive behavior dismissal). Be careful to record exactly what happened and when it happened. It is also important to protect the confidentiality of the situation for both the organization and the individual. When you meet with the player, be professional and sensitive, but do not get into a debate or prolong the process. Termination is difficult for everyone involved. Do it quickly, try to treat people with respect, and allow them every opportunity to save face.

IMPLEMENTING THE ARTISTIC PLAN

Planning Cycle and Deadlines for Programming

As a music director, there are certain things that you must do in order for everyone else to do their jobs. If you do not complete your tasks in a timely fashion, no one else will be able to proceed with their responsibilities. One of the most important things you are responsible for is the programming. Programming for the following season should be sketched out at least a year to a year and a half in advance. Planning this far in advance is important even with youth and community orchestras. If you are applying for an NEA grant, you will have to plan even further ahead. During the early spring you should gather information regarding possible guest artists and begin to select the repertoire. (The season starting in September is already printed; you are now planning for the following September, a year later.) Sometimes you will hold guest artist spots open for concerto competition winners and student soloists that will be chosen at a later date, but by early summer you should have a short list of guest artists who can be researched further. By October or November, contracts or letters of agreement should be negotiated and signed. All of the repertoire should be completely finalized by January and a copy should be sent to the person designing the season brochure which should be printed and available to the public in March to allow multiple opportunities for ticket renewals. It is good to sketch multiple years at once to insure artistic continuity and to provide information for multi-year grants. This allows you to establish educational cycles such as eventually playing all of the Beethoven Symphonies, or to gradually increase the difficulty of the repertoire that you are performing.

Programming Deadlines

March—June	Make preliminary plans for the following season
June—September	Select guest artists and repertoire
September—November	Finalize all repertoire
November—January	Sign contracts with guest artists
January	Provide information for brochure
March	Distribute the following season's brochure to public

If you are working with a university orchestra, the planning cycle may be delayed slightly as you assess what students are returning, what new students might enroll, and what dates are available at the university concert hall. It is important, however, not to get behind in the process. All programming should be completed by May for the season that starts in September to allow time for the music to be ordered and marked, and for the publicity materials to be prepared. It is also useful in recruiting new students to know what repertoire is going to be performed the following school year.

Make sure that you have checked every detail before the program is finalized. Do not program pieces that you do not know, or pieces that you have never seen a score for (except for world premieres). Make sure that all of your programming is playable by your orchestra in the amount of rehearsal time you have and that it fits within your budget structure. By planning in advance, you will be able to fit the budget to the programming. The artistic goals should always drive the budgeting of the organization, not the other way around. It is dangerous to continually force programming into smaller instrumentation requirements because you've been told that it is "all you can afford." In difficult times, think outside the box and dare to do things bigger and better than you have done before. This will create the momentum to move the orchestra to a more stable footing.

With a regional orchestra, often the detailed programming for the education concerts and pops concerts is done after the regular subscription programming is finished. Try to avoid putting these off. It is best to have your educational programming finalized a year in advance so that the educational materials can be properly prepared. The timelier you can be in finalizing *all* of the programming, the easier it will be for others to do their jobs at the highest level.

Organizing Your Rehearsals

Each concert will require information from you to assure that every detail will be taken care of. This information needs to be distributed to the people involved at least four weeks before a concert.

You should prepare the following for each concert:

> Specs sheet
> Rehearsal schedule
> Tempo sheet or special instructions
> Seating for the strings
> Stage set-up diagram
> Demo tapes or CDs of unusual works

Specs

I usually create a specs sheet for each concert, with information that needs to be communicated. When I prepare this, I try to anticipate any problem or any detail that might be unusual about this concert. The top of the page includes each piece on the program, the individual orchestration for each piece, and the overall orchestration (personnel requirements) for the concert. You should also include the timings for each piece. David Daniels's book *Orchestral Music* is extremely valuable for gathering this information. The specs sheet usually includes a section for the librarian, personnel manager, stage crew, and the general office. In each area, I list everything that needs to be anticipated. These might involve drawing the personnel manager's attention to the fact that the contrabassoon player is only needed at three rehearsals, not four; or to let the librarian know that the English horn part that appears on the second oboe part in one of the pieces should be photocopied and given to the English horn player. Perhaps there are both trumpet and cornet parts, and you either need to tell the librarian to whom to give which part, or to remind the personnel manager to contact the principal of the section and have them assign the parts. Failure to take care of these details can cause huge problems later on. Notation of other essentials, such as reminding the stage crew that the celeste is needed, or that you will need the solo piano at three rehearsals, not just the standard two, helps everyone to do their jobs correctly.

After you write down everything you are concerned about, you can go over this information with the people involved to make sure they understand what they need to do. I find that by thinking these things through in advance, I am able to help anticipate problems and solve them before they occur. I always tell them to add details to the specs sheet that I might have forgotten. This way, everyone begins to think more proactively throughout the organization.

Rehearsal Schedule

Preparing a rehearsal schedule for a concert that is months away is a difficult challenge. Somehow, you must accurately guess how much time you will need for each piece in order to produce the highest quality performance. This rehearsal schedule should be sent out with the music at least three weeks in advance. Players will use this schedule to help them plan their time. It is important that once the schedule is set, you stick with it. If you need to make a change, make sure you announce it clearly at a rehearsal, when everyone who is involved with the change is present. The change should also be posted in the rehearsal area. If someone is not present to hear the change, they should be called and notified personally.

When assessing how much time is required to rehearse a piece, you need to know the piece thoroughly. You need to be able to identify what sections are difficult and which sections will "read down." You should be familiar with the retention level of your orchestra. Some orchestras have to play each piece at every rehearsal. Other orchestras can read through an easier piece at the first rehearsal, and then not see it again until the dress rehearsal. Your ability to determine how to spend your time during your rehearsals will make your concerts better. I often plan for double the length of the piece when I am rehearsing a work that is fifteen minutes or shorter. With longer compositions, you might want to look at each movement and subdivide the time, using the lengths and difficulty of the movements as your base.

You will probably not have the luxury of rehearsing every movement at every rehearsal. Concertos usually need one hour on each of the last two rehearsals. Before that, however, plan enough time to at least read through the entire piece, (this could be split over two rehearsals). No soloist should be subjected to the orchestra "reading" the concerto when they appear. The better you can anticipate the strengths and weaknesses of your orchestra and how much time they will need, the better your planning will become. As you organize your scheduling, try to work around issues that might make you lose rehearsal time, such as piano moving. If possible, make these changes during a break, or pre-set the piano before the beginning of the rehearsal. Every minute of rehearsal counts and you certainly do not want to lose expensive minutes because of stage changes.

Tempo Sheet

In order for musicians to prepare for the concert accurately, it is helpful to provide a tempo sheet that will go out with the music in advance that lists the metronome markings for every major tempo change in each of the concert pieces. This is especially useful if any of the pieces are not standard works. Players can simply set the metronome for their at-home practice and be comfortable that they are going to be able to play the difficult passages at the tempo you expect. These tempo markings should be as accurate as possible, but there will always be room for some mild variation.

You also should include information regarding unusual terms or unique compositional markings. Anything that might be unclear to the players should be explained in advance on this information sheet. It is also important if there are a lot of critical divisi parts (such as in Debussy's *La Mer*) to include information, either marked specifically on each part or on the information sheet, regarding how divisi parts will be handled. The string players want to make sure that they are practicing the correct line of music. Work closely with your principal string players and your librarian to clarify these issues in advance.

Seating for the Strings

Seating is handled many different ways from one orchestra to another. Seating can be: (1) fixed—the same for each concert; (2) rotated—players move through the section in a specific pattern; or (3) assigned for each concert—players are seated differently for each concert and there is not a definite pattern. Sometimes a music director might pair a strong player with a weak player to improve the overall section, or put a stand of very fine players in the back to help the sound. Any of these seating methods can be used effectively. Seating can be coordinated by the conductor, the section principal, the personnel manager, or through an audition process. It is important to analyze what is right for your orchestra. In evaluating seating, you want to figure out what is going to give you the best sound and blend of the section; then take into account what will keep the players happy, comfortable, and motivated. When you come into a new situation, check the organizational history to see how seating has been done in the past, and then wait until your second year before making any changes. Talk with the musicians involved to make sure that they understand what you are trying to accomplish artistically to justify the change.

Seating for some players is very personal, especially in a youth orchestra situation in which you have the ego of not only the student but that of the parent to contend with. It is good to research the people dynamics within your string sections and to incorporate their individual situations. Some might have violent personality conflicts with certain players. Once you are aware of the issues, you will probably not want to seat them together. Other people enjoy playing on the outside, or vice-versa; some need to sit in the front because of sight issues; or some are highly competitive and want the chance to advance in the section. Try to be flexible as you work with the individuals in your orchestra.

If someone is consistently unhappy with their seating in the orchestra, provide them the opportunity to play for you and the principal of the section or a small committee; it is possible that you have misjudged their abilities. Just knowing they have the opportunity to prove themselves will make some musicians happier. Others, afraid of having to play by themselves, might suddenly be quite satisfied with where they are in the section and they will cease complaining about the new system.

The seating chart for each concert should be prepared at least three weeks in advance and should be included in the packet of music sent out. Last-minute changes can be posted at the rehearsal, but it is best to seat a newly added player in the same chair as the musician who cancelled. This way you are moving as few people as possible and you don't open yourself up to the criticism of moving your "favorite" player up in the section.

Stage Setup Diagram

To avoid problems and confusion, it is best to prepare a basic stage diagram for each concert. Some concerts may require two diagrams, one for the first half and one for the second half, if the stage set up varies dramatically.

At the top of the diagram, list the concert date and the total instrumentation. It is also good to include a short list of technical needs. These might be unusual items such as a cello riser, or a microphone for a short talk from the stage. This list is especially important if you are doing a concert with extra technical requirements.

The diagram should be very clear regarding the riser format that you would prefer and the positioning of these risers from either the front of the stage or from the back wall. No conductor or player likes to walk into a situation in which the entire orchestra setup is pushed too far back in the shell, with the horns' sound bouncing back into their instruments. If you are very clear that you want the back risers set at least six feet in front of the back wall, you will avoid this problem. Make sure that you understand the dimensions of your stage so everything will fit properly. It is good to have a master diagram done to scale of the basic setup for your risers and string members. Then you can just add the particulars for each concert. Here is a sample of a master diagram, and one that is filled in. After you have worked consistently with the same stage crew, you may only need a diagram when it is different from your standard setup.

Blank Stage Diagram

Filled-in Stage Diagram

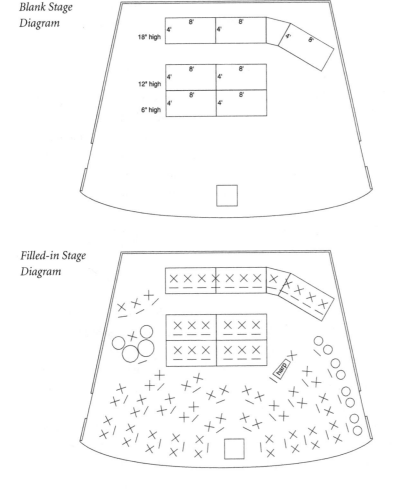

Demo Tape of Unusual Works

If you tend to program new music or unusual works, it is recommended to make recordings of these works available to the orchestra. Some players would find them on their own, but others might not. Just being able to hear how their part fits within the context of the whole can bring a higher level of performance to the ensemble. I try to make sample tapes or CDs of the music for each concert for study purposes. I make these in the summer and leave them at the symphony office. These master tapes can then be used to make copies of either the entire tape or selected pieces. You may choose to focus on the pieces that are difficult to find. All of the tapes or CDs should be clearly marked that they are for study purposes *only*. If you have a player in the ensemble that is willing to take responsibility for duplicating and distributing the tapes, this is the best way to do it. The other musicians can give them a preaddressed envelope and a blank tape or disc. With this system, you ease the pressure from the office, and the push for the better preparation for rehearsals is coming from inside the ensemble.

Working with Staff or Volunteers

Within an orchestral organization, there are specific staff members or volunteers who you will depend upon constantly. Learning how to best work with these people is to your advantage. In the hierarchical structure (except for at a university), these people will usually report to the executive director, but often you will be the person who explains what you really need from them in terms of their job duties. It is good for you to be familiar with each of these positions and the normal expectations placed upon staff in these roles. This will help you to be more effective in expressing how you would like things accomplished and make it easier for you to achieve your musical goals.

Working with the Librarian

Regardless of the budget size of the orchestra, you will probably be working with a music librarian. If you don't have one, get one! A good music librarian is critical to your success as a conductor. Sometimes you will inherit a wonderfully trained music librarian; other times, you will need to train them regarding which areas are important to you, and how you would like certain items handled.

It is customary to sit down with the librarian to go over the programming for the following season. At this time, you will need to explain how to locate any music that might be difficult to find. (This is especially true for new pieces or unusual repertoire from other countries.) You must be very clear which specific editions you would like to use for each piece. If soloists are involved, the librarian will need to contact them to confirm editions and, with vocal soloists, to confirm keys! Opera arias are often available in multiple keys. It is difficult to obtain or change music on short notice if the key you have ordered is not appropriate for the singer.

To order the music, the librarian must understand how many performances will take place, the specific dates, and what the string count will be for each concert. As you are reviewing the list, ask them to locate all of the music and to provide an estimation of the cost for the music for the next season. You will need to know the total amount, and the amount per concert. By researching this early, if any pieces are completely unreasonable in price, you will still have time to make a change before the programs are finalized. The amount for the music rental (including postage) should be included in the overall budget of the organization. This is why it is important to have the programming done early; it affects so many other aspects of the organization.

Next, the librarian should order a quintet of string parts for every piece that you are performing the following season. All of the standard pieces are easily available, but rental music is another matter. The librarian will need to convince the publisher to send a quintet of strings early (or a photocopy of these parts) so that bowings can be marked in advance.

After the parts are delivered, they will be sent out for bowings. Sometimes this is done where all the principal string players get together, play through the piece, and decide the bowings. This can be very effective, but it tends to take excessive time and might be too costly for the organization. More often, the parts or the score will be mailed out, first to the concertmaster and then, after they have finished their bowings, to the other string principals. You may be asked to help contact a principal player if a player is slow in returning their bowed parts. Work with the librarian to make sure that this is accomplished in a timely manner. If the players are late in returning their bowing, then the music might be delayed in being distributed to the orchestra members. If you are working with a youth orchestra or a university orchestra, you might need to prepare all of the master bowings yourself. If you are not a string player, it is critical that you have your bowings checked by a string player before they are finalized. Make sure that you prepare your parts well in advance so that the librarian has enough time to transfer the bowings. Properly marked parts are *essential* to a quality concert experience for the string players.

It is also very important for the librarian to check the parts for uniform rehearsal numbers or letters. These must be matched with the conductor's score with the parts, or your own personal score. There is nothing more embarrassing and difficult than trying to rehearse an orchestra where you don't have the same reference markings. You can save yourself a tremendous amount of time and frustrations if you make sure that this is taken care of in advance. Also, don't just check the first movement of a piece. Sometimes, the numbering system will change in later movements. I remember a time where my third movement started the numbers over again, and the player's parts continued the measure numbers from the second movement. Be sure to check both the wind and the string parts because they differ in some editions. Work with the librarian to solve these problems before rehearsals to maximize your time on the podium.

Duties of the Librarian

> Ordering the music
> Organizing the bowings with the concertmaster and principal string
>   players
> Marking the master bowings into the parts
> Erasing bowings or markings that are not relevant
> Mailing out the music
> Collecting the music after a concert
> Reordering lost parts
> Sending the music back

Some other areas that the librarian must cover are:

> Checking all pieces for uniform rehearsal numbers or letters
> Making sure that the letters are not too far apart
> Adding measure numbers or letters if necessary
> Preparing cuts and inserts when necessary
> Checking for page turns to make sure they are possible
> Making a photocopy insert if the page turn is bad
> Checking each part of a new composition against the score
> Marking divisi instructions into the parts
> Hand-writing out introductions, endings, or inserts as necessary
> Making sure that the conductor's score matches the parts

Locating Music

In order to really help your librarian, you will need to have a thorough knowledge of the music publishers and music sources in the United States. Publishers for classical programming are standard. A detailed list and contact information for the most common music publishers and sources are included in the Resource section. You can contact each of these publishers individually; they will be happy to send you a catalogue. You should collect catalogues from all of the major music publishers.

New music is somewhat harder to find because, more and more, young composers are establishing their own music publishing companies. These self-published composers can usually be found by searching the Internet. Almost all young composers have Web sites that they keep up to date with information about their compositions. Another important resource for new music is the *New Music Juke Box* from the American Composer's Forum (NewMusicJukeBox.org). This free Web site allows composers and publishers to post bibliographical information about works, contact information, biographies, and digital scores and sound files. With the click of a button, you can use the search engine to find scores, sound samples, and biographical information on works and composers.

Among the hardest things to locate are good pops charts or good arrangements that will work on Christmas shows and other types of lighter concerts that are not standard. Many of these types of arrangements are available from an assortment of smaller, independent publishers. Often these publishers will send a one-page flier listing available works. Keep these in a file or notebook, because you never know when you might need a specific piece. A list of pops sources is also available in the Resource section. When you are programming pops and Christmas concerts, you will need to be very clear with your librarian regarding where they should start looking to find the pieces you want, especially if you have specific arrangements in mind.

A good music librarian is worth their weight in gold. It is a difficult job with extreme pressure from many different people. Make sure that you give your librarian support and praise. This is especially important if they have many concerts to prepare for in a row. Do everything you can to try and make their job easier and less stressful.

Working with the Personnel Manager

As a conductor, you will rely heavily on your personnel manager or contractor. This is the person responsible for hiring the orchestra, replacing people who are not available for a specific concert, and dealing with all of the emergency situations that will occur during any concert season. In situations in which the orchestra is not paid, you will still need a dependable person to coordinate the attendance of the members; communicate rehearsal schedules; and to coordinate the number of players in each section required to perform the repertoire selected. This person will be responsible for documenting all issues, and often they also will be in charge of coordinating the auditions for new personnel and substitutes.

As soon as the instrumentation is finalized, you should meet with the personnel manager to go over the needs for the next season. This meeting usually happens between March and May, depending on when you have to have your contracts or commitment letters out for the following year. At this time, you will give them the repertoire/instrumentation lists for the entire season. I usually submit them in the following format. The instrumentation code is from David Daniels's book *Orchestral Music—A Handbook*. The numbers appear in score order and the * refers to instrument doubling or alternate instrument parts (i.e., flute doubles piccolo, oboe doubles English horn, clarinet doubles bass clarinet, bassoon doubles contrabassoon).

DATE: TBA

TITLE: "MUSICAL IMPRESSIONS"

SOLOIST: Organ Soloist—TBA

TOTAL INSTRUMENTATION:

*3,*3,*3,*4, - 5,5,3,1   timp+3, 2 harp, strings   STRINGS: 12,10,8,8,6

Minuet Antique	Ravel	7'
*3,*3,*3,*3, - 4,3,3,1 timp, harp, strings		
La Mer	Debussy	23'
*3,*3,2,*4, - 4,5,3,1 timp+3, 2 harps, strings		
———		
Symphonie Concertante Organ Solo	Jongen	37'
*3,*3,*3,*3, - 4,3,3,1 timp+2, strings		

From this information, they should understand exactly which personnel to hire or assign for each concert. (Note the use of the assistant horn in the "total instrumentation" numbers.) They must be sure to communicate doubling needs so that the players will know which additional instruments they will be playing. Usually the tenured or regular players are contacted first. After they have selected which concerts they are available for, then positions will be filed for single concert by musicians from the substitute list. The personnel manager is responsible for maintaining the substitute lists. Ranking of the substitute list is usually defined by the music director, the principal of the section, and the members of the

audition committee. It is best that you set up a policy in which the personnel manager checks with you before hiring substitutes for critical positions. You must be
very clear on which particular decisions you want to be involved in, and which
they should take care of on their own. A good personnel manager has an extensive network of musicians to work from so that if all the names on your normal
substitute list are exhausted, they are still able to fill the position before the first
rehearsal. They should provide a copy of the complete personnel for each concert
at least two weeks before the first rehearsal. If a personnel manager consistently
has difficulty filling all of the required openings before the first rehearsal, you
may need to find another personnel manager.

The general duties of the personnel manager break down into specific categories:

Orchestra Policies

     Prepare all contracts or letters of agreement
     Hire or arrange for all players for each concert (regulars and subs)
     Maintain accurate substitute lists
     Obtain appropriate tax documentation as necessary (IRS forms)
     Handle attendance and payroll as necessary

Production

     Provide personnel list for concert programs
     Facilitate and post seating for string sections

Rehearsals

     Keep track of time at rehearsals—starting time, break time, ending time
     Log significant events, complaints, tardiness, appropriate dress
     Respond to musician problems and issues as needed
     Communicate information regarding dress, parking, and concert times
     Inform musicians of "house rules"

Auditions

     Identify and post openings
     Coordinate audition dates with music director and the audition
        committee
     Handle all publicity for auditions
     Schedule and coordinate all details for auditions (space, screen,
        handouts)
     Follow up all auditions with results in writing

Administrative/budgeting

> Assist with the development of budget projections for orchestra
>   personnel expenses
> Ensure that musicians and substitutes receive timely compensation

As you work with your personnel manager, you will develop a rapport and they will know which discussions and decisions you want to be involved with. If you are having private conversations with a player regarding the quality of their playing, it is helpful if the personnel manager knows that this is going on. Sometimes they might be asked to sit in on these conversations. They will also be your eyes and ears in the orchestra to identify problems and concerns before they escalate.

The personnel manager is a person who will be vitally important to your success. Discuss with them ahead of time the types of values you want reflected through the orchestra—positive attitude, attention to detail, quality performance, and proper preparation. The personnel manager can be instrumental in encouraging these attitudes. It also helps if your personnel manager has a sense of humor. Many tense situations can and will occur within an orchestra. The ability to smile, or even crack a joke and go with the flow, is critical during these times. Even in pressure situations, the show must go on.

Working with the Education Director or Education Committee

If you are the conductor of a regional orchestra, your work with the education director or committee will first center on the youth concerts you are scheduled to conduct. The programming for these should be done as early as possible after the subscription concerts have been finalized. Once the program has been chosen, it is good to meet with the education committee or staff to talk them through each program. During this conversation you can let them know what educational points are being emphasized during the concert, and what information might be good for preconcert and postconcert learning. You will want to prepare a sample tape or CD for the office of each of the pieces that will be performed. This tape can then be duplicated as a learning tool, both for the teachers, volunteers, or the staff writing the educational materials, and for distribution to the teachers who are preparing the students to attend the concerts.

As you get closer to the concert, you will need to distribute the following to the staff:

1. A script with timings for the pieces and the dialogue
2. A cue sheet of cuts and demo information for the orchestra

3. A standard tempo sheet for orchestra preparation
4. A list of the props you need
5. A riser diagram that includes all technical requirements
6. A specs sheet which will point out anything unusual
7. A sample tape or CD of all the pieces
8. Seating for the strings

If your concert involves numerous technical issues such as lighting changes and stage setup changes, you may want to have a separate meeting with the stage crew one to two weeks before the performances. This will depend on the quality of your stage crew and the capacity of your hall for additional technical equipment.

Regardless of the size of your orchestra, you will probably work closely with volunteers on educational outreach programs such as ensembles in the schools, or a traveling musical petting zoo. More and more, orchestras are being asked to produce school programs to encourage young people to learn more about classical music. Even the college students are now being trained to perform these types of concert activities. Because of this, you may be directly involved with the planning, scripting, and implementation of music outreach programs. All educational outreach programs should have specific goals that fit the parameters of your artistic mission. (For more examples of community outreach, see pages 200–202.)

Sometimes, organizations fall into the trap of doing educational programs simply to qualify for the grant money available. This is not the right motivation. Your orchestra needs to be clear on how these programs impact the quality of life in their community, and how they help support the overall artistic directions of the organization. If you cannot make this connection and commit to doing these programs at a high level, then you should not do them at all. Effective and high-quality educational programs are important to the community; they should have an equally high value within your orchestral institution. As a music director, you should be a catalyst for encouraging outreach programs. All outreach programs need to be structured to engage and excite people about classical music and the orchestra. All programs should also lead back to the concert hall and a performance of the symphony orchestra. Over time, it has been proven that multiple exposures are more effective than a single exposure, but single exposures are certainly better than nothing. Because so many schools have reduced or eliminated their music programs, sometimes one exposure is all these students will ever have. Let us never forget that for some, this one-time experience might be life-changing. Because of this, we must make sure that extreme effort goes into making every children's concert performance excellent and exciting. We want to turn students "on" to music, not turn them off. Take the time to write interesting and fun programs that feature quality music. It will be time well spent.

Working with the Operations Manager or Stage Crew

Most symphony concerts involve very little technical equipment. For the majority of the concerts, a simple diagram of the chairs and risers is all the stage crew needs. You do need to be clear on your rehearsal schedule regarding when you would like the stage changed for the soloist and when you would like the soloist on stage during the rehearsal.

Other things you might want to anticipate with the stage crew are extreme heat and extreme cold. Both of these conditions are very bad for orchestral players to work within. Anticipate major weather changes by contacting the hall in advance about the possible problem so that the temperature in the building can be set accordingly. In addition, it is good to always have a backup plan—like portable electric heaters or fans—in case of an emergency.

If you are performing pops concerts, the stage issues become more involved than a regular subscription concert. When you need a sound system, be certain that you obtain the *right* type of sound system. Never scrimp or try to save money on sound. If you do, you will run the risk of crashing the entire concert. There is nothing worse than a concert with feedback. It is important to have the right quality equipment, but also that the person running the sound board has orchestral experience. The last thing you want your orchestra to sound like is a rock band. Unfortunately, this is sometimes the experience level of the person who is hired to operate the sound equipment.

If you are performing a special concert that uses dancers, actors, special lighting, or audio-visual effects, you may want to plan a separate tech rehearsal on the stage. This will enable everyone to become accustomed to the space and to work out problems. It is well worth the extra effort and money for this rehearsal to ensure that orchestral time is not wasted. Inform everyone of your desire for a tech rehearsal way in advance so that it can be included in the contracts and schedules, and added to the overall budget for the year.

Guest Artists

When arranging for guest artists, you may be working with someone on the staff like an operations person, artistic planner, or the executive director, or you may be arranging for your soloists personally. As you develop your short list of guest artists, be sure to include information about repertoire and the number of rehearsals that the soloist will be required to attend. If you have a total of four rehearsals, usually the guest artist attends two. If you are doing a Brahms piano concerto, you might want them to participate in three rehearsals. If it is a short concerto that the orchestra has played many times, one rehearsal might be sufficient. Take time to work this schedule out before the contract is negotiated. Everything should be spelled out very clearly to avoid problems later on.

Before the first orchestral rehearsal with the guest artist, reserve an hour to meet with them privately to go over their interpretation and tempos. For a vocalist, you might need to hire a pianist for this rehearsal. This prerehearsal meeting is very important so that any discrepancies in interpretation and tempos can be discussed and settled before getting together with the orchestra. Most guest artists are very easy to work with, and they enjoy spending this time talking about and demonstrating the piece they are going to perform.

Working with the Marketing Staff or Committee

When you have finished your programming for the following season, it is advisable for you to meet with the people who are going to design the brochure to talk them through the programs. Often, they will want to assign snappy titles to each concert for attention grabbing purposes. You need to make sure that these titles really fit. Nothing is worse than a marketing title that has nothing to do with the music. Often, the people writing the copy for the brochure or doing the design will not have a musical background. It is your job to make sure that the musical integrity of the program is not compromised by the marketing.

In addition to talking them through the programs and the mood of each of the pieces, it is helpful if you also take the time to write a short paragraph about each program. Try to list four or five specific descriptive words that are appropriate for each of the pieces. Try to convey what you are trying to accomplish artistically with this program, why these pieces fit together, and how. This document can be circulated to the volunteers, the staff, and the board. Everyone involved with the organization needs to be comfortable talking about the upcoming concerts, and they should be able to answer questions about the music that will be performed.

The other way you might be involved with the marketing aspects of the organization is in regards to organizational "branding." This branding must reflect the mission and vision of the organization. Your name will be actively associated with it and you need to be a part of the process in deciding the direction. Within the process, be careful not to let marketing drive the programming. It is good to be aware of ticket sales, both subscription and single tickets, and to be involved in discussions regarding what sells and what doesn't. You should regularly ask for these statistics from the office or your committees and be aware of trends in your audience base. It is however, very dangerous to start making programming decisions just to provide the marketing committee with something more saleable. Try to keep the artistic vision clear in your mind and create balanced programs that further the artistic goals of the organization and that you are pleased and proud to put your name on.

Music Director's Role with the Board
Working with People on the Board

As a music director, you will be responsible for selecting the programming for the orchestra and presenting it to the Board of Directors. (If you are at a university, you might be presenting this information to the department chair or the other faculty members.) Before finalizing the concerts, presentation, you should meet with the artistic committee (if you have one) and the executive director to flush out concerns and to adapt things as necessary. During this process, it is important to stay true to your artistic ideals, but also to be perceived as being open to input. Demonstrating flexibility and the ability to come to solutions that work for everyone is critical at this stage.

"Selling" Your Programming

As you present your programs, invite the board into the discussion. This is an ideal opportunity for them to ask additional questions and for you to sell them on the value and excitement of each concert. As with the marketing committee, use descriptive words that will help everyone understand the focus of these programs. The board needs to buy in to the season and to be able to talk excitedly about it with their friends. This is very helpful in creating the "buzz" throughout a community.

Be prepared to face some direct questions and even opposition. The amount of this will depend upon the trust level you have developed over time. If you have programmed exciting, stimulating concerts in the past, they will trust that, even if they do not know all the pieces selected, your programming ideas will be successful. It is when the level of trust is thin that problems occur and you might find yourself in a "tug of war" over the artistic direction of the orchestra. It is best not to fight with, or divide, the board. Instead, find a medium ground of programming while the trust level is rebuilt. This is probably your best course of action. In doing this, do not think of it as sacrificing your ultimate artistic goals. Remember: life is a process. An organization has a natural level of growth and change. Perhaps you were just trying to move it forward too quickly.

Working with the Artistic Committee

Sometimes you will inherit an artistic committee. This committee might serve a variety of purposes, depending upon how it was setup in the past. When properly channeled, this group can be an excellent sounding board for ideas. The makeup of the committee is important. You really want people involved who are knowledgeable about musical quality and who can also see the big picture. These people should not be afraid of growth, and they should have enough power within the orchestra to convince people of the importance of artistic quality.

I usually prefer to keep the committee focused on guest artists and on overall concepts, projects, or ideas. It is wonderful to know that you have the active support of a group of board members before new ideas are presented to the entire board. It is advantageous to have the chair of the committee actually present the new artistic ideas at a board meeting if these ideas involve a financial stretch for the organization. These might be concepts such as performing a Mahler Symphony or presenting a semi-staged production of an entire opera.

Throughout the year, you will be approached by members of the community to participate in collaborative efforts or projects. As a music director, you will not always have the background on the politics of the situation to know whether this would be a positive thing for the organization or not. It is good to have a committee with which to discuss these issues. This committee should spend time developing criteria regarding which types of extra activities fit within the mission and vision of the organization. This way, they will have something to measure each decision against. In addition, if you need to say "no" to some of these community proposals, it is not a "no" that is coming from you as the music director alone, but from a strong group within the organization.

Members of the artistic committee are the ones who must keep the board focused on the total artistic vision. They are the catalyst for moving the organization forward in an artistically positive direction. Spend time during the meetings discussing where you are currently and where you hope to be in five years. Analyze what needs to be done for the orchestra to achieve the next level and have the committee help to develop the plan to get there. Notes from these meetings should be distributed to the entire board so that others can be included in the discussions. It is helpful if your executive director is also involved with the artistic committee. This way, you will both be on the same page.

It is best to keep the artistic committee out of the "formal" programming for the organization. As the hired musical expert, your job requires you to select and perform the music for the organization. The organization chose you for your musical expertise. If they are not satisfied with the programming, you need to see if there is anything that you can subtly change that would make the board and audience more comfortable. Ask for, and incorporate when possible, repertoire suggestions from the artistic committee but remember that ultimately, you are responsible for the programming. If you cannot come to agreement with the board on this issue, then it might be time for you to look for another position.

An artistic committee can be a strong advocate for you with the board. If you accept a job that already has this type of committee, do not be fearful of it—embrace it. A properly managed and inspired artistic committee will make it easier for you to do your job.

Board Structure

Depending on the size and structure of the organization, the board might meet monthly, every other month, or quarterly. If your board only meets quarterly, then your executive committee will probably be meeting monthly or bimonthly. It is good to attend as many board meetings as possible. If you are a traveling conductor, try to convince the administration to schedule these meetings when you are in town for concerts. If you live in the area, try to make sure that meetings are scheduled when you are able to attend.

Size and Makeup of the Board

The number of board members for the orchestra might range anywhere from seven to one hundred. Sometimes, these board members are divided into different categories, depending on how long they have served on the board and how active they are at present. Some of the categories you might encounter are:

> Trustees
> Board of Governors
> Board of Directors
> Advisory Board

Many American boards for orchestras are composed of between thirty and forty people. It is desirable to have a balanced selection of board members who represent your community. You usually need people who can bring at least *two* of the following qualities to the board: wisdom, wealth, and work. It is common for the board to have representation from different professions. This is helpful if you are in need of pro bono advice in specific areas. Some of the occupations that might be covered on your board are:

Law
Public Relations/Marketing
Computer Specialist
Banking
Accounting
Planned Giving
Graphics/Printing
Music Education

You also will want to have major representation from the top leaders in the business community. Sometimes with smaller orchestras, because these business leaders are so busy, the nominating committee might try to get the community leader's wife on the board instead. This can work successfully, but it is usually more effective to go straight for the person with the clout.

Your board also will need a group of people who are simply lovers of music and philanthropists. These people are individually capable of writing a large check for any project that takes their fancy. It is good to develop a strong relationship with these members right from the beginning.

Board Committees

Most boards function between meetings through committees. Some of the normal board committees you should be aware of include:

Executive
Nominating
Finance
Development
Marketing
Education

Additional committees that are formed as needed might include:

Tickets/subscription sales
Artistic
Special events

Strategic planning
Board operations
Human resources
Hospitality

Every organization will have its own committee structure. Each of these committees should be accompanied by a job outline. It is good for the music director to read through the committee job descriptions so that they know the responsibilities of each committee. This knowledge will enhance your understanding of the entire organization. As you outline your artistic vision for the future, the chair of each committee should be consulted regarding the requirements of their committee to move the organization forward in this manner. Their feedback must be incorporated into the plan. If you do not ask for their input early on, you might have problems later when it comes to actually accomplishing the goal. The executive director should be actively involved in this process.

Board Meetings

Most board meetings will last around one and one-half hours. You must always be on time to board meetings. If fact, you should really try to be about fifteen minutes early, giving you time to chat with two or three board members individually. Try to talk to different ones each time. This is an excellent way to strengthen relationships and to build alignment.

Usually board meetings will be held at a very large table. There will be a perceived place of power at the head of the table. The board president, executive director, and music director should sit together at the head of the table. This subconsciously presents a united front to the rest of the board. When you start to see these three people separated around the table, it might be a sign of other problems within the organization.

Most board meetings and musician meetings will follow *Robert's Rules of Order*. It is advisable for you to purchase this book for reference and to keep it in your library. This book outlines the process by which the decisions are made at a board meeting. New topics will usually be introduced, then, a motion might be made to approve this new idea. Someone on the board must "second" the motion. After that, the president will ask for discussion. Then before the vote, someone must call the question. Then the vote is taken, usually in the form of a verbal "all in favor" and "all opposed." The secretary will record all of this in the minutes. The music director is usually a nonvoting member of the board. You are allowed to take part in the discussion, but you are not allowed to vote.

On the agenda for the regular meetings, there will be a spot for the music director to speak. Come to each board meeting with a prepared set of bullet points regarding upcoming concerts and the overall season. You also might want to talk about the audition procedures and distribute information regarding concerts and recitals that orchestra members are performing. You are the board's window into the world of the orchestral musician. You should demonstrate enthusiasm and excitement whenever you talk to the board. Your talk should be kept to about three minutes, unless you have something that needs further discussion for a vote, or when you are presenting the repertoire for the next concert season. When at all possible, have the chair of the artistic committee or the education committee present ideas that have been discussed and approved of by those committees. This encourages others to take a leadership role.

Musicians on the Board

Some symphony boards have musicians as either voting or nonvoting members of the board. This is excellent for keeping communication open within the organization. If you do not have musicians on the board, encourage the organization to form a committee to meet regularly with members of the orchestra. This is not a negotiating committee for the Collective Bargaining Agreement but, rather, a committee that allows musicians to air concerns, makes sure that all ideas can reach the administration, and works throughout the year to resolve issues before they become problems.

Board Training

It is important for the success of an arts organization to have a strong board. Even if you have a board full of people who mean well, they must be trained in how to be effective within the orchestral structure. As a music director, you should offer to be involved with board training for new board members. These new board members need to be introduced to the mission and priorities of the organization right from the beginning. That means that, first and foremost, they must be introduced to the artistic goals. Who better to present the artistic goals than the music director? As a music director, you are considered a leader in the field. Your board will be looking to you for guidance. Talk to them about national trends in the industry; get them active in national organizations such as the American Symphony Orchestra League (ASOL); encourage them to attend conferences that will increase their knowledge of their responsibilities as a board member. All of these efforts will make your organization stronger for the future.

Union and Orchestra Relations
Orchestra Policies

All orchestras, whether union or nonunion, will have guidelines and policies that must be followed. These polices define the working structure and expectations between the orchestra members and the administration. Most orchestras will already have these in place when you accept the job, but sometimes they will be created during your tenure. Orchestras may also change from being nonunion to being unionized. Don't be afraid of this change. All orchestras when they reach a certain budget level or quality level will probably become unionized. It is like going from high school to college—although scary, it is just a part of growing up.

It is important for you as a music director to be familiar with the policies of your organization. The titles of these policies vary. Some of the more familiar titles are:

Nonunion

> Orchestra Guidelines
> Orchestra Policy

Union

> Collective Bargaining Agreement (CBA)
> Master Policy
> Master Agreement

These documents can range in length from just a few pages to more than sixty pages. Most of them include the same basic categories, but the actual details often differ tremendously. It is important that you become familiar with the documents of your orchestra as well as understanding what is standard in the industry. You will not (and should not) be involved in the actual process of negotiating, but you will want to be a voice behind the scenes to help educate your board, and to stand up for the things you need to do your job effectively.

General Categories

Here is a listing of the basic items included in most orchestra policies or collective bargaining agreements. This list will vary in detail depending on the budget size of your orchestra.

Terms	The starting and ending dates of the document

Definitions	Defining terms within the document (not always used)
Schedule of services	Duration of rehearsals and breaks, cancellation policies, defining different types of services
Engagement of musicians	Contract issues and deadlines: tenured, probationary, substitute; and extra musicians' procedures
Wages and compensation	Salary scale, per-service pay, travel, overtime, doubling, cartage, audition honorariums
Attendance	Absences policy, tardiness policy, concerts required to maintain tenure, leave of absences
Auditions	Policies, committee structure, compensation, role of the music director in the process
Working conditions	Type of environment that must be provided for the orchestra to rehearse and perform
Dress code	Orchestra dress requirements for each type of concert
Nonrenewal	Process outlined for not reengaging tenured musicians
Grievances	How complaints are officially filed
Bowing and music	Policies on how bowings are handled, when music must be sent out, penalties for non-returned music
Electronic media	Policies on recordings, archival recordings, two to three minutes for promotional purposes, web streaming, and live broadcasts
No Strike—No lockout	Clarifies that there will be no work stoppage by either party during the term of this agreement

There are additional categories that might be included in these documents. For a further study of master policies, I recommend that you contact the resource center of the ASOL. They sell a CD disc that includes 110 different master agreements from orchestras of varying sizes from across the United States. You, or your orchestra, will have to be a member of ASOL to purchase this CD.

As a music director, you should be familiar with all the policies from your own organization, but the four sections that you really need to understand and influence are: attendance, wages and compensation, auditions, and nonrenewal.

Attendance

Attendance at rehearsals is critical to produce a uniform concept of sound and interpretation. Be sure you stress that complete attendance is required for each concert. Sometimes a section of a piece might only be rehearsed once and the nuances and changes that a conductor might specify will be lost if the player is absent. Emphasize to your orchestra members that the strict policy for attendance has nothing to do with whether they are individually capable of playing their part. The ability to play the part is assumed before the rehearsals begin. Rather, it is about the interpretation of the music. This can only be communicated through the process of the rehearsals with everyone present. A substitute tone color in the woodwind section can totally change the sound and intonation of that section. The basic notes might still be there, but the quality of the music making may change dramatically. If a person is not available for all rehearsals, then you might want to hire a qualified substitute.

The next goal is to try to have the same personnel at each concert throughout the year. This is much harder to accomplish with the smaller per-service orchestras, and probably impossible at a university where it is important to rotate the wind students through the different ensembles. Continuity of players is important to the overall quality of the ensemble. The more an orchestra plays together, the better it will become artistically. If you are programming exciting music and producing musically stimulating concerts, most musicians will want to play as many concerts as they possibly can.

Two other items that must be taken into consideration when talking about attendance are scheduling and pay scale. Both of these can work against you if there are multiple demands on your players' time. Strive to coordinate schedules with neighboring orchestras to reduce conflicts for the musicians. This way everyone wins. Also, if you are a paid orchestra, strive to make the pay scale competitive with neighboring orchestras. Otherwise, even if artistically the musicians would rather play your concert, they might be forced financially to take another job.

Wages and Compensation

Providing a competitive wage for your musicians is very important. As a music director, you must communicate to the board the importance of the orchestra members to the organization, and the discrepancy between their intrinsic value and what they are actually paid. Sometimes board members will believe that because a musician is doing something they love, they should sometimes do it for free. This thinking is usually expressed by board members who are volunteering extensive amounts of time and money to the organization and think that the musicians should do the same. It is difficult to explain to them that musicians perform for a living and are usually not in a position to volunteer their time in this manner. They need a stable income to be financially able to dedicate more of their lives to music making. A respect for this will keep the musical quality and attitude high throughout your orchestra. Orchestra members have spent a lifetime perfecting their musical skills. Their instruments alone can cost more than most people spend on a house. If your orchestra is a professional orchestra, asking musicians to perform for free can create animosity and tension. If you cannot adequately pay for their time, they are economically forced to find someone else who can. Honor your musicians by paying them as much as possible within the parameters of your budget. If you want to retain your level of quality, it is important that you strive to be the highest-paying orchestra in your region, not the lowest. The orchestra that pays the best will be able to attract the best musicians and to keep them. If, indeed, you put musical quality at the forefront of your institutional values, you will always keep your orchestra pay scale competitive.

If your orchestra is a nonpaid, volunteer orchestra, try to feed them well. We always joke in the industry that musicians will do anything if a little food is provided. This is not far from the truth. Anything you can do to help show appreciation to your musicians for their hard work and dedication will go far towards increasing their commitment to the organization.

Auditions

For a regional orchestra, the makeup of your audition committee will be specified in your orchestra policy, collective bargaining agreement, or master agreement. Usually, the audition committee will be composed of between three and five people in addition to the music director. In a strict voting system, the weight of the music director's vote will vary with the orchestra. Other systems might involve discussing the candidates and deciding together who should be moved to finals status. With any audition process, it is best to have a committee of orchestra members involved. I have found that orchestra members are excellent at analyzing the talents of those they are hearing and rarely do I need to control the situation. It is a wonderful way for them to demonstrate leadership and, as members of the orchestra, they are vested in creating and upholding the musical standard.

Screened Auditions

I must say that, years ago, I was definitely against screened auditions. As a young music director, I wanted to be able to assess not only the playing but also the personality of the person who was auditioning. I have changed my mind. After sitting though many auditions both ways, I really appreciate the screen. When the committee is not able to see the person auditioning, many positive things happen.

Benefits of Screened Auditions

1. The screen takes away any of the issues that arise when someone on the committee knows the person auditioning.
2. The screen is very helpful if a person who is currently a member of the orchestra auditions for a new position and does not get selected. No one except the personnel manager knows who auditioned.
3. The audition committee listens better with the screen and is actually much more critical. This creates a higher standard when the winner is selected.
4. Having a screen is usually less stressful for the candidate, so they perform better.

My initial concern of wanting to know about the candidate's personality is easily taken care of, either by having an unscreened finals round or by asking the finalist(s) to perform a concert with the orchestra. This way, everyone in the orchestra hears the candidate's playing and can see if his or her personality will fit on the team. If you have the finalists play in the orchestra, it is advisable to have a survey completed by the principals of the sections involved regarding each candidate's playing. If the finalist is a string player and you have multiple openings, a finals round might not be necessary. You may decide to go straight to the "probationary" year to assess the player's musicianship and personality. Most regional orchestras have a time period of between one and three years in which a person is on probation and evaluated before they are granted tenure.

Nonrenewal

This is an area that you *must* make sure you understand in the orchestra policy or master agreement. Following specific procedure and timelines is critical in the area of nonrenewal; failure to do so might jeopardize your relationship with the entire orchestra and prevent you from accomplishing your artistic goals.

Most policies require a general set of steps for dealing with the nonrenewal of an orchestra member. These basic steps can be adapted to any orchestral situation. Nonrenewal for excessive tardiness or extremely disruptive behavior is usually clear-cut and handled by the personnel manager. In improving your orchestras, however, you are going to be faced with musicians who simply are not performing up to the standard of other orchestra members. Failure to address these problems is to fail to do your job as a music director.

Before you meet with any player individually, you must make sure that you have full documentation of the issues and specific examples where they were not playing up to standard. Therefore, it is recommended after rehearsals to make notes of issues, positive and negative, as they happen, and to keep them in an on-going notebook. When you have worked with a regular orchestra member over a period of time and you realize that they have artistic problems that need to be addressed, the steps below should be followed:

1. Meet with the player privately and informally communicate to them your concerns about their playing. Try to be as specific as possible. Follow this up with a written letter confirming what was discussed. Sometimes you will want to talk informally more than once. If things do not improve, you will need to move to the next, more formal level of notification.

2. Send a letter from the association to the musician, with copies to the orchestra committee, personnel manager, and executive director (as necessary), detailing the problem and placing the person on "artistic probation" with the possibility of demotion or non-renewal. If you are a union orchestra, these types of letters must be sent by a specific date notated on the orchestra policy or collective bargaining agreement. Make sure you know what these dates are or you might have to wait another full year to deal with the issue.

3. Usually, the musician is then encouraged to meet with the music director. The union requires that a union member or orchestra representative be present. If you are dealing with a nonunion situation, you will probably keep this meeting private, but you should carefully document what was discussed.

4. Next, there is a period (usually specified by the policy) in which the orchestra musician is given time to improve. This can range from one concert to an entire year, depending upon your organization.

5. After this, the music director will make a decision regarding the player's performance. Usually, this also has to be done by a specific date. Never miss your deadline. At this time you have four choices:

   a. The player has improved and he/she is renewed for the next season.
   b. You see signs of improvement, but are not sure, so you extend the probation period with consultation from the orchestra committee.
   c. The player has not improved enough for their current chair but can remain a member of the orchestra. They are demoted in the section.
   d. The player has not improved, and therefore you do not renew their contract. They are dismissed.

After this happens, the player can either accept this decision, or appeal. It they choose to appeal, a review committee can be set up for this purpose as specified in the collective bargaining agreement or orchestra policy. The makeup of this committee will vary, but it is usually composed of orchestra members and perhaps members of the administration. The player is then allowed to present his or her case. They are usually given the opportunity to perform to prove their ability, but they are not always required to do so. The music director is also asked to present his or her side of the issues. This is why accurate documentation is so important. The committee will then vote. Most organizations require a super majority vote to overturn a music director's artistic decision.

Nonrenewal is one of the most stressful processes you will go through as a music director. Anytime someone in the orchestra is placed on artistic probation there will be a ripple effect of distrust and fear. This is only normal because people are now worried that they might be next. Try not to initiate too many artistic probations in one season. More than two or three is likely to create a tension within the orchestra that will interfere with your music making. Sometimes, growing an orchestra slowly is much more effective and successful in the long run. Above all, as you go through this process, make sure you treat everyone honestly and fairly. Remember, it is not so much *what* you do, but *how* you do it that counts. Everyone deserves appreciation and respect.

Contract Negotiations

When your collective bargaining agreement is up for renegotiation, it is important for the music director to remain in the background and not become actively involved. The terms of this type of negotiation are handled by management, represented by the executive director, perhaps a board member, and a lawyer. If, as a music director, you have any issues that you would like changed in the collective bargaining agreement or orchestra policies in order to increase the artistic potential of the orchestra, it is important that you discuss these with the management side of the negotiating team long before the contract negotiations begin. You should divide your list into things that are critically important, and items that you would like to see changed, but that you are flexible on. Once the actual negotiations begin, it is best if you remain completely out of the picture. If the negotiations become difficult and the press tries to bring you into the situation, refrain from taking sides or making any public statements. If you must say something, try a positive statement, such as, "I have great confidence that the musicians and management will find a way to work this out so that we can continue to bring quality music to this community." No one wins when a lengthy negotiation is played out negatively in the press.

Working with Musicians

Orchestra Committee

Almost every type of orchestra has some sort of committee that represents the orchestra and handles issues. Usually these members represent the different families of instruments. An average-size orchestra committee has five members. Often this committee will have its own set of bylaws and operating procedures. Their meetings will follow *Robert's Rules of Order*. You will want to become familiar with the orchestra committee's bylaws and you will need to work closely with this group as changes are made that affect the orchestra. Often, proposed changes will need the approval of the orchestra committee *in advance*, or the committee might want to have the entire orchestra vote on an issue. Make sure if you, or the administration, have requests that would require adjustments from the current policy, that these requests are presented in advance. Most committees only meet when the orchestra is rehearsing. This might require you to work a month or two ahead of your deadline.

Orchestra Representation on Board Committees

The more you can involve your orchestra members in the overall structure of the organization, the better. One way that orchestra members can be encouraged to volunteer and become more involved is through board committees. Committees such as the education committee and the artistic committee are excellent vehicles for orchestra participation because the musicians have a vested interest in the results. An expansion of your educational outreach programs usually means more work for the musicians. It is wonderful to have the feedback immediately regarding which types of outreach programs are of interest to the players, and what they think their time is worth to perform educational outreach. By being active on these committees, they can help shape the future of the organization in a way that relates to them personally.

Remember that orchestra members are also the best people to help sell the importance of the orchestra to the community and to thank donors. Encourage the musicians to participate in fund-raising calls for the organization or to make thank-you phone calls, sign letters, or write personal notes to donors. Orchestra members can speak with passion and excitement about the concerts that they are presenting. It is often a very eye-opening experience for them to realize just how difficult it can be to raise money. Musicians also can be involved in phoning for the annual campaign or yearly subscription ticket renewals. Often, the subscribers have developed personal relationships with the musicians in the orchestra; they will respond better to them than to a board member. The important issue is not how the musicians are involved, but the fact that they *are* involved. Encourage ownership and responsibility on an institutional level. This will pay off in the long run and create a stronger foundation for your organization.

Socializing with the Orchestra

Socializing with the members of your orchestra can be a risky situation. Stories abound about conductors who have been caught in compromising situations by drinking with their musicians after a rehearsal, or by dating a member of the orchestra. As a music director of an organization, there is a line of respect that *must* be honored at all times. If your behavior crosses this line, you will run the risk of losing the respect of some of your orchestra members or your board. There have been situations in which this type of behavior has eventually cost conductors their jobs. It is always best to maintain a totally professional relationship with the musicians in your orchestra. You should be friendly, and tremendously supportive, yet you should *never* place yourself in situations that could compromise the integrity of your position.

Communicating the Vision

Because the interaction between the general orchestra members and the board members is usually minimal, it is sometimes hard to get everyone on the same page. In order for the organization to be successful in its artistic mission, everyone must understand the mission, and understand the role they play in accomplishing each goal. I would encourage you to invite the president of the board to attend some rehearsals and take a few minutes to update the musicians about issues that are happening within the organization.

If you are working on a long-range strategic plan, it is useful to have musicians involved in this process. Even after you have narrowed the planning down to a small group, make sure that you have someone report back to the musicians regarding potential plans for the future. Often, the musicians are the last to find out. It also helps to have an informal, combined lunch or dinner before or after a rehearsal, during which the board members can sit on stage during the rehearsal and mingle afterward with the musicians. Encourage everyone to talk freely about the goals of the organization and what it will take to accomplish them.

Once the strategic plan is finalized, copies should be distributed to the musicians and short-term goals should be posted backstage. As the music director, be sure to take a few minutes here and there to talk about some of the future repertoire plans and the exciting things that the board is working on. This will help to keep the excitement level high within the orchestra.

Rehearsal Techniques

There are many ways to approach working with the musicians in a rehearsal. Some are more effective than others. All conductors have had the experience where they said something as a sort of joke, and suddenly the attitude of the entire orchestra changed from comradeship to sullen distaste. Once something is out of your mouth, you cannot take it back. That is why the best policy is to show as much as you can with your hands, and to talk as little as possible.

It is important that you trust your orchestra. You must truly believe at the first rehearsal that everything will be perfect. Even though in your preparation, you will want to anticipate trouble spots, you must avoid correcting problems at your rehearsals before they happen. As you are rehearsing, make sure that you keep your eyes to the back of each section so that everyone feels included. In general, you want to create an atmosphere of inclusion and respect. The rehearsal should be a collaborative effort, as if you are preparing a chamber ensemble to perform a concert without a conductor.

As you are rehearsing, you will be in a hurry to solve problems and to cover a lot of material. You will want to be short and effective in your communication with the orchestra (one or two sentences, reinforced by facial expressions and hand cues). You probably know the old saying: all the orchestra really wants to know is, "Do you want it higher or lower? Softer or louder? Faster or slower? Shorter or longer?" These words basically cover everything. Don't be afraid to use them, but avoid just telling the player what is in the part already. For example, if they already have a mezzo-forte (*mf*) marking, don't just repeat this fact. Instead, tell them whether they need to play it louder or softer. Or better yet, develop a vocabulary of descriptive words like forceful, determined, incisive, or elegant, delicate, wispy—that give you a much broader range of emotions and sounds on which to draw. If there is a crescendo or an articulation that an orchestra member is not playing, you might want to clarify if it is actually in the part before you question the fact that they didn't play it. Sometimes, there are large discrepancies, missing articulations, and actual mistakes between the score and the parts, especially in Kalmus editions and Luck's reprints.

As you make your comments to the orchestra, look at them and be careful not to embarrass or insult people. This accomplishes nothing. An unhappy person will not work for you, and this will get in the way of your music making. Also, do not control people through fear; fear of failure is one of the worst motivators. If people are afraid, they are more apt to make a mistake, and you will see the energy of the music-making just shrink up.

As I work with an orchestra, there are a few things that I try to remember. I call these universal truths because they are always applicable. One of my favorites is: "*Tell them what you want; don't criticize what they did.*" Ultimately, the musicians want to play everything correctly, but sometimes they are not properly prepared; or, due to poor conducting technique or inadequate knowledge of the score, the conductor sends mixed signals. If they misinterpret your gesture or make a mistake, don't berate them for trying—just tell them what you want. If you keep this in mind for every comment you make to the orchestra members, you will always have a positive, productive rehearsal. Here are some examples of how this can be applied.

Instead of saying	*Try saying*
That note was flat!	Could you play the "G" a little higher?
That chord was out of tune.	Let's tune that chord.
Don't play it so short and staccato.	Let's try that a little longer and more beautiful.
We're not together.	Can we try that section again and listen more?
You're behind.	Please lead more.

Remember, anything you say to a player or a section is being heard by the entire orchestra. Try to build up the orchestra with your comments, not tear them down. An effective rehearser can motivate an orchestra to play well beyond the individual talents of its members. It is a very valuable skill to master.

Below are some other universal truths and useful techniques for rehearsing your orchestra:

- Keep the music at the core of the focus, so that the personalities get out of the picture.
- Invite the orchestra to play, don't demand.
- Know the quality of the sound you want; take the time to hear it in your head; show it; listen to the placement; and never let it go.
- Do not substitute tension for intensity. Tension will squeeze the sound—Intensity will release it.

- The less interesting the part, the more energy and initiation is needed. Encourage players to sustain the energy of the slow moving notes.
- If you are having trouble balancing the soloist and the orchestra, ask the orchestra to "play into the color of the soloist" as opposed to asking them to "play softer."
- Low instruments need more clarification of sound—encourage them to play with slight sound attacks or "consonants." Emphasize the beginnings of the notes.
- When playing legato, listen to the ends of the notes; make sure that the musicians continue the energy to the end.
- Help the orchestra members establish aural focal points to develop better ensemble. A single player on a part will provide a clearer focal point than a section; and a higher part will be easier for others to focus on than a low part.
- When tuning chords, begin with the musicians playing the tonic and the fifth, and then add the third of the chord. This helps the players understand the placement of their note. Keep the third high in a major chord and low in a minor chord.
- If there are intonation problems in the winds and brass when they are playing doublings or octaves, always ask the second player (lower part) to play softer.
- Always give wind players a very precise breath and entrance attack. Give more *breath* for horns, trumpets, trombones, and tuba; and more *attack* for bassoons and oboes.
- When the orchestra rushes, beat smaller to catch them, then beat larger to get them back in your tempo.

When planning your rehearsal time, it is wise to start with something that the musicians are more familiar with. This allows you to focus on musical details right from the beginning without having to worry as much about the notes. Beginning with the most difficult piece on the program can create tension and stress. It also tends to bog down the rehearsal and disrupt the positive flow of energy. Neither should extremely difficult pieces be scheduled at the end of long rehearsals, when people are physically and mentally tired. This will just create frustration and people will leave the rehearsal feeling discouraged.

It is also good to plan your rehearsals from either the largest instrumentation to the smallest, or vice versa. Players really appreciate it if they do not have to sit around for forty-five minutes while a piece is being rehearsed where they do not perform. Some of this cannot be avoided, but when possible, adjust the schedule to get the players out of there as soon as possible. They will really appreciate your efforts.

The first rehearsal is usually dedicated to playing through each of the compositions. This will let you know where your time needs to be spent for the other rehearsals. The middle rehearsals are where you can break things down and work out problems, and the final rehearsal is to achieve continuity and conviction of interpretation. After each rehearsal, it is advisable to make notes of what went well and what still needs to be rehearsed. This will enable you to use your time more effectively. You should have a specific goal of what you need to accomplish each time you work with the orchestra. I often mark my score with Post-it notes to remind me to announce things like, "Yes the repeat is good" or to clarify specific cuts, before we begin each piece. Without these little reminders, it is easy to forget a detail that is critically important to clarify.

At the beginning of a rehearsal, let the orchestra play a while before you start rehearsing. They need time to warm up and get into the musical flow. When you do start rehearsing, try to work within larger sections and longer phrases. No one enjoys a rehearsal that goes bar-by-bar. Always give the musicians the pleasure of finishing the phrase, then go back and announce the list of things you want them to consider differently before you ask them to play it again. Never ask an orchestra to play something again without telling them what you would like to change. They want to know why they are doing it again. Never make them play it again just because you conducted it badly. Mark the passage and study it on your own before the next rehearsal.

When you speak to the orchestra, wait for that moment of absolute quiet after you stop before you continue with your instructions. I call this magical moment the "pause." This silence is critical to focusing the attention and energy of the group. If they are having trouble becoming quiet, never "shh" them, rather, just wait. The first time, it might take a long time, but after that, the standard of what you expect has been set. Once they are quiet and you speak to the orchestra, make sure that you speak slowly and loudly. It is sometimes hard for the players in the back of the orchestra to hear.

When you are instructing an orchestra where to start during a rehearsal, announce the instrumentation that you want to rehearse (i.e., trumpets) then say: "After Letter T—six bars." Once you have announced the letter and the number of bars to count, give them time to find the right place before you start again. This will go far to avoid that annoying question of "Where are we starting?"

When problems occur in rehearsals, you often will rehearse an instrumental section separately from the rest of the orchestra. Keep in mind, however, that everyone else is sitting and waiting. If the problem does not solve itself with three attempts, you might want to ask the players to work on it themselves as a section during the break or after the rehearsal. Sometimes, when working continually on an exposed passage, it gets worse, not better. A good conductor knows when it is best to just move forward. When tension is high, a problem will often miraculously be fixed if you leave it and come back to it during the next rehearsal. In pacing your rehearsal, you should vary how much is full-orchestral playing, and how much is "spot" rehearsing with specific players. Make it a goal during every rehearsal to spend some time working specifically with each section in order to encourage them on their hard work and progress. This helps to make each person feel valued and heard within the orchestra. At the same time, however, you must be cautious of having the rest of the orchestra sit too long on the stage with nothing to do while you are rehearsing other sections.

Most important, keep to the schedule that you have planned and announced in advance. Even though there may be more things to correct in the first movement, if you don't continue on through the piece, you run the risk of jeopardizing the total performance because you ran out of time to rehearse the last movement. Trust your orchestra and know that many things will solve themselves on the second time through. A truly experienced conductor knows what to stop for and what will solve itself. If someone misses a note, try to catch their eye to see if they are aware of it. If they are, then there is no reason to do it again or to even mention the mistake publicly. Remember, every time you stop the orchestra for something, you lose about three minutes of precious rehearsal time. If you can solve the problem by conducting more clearly, or by whispering a word about a bowing without stopping, then you will ultimately accomplish more during your rehearsals.

At your dress rehearsal, you will be playing through large pieces, and you will usually have a little time at the end to rehearse trouble spots and to make specific comments. It is important for you to be able to remember the spots that had problems and to be able to find them quickly in the score. I have used two different techniques to help with this. One is to have a stack of index cards handy to place in the score when problems occur. When you quickly refer back to these after the run-through, you will remember what the issue was and you will be able to announce a specific measure number for the orchestra to begin or speak to a specific player about doing something differently. Another, less obvious technique is to fold over the corner of the score page. At the end of the run-through, you can identify all of the bent pages and rehearse those spots. It is important, however, after each run-through to "unbend" the pages, so that the next time you conduct the piece you are starting fresh.

Effective and efficient rehearsal technique is critical to success as a conductor.

Keep the talking to a minimum and make sure that your comments are specific and clear. I encourage you to give analogies, or to sing examples of phrasing. Often the best music-making occurs at this intangible level. And, most important, be passionate about the music. The joy of music-making should show on your face. The integrity and the emotion of the composition should be embedded in your demeanor on the podium. Be honest and truthful with your orchestra and they will return the courtesy.

Developing Your Network
The Importance of Networking

Even though we would like to believe that we can make it on our own, the truth is that everyone needs a network of colleagues, not only for support and feedback, but also for advancement. Most of the time, when organizations are looking to hire someone, they immediately think of whom they already know who shares a like set of values and work ethics. They try to identify those who they already feel will "fit in." When they cannot personally think of anyone who is "right" for their position, they immediately call up their friends and ask if they know of anyone. Even if you object to this system, you have to recognize that this is usually how things are handled in the United States. This is not to say that quality is not an issue; organizations still want to hire the most qualified person for the job. It is just that they trust someone they know more than someone they do not know.

Although knowing someone might help to get you into the final round for a job, it will not actually get you the job. Getting the job is dependent on a high-quality, exciting performance through an audition or guest-conducting experience, and a kinetic chemistry or relationship with the organization. (See pages 45–58.)

At the beginning of your career, it is important that you *never* turn down any opportunity to conduct, no matter how small or inconsequential it might seem. You never know who might be in the audience or whom you might be working with that could recommend you for something in the future. Also, as you build your career, be careful not to alienate anyone, or to treat them disrespectfully. You never know when they might be in a position to help or hurt you in future job applications. The music industry will become "smaller and smaller" the longer you are in it.

Developing your network is an ongoing task. The important thing is to develop your relationships with people over a long period of time. The music world has often been compared to the game of musical chairs. Someone that you know now as an operations assistant at a mid-size orchestra might eventually be the executive director of a major orchestra. Someone you went to school with years ago might now be the chair of a search committee for a job that you are interested in applying for. It is important to stay in touch with these people and to follow them in their career paths.

Develop a database of the names and addresses of colleagues and periodically let them know how you are progressing as a conductor. You can increase this list by attending the major conventions of both the ASOL and the Conductors Guild, and by trying to meet as many people in the industry as possible. Once you have developed your network you can send out yearly season brochures or reviews of your concerts to keep your name fresh in everyone's mind. It is also helpful to solicit your colleagues for feedback and advice on a regular basis and to send them notes of congratulations when they move up in the field. Whenever you get a new job or receive an award, distribute a press release to publications such as union papers, ASOL, Conductors Guild, college alumni magazines, local newspapers where you currently work, and the newspapers where you grew up. Often these publications are eager to print these types of articles and announcements. Their distribution will reach thousands of people who would otherwise not be in your network. Regular publicity is important for creating the "buzz" that helps to build your name recognition as a conductor. Make it a goal to do something every day that reminds someone that you are pursuing your conducting career.

Never Burn Your Bridges

As a conductor, it is important that you guard your professional reputation in everything that you do. As with all occupations, you will experience conflicts and disagreement along the way with those with whom you work. Always resolve these conflicts in a professional manner, or your past actions may resurface and haunt you later on. Remember the old saying, "Be careful how you treat people on your way up the career ladder, because you will most likely meet them on your way down." The music industry is very small. Everyone knows each other and, with e-mail, the word spreads very quickly throughout the country—and even the world. Control your feelings and actions so that you avoid creating personal confrontations that may hinder your career progress. Remember to choose your words and your actions carefully and never put anything in writing that you might later regret. In my dealings with difficult people, I try to remember that the Miranda warning applies "anything you say, can and will be used against you." Make sure that you don't give anyone ammunition to shoot back at you.

When ideas do conflict, recognize whose interests you represent and whose goals you are being paid to meet or fulfill. In the position of music director and conductor for an orchestra, you are considered as part of the administration and you report directly to the board of directors. If you are forced to choose a side in an argument, it should be with the people that sign your paycheck unless you are ready to look for another job. It is important to protect this relationship and to calmly work through conflicts. Never let your emotional side dictate your response to difficult issues, and never draw a line in the sand to make a point. If you desire a long-lasting career as a conductor, never burn your bridges!

Chapter 7

Funding the Artistic Vision

Getting to Know the Numbers

Understanding Your Community Assets

Every community has a limited number of resources that will be available to support the nonprofit organizations within that community. The amount of this funding is dependent on whether major corporate offices or simply satellite offices are located in your area. How many large businesses, banks, and foundations are you able to draw on? What is the financial makeup of the majority of your community? How large is the community, and is it growing larger or smaller? Of this number, how many currently attend your concerts? How many might be persuaded to attend in the future? If you offer more concerts, you need to be sure there is an audience to fill the seats. If you offer larger concerts, you need to identify donors who are excited about artistic growth and willing to fund it.

Growing the Orchestra in a Fiscally Responsible Manner

One of the problems that many music directors help to create is that they develop a plan for growth that doesn't take into account the actual funds available. Instead, they take the "build it and they will come" approach. Although you need to be a dreamer and a person of vision and big goals, you also need to be realistic as to what type and size of orchestra is appropriate for a specific community. A small community of one hundred thousand people would probably not have the resources available for a thirty-five-week, core orchestra. Do not try to move them in that direction, even if you think it would improve the quality level of the orchestra. I do, however, encourage you to challenge the board to do more than they are accustomed to doing. Every organization needs to be faced with challenging goals to stay current. Build your orchestra and organization, but do it slowly and wisely. Slow growth is the only type of growth that will really maintain itself. Take the time to develop relationships and to build consensus with the orchestra members and the board. You will need to prioritize your growth according to what is most needed in the community and what will help the orchestra improve in quality. These two areas should always be the focal points of your growth.

You may reach a point where you have grown the orchestra both in quality and size to something that is an ideal fit for a community. If, because of the location and the inability to draw better players, you are still not satisfied personally, it is better for you to find a larger orchestra closer to a major metropolitan area; than, to try to push the board to build, build, build, only to see the organization collapse later because the funding in the community just was not available. Always remember, the orchestra was here before you, and will be there after you are gone. It is not "your" orchestra to simply build your career. It is a community organization that has entrusted to you the leadership role of taking it to the next level and moving it forward on its organizational path. It is a major responsibility that should not be taken lightly. Every decision you make regarding the artistic direction of the orchestra should be in light of what is needed by the community it serves. That is the reason for its existence. If your idea of growth takes it beyond or away from what the community wants and needs to directions that only help you, then you will have failed as a music director.

The Budgeting Process

Budgeting within a symphony orchestra has many different levels and components. Your orchestra might have a finance committee that is ultimately responsible for creating and presenting the budget or the budget might be done by the executive director or yourself. The important thing is to establish priorities regarding how the limited resources will be spent. One of the major reasons that the music director must program well in advance is so that the budgeting process can be driven by the programming, not the other way around. Before you select the music, you will already know the basic parameters that have been established by your long-range plan regarding orchestra size and the number of concerts. Try to stay within these parameters. If you are considering any large projects or works, they should be approved before you complete the programming. No one likes sudden surprises that cost money, no matter how exciting they might seem to you. Once the music has been selected, then the numbers can be "crunched" regarding the exact costs of the orchestra for each concert, based upon the instrumentation for the concert (which will vary). Technical expenses and equipment will also have to be anticipated. Once the guest artists have been selected, their fees and travel expenses will be added to the budget. The amount of money needed for the rental or purchase of music will be provided by the librarian. This amount may vary quite a bit from year to year depending upon the programming. Outreach programs that involve musicians will also need to be considered and a budget number assigned. As the music director you will want to be informed regarding these numbers are so you can help keep the artistic side of the organization fiscally responsible.

Do not allow the organization to simply add a percentage number to last year's budget and force you to work within these parameters. This will stifle programming and puts the focus in the wrong place within the organization. The goal is to set your artistic mission, define your artistic programs with carefully calculated growth, and then to find the money to make these things possible. If you do budgeting the other way around, when times are tough, it is too easy for the board to say, "Let's take 5 percent off the music budget." In doing this, the board does not even know what they have given up. Stress to the board the importance of deciding what should be accomplished with the artistic programming; then help them raise the money to do it.

Budgets

There are many different ways to organize a budget. You should be comfortable reading the budgets from your organization, and you should know how to find discrepancies that might lead to problems down the road. Most budgets have the same main categories. Often the financial reports presented at the board meetings use the simplest form of the budget with the largest categories. In all budgets, there will be areas for income and expenses. Within the expenses, the amount allocated for artistic expenses is normally between 30 percent and 50 percent of the total budget, unless your orchestra is composed totally of volunteers. If your organization is spending less than 30 percent on its artistic product, you may need to reevaluate the priorities. Below is a sample of the budget categories you might see at a board meeting:

Earned Revenues

Concert tickets	Program ads
Fund-raising events	Investments

Contributed Revenues

Individual gifts	Trusts
Board giving	Government grants
Corporate sponsors	In-kind gifts
Foundation support	

Expenses

Personnel	Publicity/Marketing
Staff	Insurance/Workers' compensation
Musicians	Fund-raising expenses
Production, office expenses, travel	

The artistic side of the budget can be further broken down into the following types of categories:

Personnel

Music director/Conductor	Personnel manager
Orchestra members	Librarian(s)
Guest artists	Stage manager/Stage crew
Assistant conductor	

Production

Hall rental	Travel expenses for guest artists
Music rental/Purchase	and musicians
Equipment rental	
Concert recording	

The organization will define how many and what kinds of concerts you will perform. To be a successful conductor with a community or regional orchestra, you will need to be flexible in the types of concerts you are willing to program and conduct. A community orchestra might have only three concerts per year and they will rehearse weekly in preparation for these events.

Many regional orchestras will have the following combination of concerts:

Five subscription concerts (singles or doubles)
Holiday concert
Youth concert series
One to three pops concerts

Once the budget for your orchestra has been established, it is your job to stay within it. Do not come back to the administration and suddenly say you want to add ten extra string players, or an additional rehearsal. Overtime is not an option to save you because you did not plan carefully enough in selecting your music or because you did not use your rehearsal time effectively. If you plan accurately, you should be able to stay within your budgeted amount. This is appreciated by both the board and the executive director, who are always trying to make ends meet.

Keep in mind that once the budget has been set, if there are ways you can save the organization money, you should do it. Sometimes, in planning the rehearsal schedule, you discover that you can creatively schedule so you do not need all the players at all the rehearsals. This might save the organization $1,000 or more per concert. Other times, a string player might cancel at the last minute because of an emergency, and you choose not to throw a new player into the mix. This will also save money. Treat the organization's money as if it were your own. Spend it wisely and save it when you can. Remember that you are a steward of the donations that are given to support the orchestra.

THE MUSIC DIRECTOR'S ROLE IN FUND-RAISING

Types of Fund-Raising

In addition to spending money, as a music director, you may be asked to participate in the process of raising it. This is a part of the job that you might not have been trained for. With fund-raising, you will probably be asked to participate in four ways: (1) attend official fund-raising meetings, lunches or dinners, to ask a specific benefactor to fund a specific project or concert; (2) help slant prospective artistic projects to fit the guidelines of a foundation or granting organization; (3) "sell the vision" to a group of community leaders that will be contacted separately by board members at a later date; and (4) attend informal lunches, dinners, and community events to provide long-term donor cultivation. In each of these areas, you should try to help in any way you can. As the music director, you are the best person to communicate the artistic vision of the orchestra. Fund-raising is simply telling people what you are excited about and then inviting them to join the team to make it possible.

Fund-Raising Meetings

Most fund-raising meetings should be attended by at least two members of the organization. When you are involved, you should be accompanied by a member of the board or a member of the staff so that the relationship does not rest on you alone. Before you attend any meeting, try to get as much information about the individual you are meeting with as possible. Do they currently attend concerts? Have they given money in the past? Do they like classical music or do they prefer pops? Do they have children or grandchildren? Do they, or any of their relatives, play a musical instrument? Do they support other endeavors in the community? If so, what in particular do they support? The better prepared you are, the easier it will be to establish a relationship.

For these fund-raising meetings, you should have packets to distribute that include material about the organization. This packet should have general information about the history of the orchestra, information about its concerts and outreach in the community, press reviews, and perhaps some details of sponsorship opportunities. If you do not know the potential donor well, it is best to have a variety of types of sponsorships and amounts ready to discuss.

When you are at the meeting, it is good to spend the first ten to fifteen minutes just talking to the proposed donor to find out more about their background and their interests. People are interested in you if you are first interested in them. During this time, try to make the person feel special. As you are speaking with them, use their name as often as possible and personalize the conversation. You want to find common ground and to establish a level of trust. Use this opening time to discover the dreams and goals of this person. How would they like to make a difference in the world? What are their interests? What do they get excited about?

Once you have identified what they are excited about, you must see if you have a program that involves these types of things. Successful fund-raising is dependent upon figuring out the "right ask" for the person you are talking to. By "right" it must be both the right program and the right amount. Make sure you are able to present the features and benefits of the program so that it matches their needs and wants. As you are talking about this program or project, be enthusiastic and demonstrate your true love for the music and your own confidence in the organization's ability to be successful in carrying it out. People invest in ideas, but they also invest in people. In giving you a donation, they are trusting your ability to complete the project at the highest level. As you are speaking, anticipate questions and concerns and have the answers ready. This lets them know that you have thought through all the parameters of the project. Knowledge of both your own programs and also your competitors' programs (other orchestras or arts organizations in the area) is important. You should be aware of what is going on throughout the community.

Dealing with Rejection

Don't be discouraged if you receive "*no*" for an answer. So many people are afraid of fund-raising because they don't want someone to tell them no. Statistically, it has been said that you have to ask a person three times before they will say "yes." Persistence is the key to fund-raising. Often it takes a long time to develop a relationship of trust. If you do happen to get a "no" on a fund-raising call, then spend the rest of the time asking questions and gathering more information.

Sometimes there are other issues that you are unaware of that stand in the way of an affirmative answer at that time. Perhaps their foundation only gives money once a year; perhaps they are only interested in capital gifts, or they only fund educational projects for minority children. If you are meeting with an individual, perhaps they need to speak further with a husband or wife. By asking questions and keeping the communication open, you will eventually find the right match for each donor.

If you are speaking with someone at a corporation, you might need to spend more time emphasizing the potential benefits to them. Often, corporations are funding their charitable gifts through marketing funds. Obviously, they are very interested in marketing exposure and value. Before the meeting, make sure that either you or someone else representing the orchestra can speak in detail about the marketing value.

"Slanting" Artistic Programs

Because the interests of individuals and foundations are often so specific, it is sometimes hard to make them fit with what you are currently doing. *Do not* go out and form a new outreach program, or select music for a concert just to fit the needs of a possible funding organization. This could be counterproductive to your mission and may sidetrack the organization from its original goals and priorities. Instead, see if there are any ways of slanting what you are currently doing. Often, you can add an emphasis on minority children by having a foundation underwrite tickets for them to attend a concert, or you can partner with a local senior center to incorporate this group into your current programs. If you want to program a concert with music based on Shakespeare, slant some of your fundraising efforts toward foundations that encourage literacy. Partner with a local organization to develop a program in the schools that explores the creative link between music and the written word; have all of the outreach activities culminate in the participants attending the orchestral concert; and identify a company that might be interested in underwriting the tickets for students and families that are financially limited. Be creative with your "slanting," but make sure you are not adding things that will cost more than the grant funding amount. Usually, the staff will come to you to see how you might angle a program to meet a specific goal, yet not sacrifice artistic credibility. Sometimes you can do it, sometimes you can't. The important thing is that you are involved in the process *before* decisions are made. Nothing is worse than finding out that a commitment was made to do a special project that you do not feel fits in with the mission and current programs of the organization.

"Selling" Vision

As the artistic leader for the organization, you may be brought into larger meetings to explain the mission and artistic goals of the organization. You should take time to develop a one-page summary of what the organization is trying to accomplish artistically in the next five years. You should be ready at any time to talk about these goals in a very detailed manner. You should know why these things are important, when the organization is planning on doing them, and how much they will cost. People in the community need to feel that you are committed to the big picture, and that you don't just appear for the concerts. Being committed to the larger picture is being committed to the community itself and what the orchestra brings to that community that is special.

Donor Cultivation

Donor cultivation is the ongoing process of making people feel involved and special. You usually start with people who are already exposed to the organization from attending concerts, but other people who are philanthropists in the community can also be cultivated. The conductor's role in this process is to help make these people feel special. It is important for you to remember the names of the donors who provide support for the orchestra. Any time you write a special note of thanks for a generous contribution, it will go a long way toward establishing a bond between the individual and the orchestra. Don't view this part of your job as a hassle, or as unimportant. View it as an investment in the financial future of the organization. Take the time to have lunch with symphony supporters where an official "ask" will not be made. Attend dinner parties and social events in the community and spend the time mingling with people and talking informally about your dreams for the orchestra. It is through many of these informal conversations that you will realize what people are really interested in. Later on, the staff can follow up with a more formal meeting. Ongoing donor cultivation is critical for the success of the orchestra. It is one of the best ways to spend your time, outside of concert preparation and your time on the podium.

CREATING A VISIBLE PRESENCE IN THE COMMUNITY
Education and Outreach Programs

The type of orchestra you are conducting will have an impact on your involvement with the education and outreach programs. With a community orchestra, you will find yourself wearing many hats and you will be active in all areas. As the orchestra increases in size, you may hire an assistant conductor who will take on many of the education duties. Even if you have an assistant conductor, you should be involved with more than just conducting the subscription concerts. You should help the organization develop a philosophy of how they are going to impact more people in the community. Ideally, you should inspire the organization to develop engaging programs for people of all age groups and backgrounds.

> Preschool–3rd grade
> 3rd grade–6th grade
> Middle school or junior high
> High school
> Young professionals (ages 18–30)
> Parents with young children (25–40)
> Empty nesters (40–60)
> Active retired people (60–75)
> Seniors (65–90)

These categories divide further into:

1. People interested in classical music
2. People interested in pops music
3. People interested in music education for themselves or for their children
4. People who think they don't like classical music
5. People who have never heard a symphony orchestra

Often, community engagement focuses on just the third to sixth grade level with educational concerts because, historically, this interaction has been supported well by the schools and the communities. For these concerts, the schools bus the children to the hall, and in just a few hours, hundreds of students are exposed to classical music. To only reach out to this age group, however, is not enough when you are trying to serve the entire community. Many of your outreach activities do not have to involve large expenses. Single musicians, duos, chamber music groups—all can be trained to do wonderfully interactive programs for the various age groups. The size of your organization will dictate how much you are personally involved with the creation of these programs. I also encourage you to help create volunteer opportunities combined with musician performances so you can educate and further involve your volunteer base in these types of outreach activities.

It also is important to take time to brainstorm and research successful education and outreach programs from different orchestras around the country. Try to be current with what is going on in the field. Here is a list of some examples:

Educational and Outreach Programs

- Kinderkoncerts—(Orchestra concerts for 3–7 year olds)
- Story concerts—Story teller, pianist, and one orchestra member (performed for 100 young children at a time)
- "Meet the Musician" chamber music ensembles in schools
- Youth concerts
- Family concerts
- Composer's residencies or "Meet the Composer" concerts
- Student mentoring program
- Music scholars program
- Pre-concert lectures
- Side-by-side concerts (with local high school students)
- "Petting Zoo" (where young people can try different instruments)
- Resident musician at schools ("Adopt a Musician")
- Senior center conversations and performances
- Retirement center concerts or preconcert lectures
- High school date night
- Library concerts (chamber music or other ensembles)
- Clinics at local schools
- Master classes with orchestra members and guest artists
- Coloring books and educational materials
- Radio series with orchestra members

As you move from brainstorming to selecting actual programs to incorporate, make sure that these outreach programs fit with your overall goals and that they do not become the mission itself. First and foremost, you are a symphony orchestra formed to bring great music to the people in your community. All of your educational outreach should be designed to culminate with the targeted group attending a concert of the full orchestra. Try to create programming bonds by tying the focus of the educational outreach to the subscription concert repertoire that will be performed throughout the year. This is sometimes difficult to do and requires extra work for the staff, but it will make your programs much more effective and relevant to your overall mission.

It is good for you as a music director to have a presence at some of these outreach programs. Even if you are not involved with the actual performance, try to attend at least two to three outreach activities per year and more if you can. Say a few words at the event to welcome the audience and to thank the musicians for their participation. This type of involvement will go far towards building good will within the organization. The musicians are always excited when someone cares enough to come and see their performance; the audience will feel pleased that you felt their program was important enough for you to show up. Like the school principal who constantly walks the halls during the passing period, saying "hello" to everyone, make it your goal to have a presence within the overall organization and throughout the community.

Public Speaking

As a music director, you will be called on to be a guest speaker for civic clubs and other organizations. You should try to accept as many speaking engagements as possible, even if you are uncomfortable presenting speeches. This is an excellent way to spread the word about the projects that the symphony is involved with and to encourage people to attend concerts. Often, people need this personal interaction to finally make the commitment to hear the orchestra. What they are really doing is going to see *you*—because you have developed a relationship with them.

Most of these speeches will be about twenty to thirty minutes long, with some time for questions at the end. The size of the group might range from ten people to two hundred people. Never turn down an opportunity just because the group is small. I was once scheduled to do a talk at a library. The day before the talk, the woman from the library called and said there were only five people signed up. She asked if I wanted to cancel. I thought about it, knowing I would much rather have the time free, but then decided that since I was in town anyway, I should talk to whoever was interested in learning more about the symphony. We had a wonderfully stimulating discussion at the library that day. Imagine my surprise when, later, one of those five people sent a check for $1,000 to the symphony office. You never know when you are going to meet someone who is interested in helping the orchestra achieve its goals.

Preparing Your Presentation

When you are preparing for your presentations, ask yourself a few questions to clarify your ideas:

1. What is the purpose of this talk?
2. Who is my audience?
3. Why are they here?
4. What is their previous knowledge level? (as best as you can assess)
5. How large will the group be?
6. How can you personalize the information toward this specific group?

Some people, when preparing speeches, need to write out the entire text. Other people are more comfortable with cue cards or a page of "bullet" points. You will have to discover which style works best for you. In organizing the talk, you basically want to—tell them what you are going to talk about, talk about it, review what you have told them, and then close dramatically with a short quote, or a call to action. With most speeches, you will keep everything in the first person. This will make the speech appear to be very informal and conversational. The more little stories and personalization you can work into your talk, the better. People want to leave the room feeling that they know the real you.

Before you present the speech, make sure you check out the room in advance. If you are going to be using PowerPoint or special equipment, arrive early to test the system. There is nothing that ruins a speech faster than technical problems. Make sure you also arrive early so you can meet and greet the audience as they arrive. This should help you to feel more comfortable and relaxed, and it allows you a little time if you need to slant your points differently once you see who the audience really is.

Before you start your speech, know what time you are supposed to be finished. Nothing is more uncomfortable then having people get up and leave, or having someone come up and tell you that you are out of time. It is better to know your deadline and to make the adjustments yourself as you go along. Keep a watch handy on the podium, if possible, so you can keep track of the time without drawing attention to it.

Giving Your Speech

As you are presenting your speech, take care that you do not simply read it through. Also, never distribute handouts to your presentation in advance. Your audience will spend the entire talk reading the handout instead of listening to what you have to say. While you are speaking, establish eye contact with the audience and remember to smile. If you want to be more informal, move away from the podium and stand closer to your audience. Be animated in your delivery, and vary your voice in tone and speed. If, in the middle of your speech, your audiovisual equipment fails, just turn it off and go on. You should always be prepared to do a presentation without any props just in case. As you are getting near the end of your speech, signal the close to your audience. Use words such as "in conclusion," or "to wrap it up," or "I would like to leave you with . . . " If you would like to have time for questions at the end, allow for them within the total time allocated for the presentation. If you ask for questions and there are none, make sure that you have one closing thought prepared so that you can end on a positive note and not leave your audience hanging. It is important to bring plenty of business cards and season brochures with you so you can give people information on how to contact the organization and how they can become further involved.

Presenting speeches in the community is an excellent way to reach people in a manner that feels very personal. After a while, you will develop a couple of basic talks that can be pulled out at a moment's notice. Being available for these types of presentations is a great way to have a presence in the community.

Dealing with the Media

Once you become a music director, you will be considered a celebrity in the orchestra's community. The organization will want to capitalize upon this with as much press as possible. This will mean extensive interviews and exposure. Throughout your career, you will be involved in giving radio interviews, phone interviews, personal interviews with reporters from the local paper, and television interviews. You will need to become comfortable and effective in all of these environments in your role as a music director.

Radio Interviews

Radio interviews usually take place on either the local classical music stations, university-owned stations, or local talk-show radio stations. Occasionally, if you are performing a pops concert, you might do an interview on a nonclassical radio station. For each of these interviews, you will want to make sure that the staff sends an information package in advance. This should include your biography, information on the soloists for the upcoming concerts, repertoire for the concerts, historical information on the orchestra, information on ticket prices and phone numbers, time and date of the concert, and information on future concerts. You also should bring with you a two-page sheet of critical information that could be scanned by the eye when you are actually on the air. Often, radio announcers get busy and they misplace the original packet. When you walk into the studio, they barely know who you are, much less which organization you are with. Having a "cheat sheet" solves this problem immediately and allows them to save face. Another helpful thing is to bring CDs of the pieces featured on the concert. Do not rely upon the music library at the station to have these works. If they do have them ready to be played on the air, great! If not, you are still covered, and you will be able to get some samples of the music out to the listening audience. If the radio is a talk radio station, you will not need the CDs. Instead, be ready with some bullet-point questions that you can encourage them to ask if they have not prepared any of their own. Usually, talk show hosts are never at a loss for a question, but you may have to help steer the conversation towards the points that you really want covered in the interview. Don't be afraid to answer a question and say, "Yes, that is true, but you know what we really do best is . . . " Using these types of techniques, you can take a conversation in any direction that you want.

Newspaper and Magazine Interviews

For a newspaper article, you will either hold a phone interview or a personal interview. You will want to set up a specific time, so that you are prepared with your comments regarding the program. Before the interview, make sure you have reviewed the repertoire, that you know the dates of all of the composers, the dates the pieces were written, and the connections between the musical pieces. Be ready to talk about why you selected these pieces and what is interesting about them. You also will need to review the biography of the guest artist. It is important when the reporter asks you about the soloist that you can quickly state the highlights of their career and that you know the correct spelling of their name. It is also helpful if you know the general ticket pricing for the concert. You should have the office send the newspaper reporter a copy of the same materials as the radio interview so they have concrete information to fill out the article. Sometimes, the interviewer will have an in-depth knowledge of music and sometimes they won't.

Some reporters will be more prepared than others with their questions. Be ready to tell them exactly what you would like to have printed. Always keep your comments positive and remember that anything you say can appear as a quote for all to read. Be careful to be very clear with your statements to avoid being misquoted. Never joke or say anything off the cuff; these are the things they love to print. Sometimes they will ask a question where you will not know the answer. Never make up an answer; simply say that you do not know. Offer to research it, and get back to them.

Sometimes, a reporter is looking for an angle about nonpublic or private information from within the organization. Do not talk about private matters with reporters, even if they ask and you are promised it will be kept off the record. One way to avoid answering a question is to ask them a question in return. If they have just asked you about the looming deficit of the orchestra, you could ask them what they think of the economy across the country. When you sense trouble, talk about general concepts within the industry, not specific issues within your organization. Throughout the entire interview, make sure that you speak enthusiastically about the wonderful concerts and outreach programs that the orchestra is involved with. Try to give the reporter plenty of "quotable" comments.

A live interview varies slightly from a phone interview because it is usually longer. Most phone interviews last between five and twenty minutes. A personal interview is usually half an hour to one hour. These might be for a feature article on an outreach program or a story for a magazine. This type of interview will require a broader preparation, and often the interviewer will speak to a variety of people within the organization, not just you. Because these interviews are longer, they tend to be more informal. Enjoy the conversation, but never relax so much that you forget you are talking with a reporter. Every word you say has the possibility of being repeated—often out of context. Choose your words carefully and always represent the organization in the best possible light.

TV Interviews

If you are in a smaller market that has a network TV station, you will probably have regular TV interviews, or someone might appear at a rehearsal to do a short interview during the break. When you are being interviewed on TV, do not look at the camera; look at the person who is asking you the questions. Sometimes this person is also on the air with you, and sometimes they are to one side of the camera in front of you. Usually, they will have prepared a set of questions. Once again, do not be afraid to continue after answering their initial question to say some of the information you really want to have communicated. Usually, your on-air time will be very short, so you don't have much time to get your points across. If the interview is for an upcoming concert, and if you have a chance to talk with the crew ahead of time, see if they can have someone in the studio prepare a screen with the phone number for tickets. They can then flash this information on to the screen during part of the interview. This is much more effective than simply saying the phone number.

If you know about the interview in advance, make sure that you are dressed appropriately. Do not wear stripes, or outfits with involved patterns. Keep to bold, solid colors. Also, do not wear all black or all white. These colors do not look as good on TV as other bright colors. Usually, they will only be filming from the waist up, but dress appropriately to be prepared either way. Your clothes should be pressed, your shoes polished, and you should be sure to smile throughout the interview. As you respond to the questions, feel free to use hand gestures, but keep them smaller than normal. Television cameras tend to exaggerate everything. Your actions will need to be more subtle that what you might use in a speech presentation. Also, remember to speak slowly but with enthusiasm. Through a television interview, you have the potential of reaching a whole new audience. Make sure you put your best foot forward.

Establishing a Visible Presence

It is important for the music director to be visibly present in the community. It has nothing to do with whether you actually live there full time, or whether you commute to town. It has to do with the amount of time you devote to becoming known. Hopefully, these tasks will come naturally to you. If not, these are skills that you will need to spend time mastering. By being a community "presence," you inspire people to become involved in the organization. A music director's name and face should be familiar to most of the people who live in the area. If you are not recognized in local restaurants and shops, then perhaps you are not putting enough time into developing your community presence.

Chapter 8

CLOSING THOUGHTS

KEEPING YOUR COMPETITIVE EDGE

Continued Artistic Development

Ongoing Training for Life

It is important always to be learning as a conductor. Often, we think that study-ing new repertoire is the only learning we need, but that is just the tip of the ice-berg. Of course, you want to be constantly exposing yourself to new music and investigating lost works and composers, but you also need to grow in many other ways. Often, as conductors, we stop attending concerts because we are spending so much time conducting our own that going to others feels like work. Try not only to keep attending quality concerts at which you can observe top conductors in the field but also make it a point to attend rehearsals. Most orchestras are very open to this. You will need to call to get permission, which is granted through ei-ther the education department or the general manager of the orchestra. They will send you a rehearsal schedule and make arrangements for you to enter the hall through the stage door when the rehearsals are taking place. This is also a good way to check out new solo talent, hear interesting repertoire, and make new con-tacts. If the orchestra does need any help in the future, you might be the first per-son they think of because they already have a sense that you would fit in.

It is also important to have other people critique your work. We are isolated as conductors and there is no formalized system for us to get feedback on our conducting technique. After you have been out of school for a while, it is easy to develop bad habits: for example, things that you may think are working but are actually making it more difficult for the musicians to follow you. You will be able to catch many of these by constantly video recording your rehearsals and closely studying the tapes. You will be amazed at what you see. Through this process, you can quickly identify potential problems and correct them before they become bad habits.

Throughout your career, I would recommend attending conducting workshops and seminars to get further feedback. Some conductors think that once they have a job, they have mastered conducting. This is impossible. Conducting is an art form that you will spend your lifetime trying to master and improve. There are many master classes and conducting seminars presented in both the United States and in Europe (see the Resource section). Often, through these seminars, you will have the opportunity to work with excellent orchestras and experienced conductors in the field. It is also valuable to meet with, and study the work of, the other conductors attending these workshops. These people will become your friends and colleagues. You will be able to go to them later for feedback and to discuss ideas and trends in the field.

You also should attend conferences and programs offered by the ASOL and the Conductors Guild. The programs from the ASOL Leadership Academy offer an in-depth study of leadership, vision, and artistic programming. I recommend all of these highly. The Conductors Guild has a wonderful journal with carefully researched articles and pertinent insights into the field. They also host a conference once a year that deals specifically with issues related to conductors for all types of ensembles.

Dealing With Obstacles and Burnout

As with any field, when you work very hard at something, there is a tendency toward burnout. Conductors often take any work that comes their way, no matter how busy they might already be. There is always the lure of what this new opportunity might lead to, and the fear that if they say "no," they will not be asked again. Because of this, we are often overworked and always under a lot of pressure. It is better to say "no" than to run the risk of presenting yourself badly. You will be judged on everything you do. The saying often used in the field is "You are only as good as your last concert." If you do not think you have the time to adequately prepare without sacrificing other important things in your life, than learn to say a tactful "no." Make sure in doing this, however, that you still leave the door open for future invitations.

As conductors, everything we do is either in front of an audience or the orchestra. Your actions and words are on view for people either to approve or to actively criticize. This is very stressful. The nature of the position tends to isolate us. Because of this, it is important to develop a network of friends outside the music profession. You need to be with people where you are not always perceived to be the conductor. You need to escape and just be a regular person for a while. It is also important to schedule down time and days off into your schedule. Often, we think that we have to study all the time, every day, in order to keep up. Sometimes it is this time away from the music that allows us to bring a greater depth of emotional understanding back to the podium.

Leaving a Legacy

As we go through life, all of us want to be a part of something larger than ourselves. All of us want to leave something behind that reminds people we were here. All of us strive to contribute towards the betterment of mankind. Somehow, we are driven to leave a legacy. In order to do this, you must always be growing yourself and you must keep from burning out or becoming discouraged.

Continued Growth and Artistic Alignment

It is important as you work with your organizations that you do not become complacent. Usually, it takes at least four years to build or turn around an organization. This is because during the first year, when you enter the job, most of the activities and programs are already planned and the organization is already in motion. In the second year on the job, you will begin to make changes, slowly improving the artistic quality and challenging your audience. By the third year, you will begin to incorporate more of your larger ideas for the organization, and your relationships within the community should be fully established. In the fourth year, you will begin to see the fruits of your labor. This is the time when you need to step back, assess where you have been, where you are currently, and how you can outline and adjust the plans for the future. Often people stop at this level because they have used up their best ideas within the first four years. It is critical for you to stay current in the field and to always bring new ideas and possible projects to your executive director and your board.

Sometimes, as you work with an organization, you assume that, because you did some extensive planning with your board at the beginning of your tenure, everyone is still on the same "page" regarding artistic growth. Over the course of a few years, many board members will rotate off the board and others will be appointed. Even if your organization holds extensive training for these board members, there might still be a "gap" in their understanding of the artistic mission of the organization. Make sure that you take the time to meet with new board members during their first year to share your passion about the goals of the organization and to be sure that they thoroughly understand these goals and the philosophy behind them. Never assume that everyone is on the same page. Keeping the artistic mission aligned is a continuous ongoing process of communication.

Whose Orchestra Is It Anyway?

As you develop the vision and plans for the orchestra and the organization, always remember that it is not "your" orchestra. This is *not* your personal toy to do with what you want. As an artistic leader, you are a steward of the talents and gifts of the people involved. The orchestra as an organization belongs to the community. It belongs both to the people involved directly and to the people it serves. Never underestimate your responsibility to others as the conductor and artistic leader of an orchestra. All of your decisions should be based upon what is best for the organization and what fits with the mission and the role of this specific orchestra in its community.

Knowing When to Leave

When you have been with an orchestra for a while, there will come a time when you have taken them as far as you can. It is the same with all teachers—and a good teacher knows when it is time to pass students on to someone else. It is not that someone else will be better, but rather that they will be different. It is a rare person that can stay fresh, new, and exciting forever. When you have been with an organization for a long time, it is easy to become blind to problems, or to just accept situations because they are too difficult to change. The orchestra becomes too familiar with you and it is too easy for everyone to relax. A great leader knows when they have accomplished their goals and it is time to leave.

You want always to leave your organizations in much better shape than when you arrived. It is best to leave when you are at a high point in the organization's growth, not when things have shifted into a downward slump. If you have not noticed that the time has come, and the board approaches you about this, don't fight them in a public battle. They are only doing what they feel is best for the overall organization. Accept it and move on. There are many orchestras out there for you to work with. If you have been learning and growing as a conductor, you will have opportunities to share your talents with other orchestras and to bring them forward in their organizational growth.

Epilogue

In many ways, I feel as though I have "spilled" the secrets of the conducting world for everyone to read. Some of my words of advice come from things I did "right" along the way just by accident. Others stem from the "correcting" I had to do after

I first did things wrong. I want to offer back to new people in the field the knowledge of how to approach things right the first time, and therefore to improve the level of artistic leadership throughout the country. I hope these words of advice will be helpful for you as you move forward in your career. It is a difficult field, but also one that can be incredibly rewarding.

As you are out there finding your own way, remember one thing:

> Nothing in the world can take the place of persistence. Talent will not; nothing is more common than unsuccessful individuals with talent. Genius will not; unrewarded genius is almost a proverb. Education will not; the world is full of educated derelicts. Persistence and determination alone are omnipotent. (Ray A. Kroc, *Grinding It Out*)

So I challenge you to persist, and therefore to succeed. To perform great music and to share it is a noble goal. Let us lead our organizations toward high-quality music, exciting performances, and effective outreach programs. My personal goal is to bring quality music to as many people as possible and through this music to change their lives for the better. I hope that this will be your goal also, as you become a great conductor—and a great artistic leader.

Resources

Music Organizations

NETWORKING ORGANIZATIONS

THE AMERICAN CHORAL DIRECTORS
ASSOCIATION
Phone: (405) 232-8161
Fax: (405) 232-8162
E-mail: acda@acdaonline.org
Web site: www.acdaonline.org

THE AMERICAN COMPOSERS ALLIANCE
Phone: (212) 925-0458
Fax: (212) 925-6798
E-mail: info@composers.com
Web site: www.composers.com

AMERICAN COMPOSERS FORUM
Phone: (651) 228-1407
Fax: (651) 291-7978
E-mail: mail@composersforum.org
Web site: www.composersforum.org

AMERICAN FEDERATION OF MUSICIANS
(AF OF M)
Phone: (212) 869-1330
Fax: (212) 764-6134
E-mail: info@afm.org
Web site: www.afm.org

THE AMERICAN MUSIC CENTER
Phone: (212) 366-5260
Fax: (212) 366-5265
E-mail: amcinfo@amc.net
Web site: www.amc.net

AMERICAN SOCIETY OF COMPOSERS,
AUTHORS & PUBLISHERS (ASCAP)
Phone: (212) 621-6000
Fax: (212) 724-9064
E-mail: info@ascap.com
Web site: www.ascap.com

LEAGUE OF AMERICAN ORCHESTRAS
Phone: (212) 262-5161
Fax: (212) 262-5198
E-mail: League@americanorchestras.org
Web site: www.americanorchestras.org

ASSOCIATION OF CALIFORNIA SYMPHONY
ORCHESTRA (ASCO)
Phone: (916) 484-6744
Fax: (916) 484-0503
E-mail: office@acso.org
Web site: www.acso.org

ASSOCIATION OF PERFORMING ARTS
PRESENTERS (APAP)
Phone: (202) 833-2787
Fax: (202) 833-1543
E-mail: info@artspresenters.org
Web site: www.artspresenters.org

BROADCAST MUSIC, INC. (BMI)
Phone: (212) 220-3000
Fax: (212) 245-2163
E-mail: newyork@bmi.com
Web site: www.bmi.com

CHAMBER MUSIC AMERICA
Phone: (212) 242-2022
Fax: (212) 242-7955
E-mail: info@chamber-music.org
Web site: www.chamber-music.org

THE COLLEGE MUSIC SOCIETY
Phone: (406) 721-9616
Fax: (406) 721-9419
E-mail: cms@music.org
Web site: www.music.org

THE CONDUCTORS GUILD
Phone: (804) 553-1378
Fax: (804) 553-1876
E-mail: guild@conductorsguild.org
Web site: www.conductorsguild.org

INTERNATIONAL CONFERENCE OF SYMPHONY AND OPERA MUSICIANS (ICSOM)
Web site: www.Icsom.org

MAJOR ORCHESTRA LIBRARIAN ASSOCIATION (MOLA)
Web site: www.mola-inc.org

MEET THE COMPOSER
Phone: (212) 645-6949
Fax: (212) 645-9669
E-mail: mtc@meetthecomposer.org
Web site: www.meetthecomposer.org

THE NATIONAL ASSOCIATION OF COMPOSERS—USA (NACUSA)
Phone: (310) 838-4132
Fax: (310) 838-4465
E-mail: nacusa@music-usa.org
Web site: www.music-usa.org/nacusa

NORTH AMERICAN PERFORMING ARTS MANAGERS AND AGENTS (NAPAMA)
Phone: 518-436-4391
E-mail: info@napama.org
Web site: www.napama.org

REGIONAL ORCHESTRA PLAYERS ASSOCIATION (ROPA)
Web site: www.ropaweb.org

SYMPHONY ORCHESTRA INSTITUTE
Phone: (847) 475-5001
Fax: (847) 475-2460
E-mail: information@soi.org
Web site: www.soi.org

TEXAS ASSOCIATION FOR SYMPHONY ORCHESTRAS (TASO)
Web site: www.tasovolunteers.com

YOUNG AUDIENCES
Phone: (212) 831-8110
Fax: (212) 289-1202
E-mail: ya4kids@ya.org
Web site: www.youngaudiences.org

DIRECTORIES, MAGAZINES, AND JOURNALS

CONCERT ARTISTS GUILD GUIDE TO COMPETITIONS (ANNUAL PUBLICATION)
Phone: (212) 333-5200
Fax: (212) 977-7149
E-mail: caguild@concertartists.org
Web site: www.concertartists.org

HARMONY—SYMPHONY ORCHESTRA INSTITUTE
Phone: (847) 475-5001
Fax: (847) 475-2460
E-mail: information@soi.org
Web site:
www.soi.org/harmony/index.shtml

INTERNATIONAL MUSICIAN—AMERICAN
FEDERATION OF MUSICIANS
Phone: (212) 869-1330
Fax: (212) 764-6134
E-mail: info@afm.org
Web site: www.afm.org

THE JOURNAL OF THE CONDUCTORS GUILD
Phone: (804) 553-1878
Fax: (804) 553-1876
E-mail: guild@conductorsguild.org
Web site: www.conductorsguild.org
The Conductors Guild also publishes
*Podium Notes, Conductor Opportunities
Bulletin, and The Conductors Guild Mem-
bership Directory.*

MUSICAL AMERICA/INTERNATIONAL
DIRECTORY OF THE PERFORMING ARTS
Phone: 609-448-3346
Fax: (609) 371-7879
E-mail: info@musicalamerica.com
Web site: www.musicalamerica.com

THE MUSICAL QUARTERLY
Phone: (800) 852-7323
Fax: (919) 677-1714
E-mail: jnlorders@oxfordjournals.org
Web site: www.mq.oxfordjournals.org

NEWMUSICBOX (WEB MAGAZINE)
AMERICAN MUSIC CENTER
Phone: (212) 366-5260
Fax: (212) 366-5265
E-mail: editor@newmusicbox.org
Web site: www.newmusicbox.org

OPERA NEWS
Phone: (212) 769-7080
Fax: (212) 769-8500
E-mail: info@operanews.com
Web site: www.operanews.com

POLLSTAR
Phone: (559) 271-7900
Fax: (559) 271-7979
E-mail: info@pollstar.com
Web site: www.pollstar.com

SENZA SORDINO (ICSOM NEWSLETTER)
Web site: www.icsom.org

SYMPHONY—LEAGUE OF AMERICAN
ORCHESTRAS
Phone: (212) 262-5161
Fax: (212) 262-5198
E-mail: editor@americanorchestras.org
Web site: www.americanorchestras.org

INTERNET RESOURCES AND FORUMS

Web sites

www.choralnet.org
(Extensive resource for choral repertoire lists, reference materials, rehearsal tips, and
choral accessories and technology)

www.harryfox.com
(The Web site for the Harry Fox Agency which is the foremost mechanical licensing,
collections, and distribution agency for U.S. music publishers)

www.imusicassociation.com
(The Web site of the International Music Association; includes useful links and
contact information for orchestras internationally)

www.mola-inc.org

(The Web site of the Major Orchestra Librarians' Association; this site includes information on erratas in scores, music preparation, publisher sources, and more)

www.Musicalchairs.info

(An international listing of jobs in classical music)

www.NewMusicbox.org

(An online marketplace for new music by American composers including scores, sound samples, and biographical information)

www.songfile.com

(Lists over two million songs with access to lyrics, artists, album titles, and sheet music)

www.TNV.net

(A thematic programming resource for pops concerts)

News Services

www.classicOL.com

(News articles about classical music and performances from around the world, updated daily)

www.gramophone.co.uk

(Classical music news stories from around the world, CD recommendations, and concert listings)

The Hub—League of American Orchestras

(Condensed news clippings regarding music events and concerts from around the country, for members of ASOL only)
thehub@americanorchestras.org
www.americanorchestras.org

Forums

ARTISTIC ADMINISTRATORS E-MAIL LIST
(Artistic Administrators forum for members of the League)
Artadmin@list.americanorchestras.org (to post)
Subscriber@americanorchestras.org (to subscribe)
http://list.americanorchestras.org/cgi-bin/mailman/listinfo/artadmin

CHORAL DIRECTORS E-MAIL LIST
Choralist, ChoralAcademe, ChoralTalk, plus 14 forums
(Resource for choral conductors)
choralist-L@indiana.edu (to post)
choraltalk-L@indiana.edu (to post)
choralacademe-L@indiana.edu (to post)
http://choralnet.org/lists

CONCERTSFORKIDS FORUM
(Discussion area for educational
concerts)
http://www.danieldorff.com/
concertsforkids.htm

CONDUCTOR E-MAIL LIST
(Discussion area for conductors who are
members of the League)
Conductor@list.americanorchestras.org
(to post)
Subscriber@americanorchestras.org
(to subscribe)
http://list.americanorchestras.org/
cgi-bin/mailman/listinfo/conductor

FINALE FORUMS
(Discussion group for people using
Finale to write music)
(Notation—Windows; Notation—
Macintosh; SmartMusic; Finale Plug-In
Development; FinaleScript Plug-in)
http://www.finalemusic.com/forum

GUILDLIST
(A discussion group for members of the
Conductors Guild focusing on conducting issues, score study, publications, jobs,
competitions, and repertoire)
http://www.conductorsguild.org

ORCHESTRA LIST
(Idea exchange for conductors of all
levels from around the country)
Orchestralist@yahoogroups.com
(to post)
Orchestralist-subscribe@yahoogroups
.com (to subscribe)
http://groups.yahoo.com/group/
Orchestralist
http://www.orchestralist.net

ARTIST MANAGERS

BARRETT VANTAGE ARTISTS
Phone: (212) 245-3530
Fax: (212) 397-5860
E-mail: info@barrettvantage.com
Web site: www.barrrettvantage.com

CALIFORNIA ARTISTS MANAGEMENT
Phone: (415) 362-2787
Fax: (415) 362-2838
E-mail: Don@CalArtists.com
Web site: www.calartists.com

CENTER STAGE ARTISTS
Phone: (800) 650-8742
Fax: (734) 662-8733
E-mail: info@centerstageartists.com
Web site: www.centerstageartists.com

CM ARTISTS
Phone: (212) 864-1005
Fax: (212) 864-1066
E-mail: lymarder@aol.com
Web site: www.cmartists.com

COLBERT ARTISTS MANAGEMENT
Phone: (212) 757-0782
Fax: (212) 541-5179
E-mail: nycolbert@colbertartists.com
Web site: www.colbertartistis.com

COLUMBIA ARTISTS MANAGEMENT
Phone: (212) 841-9500
Fax: (212) 841-9744
E-mail: info@cami.com
Web site: www.cami.com

CM Artists Guild
Phone: (212) 333-5200
Fax: (212) 977-7149
E-mail: caguild@concertartists.org
Web site: www.cmartists.com

Corbett Arts Management
Phone: (415) 928-2505
Fax: (415) 928-5225
E-mail: info@corbettarts.com
Web site: www.corbettarts.com

Thea Dispeker
Phone: (212) 421-7676
Fax: (212) 935-3279
E-mail: info@dispeker.com
Web site: www.dispeker.com

Gershunoff Artists
Phone: (954) 267-0550
Fax: (954) 267-0560
E-mail: leonmax@aol.com
Web site: www.gershunoff.com

John Gingrich Management
Phone: (212) 799-5080
Fax: (212) 874-7652
E-mail: gingarts@verizon.net
Web site: www.gingarts.com

Gurtman & Murtha Artist Management
Phone: (212) 967-7350 or
(800) 66-MUSIC
Fax: (212) 967-7341
E-mail: GMArtists@aol.com
Web site: www.GurtmanandMurtha.com

Opus 3 Artists
Phone: (212) 584-7500
Fax: (212) 646-300-8268
E-mail: info@opus3artists.com
Web site: www.opus3artists.com

IMG Artists, North America
Phone: (212) 994-3500
Fax: (212) 994-3550
E-mail: artistsny@imgworld.com
Web site: www.imgartists.com

Kaylor Management
Phone: (212) 977-6779
Fax: (212) 977-6856
E-mail: hughkaylor@msn.com
Web site: www.hughkaylor.com

Ted Kurland Associates
Phone: (617) 254-0007
Fax: (617) 782-3577
E-mail: agents@tedkurland.com
Web site: www.tedkurland.com

Robert Lombardo & Associates
Phone: (212) 586-4453
Fax: (212) 581-5771
E-mail: robert@robertlombardo.com
Web site: www.robertlombardo.com

William Morris Agency
Phone: (212) 586-5100
Fax: (212) 246-3583
Web site: www.wma.com

Omicron Artist Management
Phone: (414) 332-7600
Fax: (414) 332-6473
E-mail: info@omicronarts.com
Web site: www.omicronarts.com

Parker Artists
Phone: (212) 864-7928
Fax: (212) 864-8189
E-mail: tom@parkerartists.com
Web site: www.parkerartists.com

Joanne Rile Artists Management
Phone: (215) 885-6400
Fax: (215) 885-9929
E-mail: artists@rilearts.com
Web site: www.rilearts.com

Monica Robinson
Phone: (914) 962-6062
Fax: (914) 962-6068
E-mail: MRLTD6062@aol.com
Web site: www.MonicaRobinsonLtd.com

FRANK SALOMON ASSOCIATES
Phone: (212) 581-5197
Fax: (212) 581-4029
E-mail: info@franksolomon.com
Web site: www.franksalomon.com

SCHMIDT ARTISTS INTERNATIONAL
Phone: (212) 421-8500
Fax: (212) 421-8583
E-mail: info@schmidtart.com
Web site: www.schmidtart.com

SCHWALBE & PARTNERS
Phone: (212) 935-5650
Fax: (212) 935-4754
E-mail: info@schwalbeandpartners.com
Web site: www.schwalbeandpartners.com

MATTHEW SPRIZZO, ARTIST MANAGEMENT
Phone: (718) 948-2736
Fax: (718) 984-2736
E-mail: MSprizzo@aol.com
Web site: www.matthewsprizzo.com

STANTON MANAGEMENT
Phone: (718) 956-6092
Fax: (718) 956-5385
E-mail: TDStanton@stantonmgt.com
Web site: www.StantonMgt.com

JOHN SUCH ARTISTS MANAGEMENT
Phone: (212) 926-4833
Fax: (212) 926-2928
E-mail: jsuchmgt@aol.com
Web site: www.johnsuchartists.com

ANN SUMMERS INTERNATIONAL
Phone: (416) 362-1422
Fax: (416) 359-0043
E-mail: sumintl@rogers.com
Web site: www.sumarts.com

JONATHAN WENTWORTH ASSOCIATES
Phone: (914) 667-0707 or (301) 277-8205
Fax: (914) 667-0784
E-mail: office@jwentworth.com
Web site: www.jwentworth.com

YOUNG CONCERT ARTISTS
Phone: (212) 307-6655
Fax: (212) 581-8894
E-mail: management@yca.org
Web site: www.yca.org

Music Sources

Standard Music Publishers

As you program your concerts, you will need to be able to locate many different types of music. Below are sources for purchasing music, suggestions for contacting standard music rental companies, and a valuable list for tracking down pops arrangements. This contact information sometimes changes in the industry. This list was the most current information available at the time of printing.

Music Purchasing

Colony Music Center
(Pops sheet music)
Phone: (212) 265-2050
Fax: (212) 956-6009
E-mail: questions@colonymusic.com
Web site: www.colonymusic.com

Dover Publications
(Orchestra scores)
Phone: (516) 294-7000
Fax: (516) 746-1821
E-mail: info@doverpublications.com
Web site: www.doverpublications.com

Educational Music Service (EMS)
(Assorted publishers—Mapleson Rental
Library)
(Wonderful resource for information on
editions)
Phone: (845) 469-5790
Fax: (845) 469-5817
E-mail: sales@emsmusic.com
Web site: www.emsmusic.com

Edwin F. Kalmus Music Publishers
Phone: (800) 434-6340 or (561) 241-6340
Fax: (561) 241-6347
E-mail: info@kalmus-music.com
Web site: www.kalmus-music.com

Hal Leonard Publishing
Phone: (414) 774-3630
Fax: (414) 774-3259
E-mail: halinfo@halleonard.com
Web site: www.halleonard.com

Luck's Music Library
Phone: (248) 583-1820 or (800) 348-8749
Fax: (248) 583-1114
E-mail: sales@lucksmusic.net
Web site: www.lucksmusic.net

J.W. Pepper
(Educational Music)
Phone: (800) 345-6296
Fax: 610-993-0563
E-mail: satisfaction@jwpepper.com
Web site: www.jwpepper.com

Rental Music Publishers

BELMONT MUSIC PUBLISHERS
Phone: (310) 454-1867
Fax: (310) 573-1925
E-mail: office@schoenbergmusic.com
Web site: www.schoenbergmusic.com

BOOSEY & HAWKES
(Durand, Salabert, Eschig, Ricordi)
Phone: (212) 358-5300 (N.Y. office)
Fax: (212) 358-5301 (rental library)
E-mail: usrental@boosey.com
Web site: www.boosey.com

BROUDE BROTHERS
Phone: (800) 225-3197
Fax: (413) 458-5242
E-mail: broude@broude.us
Web site: www.broude.us

**EUROPEAN AMERICAN MUSIC DISTRIBUTORS
(EAMD LLC)**
(Eulenburg, Schott, Universal,
Warner/Chappell, Belwin Mills)
Phone: (212) 461-6940
Fax: (212) 810-4565
E-mail: info@eamdllc.com or
rental@eamdllc.com
Web site: www.eamdllc.com

CARL FISCHER
(distributed by Theodore Presser)
Phone: (212) 777-0900
Fax: (212) 477-6996
E-mail: cf-info@carlfischer.com
Web site: www.carlfischer.com

EDWIN F. KALMUS MUSIC PUBLISHERS
(Music in the public domain)
Phone: (800) 434-6340 or (561) 241-6340
Fax: (561) 241-6347
E-mail: info@kalmus-music.com
Web site: www.kalmus-music.com

LUCK'S MUSIC LIBRARY
(Music in the public domain)
Phone: (248) 583-1820 or (800) 348-8749
Fax: (248) 583-1114
E-mail: sales@lucksmusic.net
Web site: www.lucksmusic.net

MMB MUSIC
Phone: (314) 531-9635 or (800) 543-3771
Fax: (314) 531-8384
E-mail: info@mmbmusic.com
Web site: www.mmbmusic.com

MUSIC ASSOCIATES OF AMERICA
(Rental: Bärenreiter Music Corp.)
Phone: (201) 569-2898
Fax: (201) 569-7023
E-mail: maasturm@sprynet.com
Web site:
www.musicassociatesofamerica.com

OXFORD UNIVERSITY PRESS
Phone: (212) 726-6050
Fax: (212) 726-6441
E-mail: music.us@oup.com
Web site: www.oup.com/us/music

PEERMUSIC CLASSICAL
(Distributed by Theodore Presser)
Phone: (212) 265-3910
Fax: (212) 489-2465
E-mail: peerClassical@peermusic.com
Web site: www.peermusicclassical.com

C.F. PETERS
Phone: (718) 416-7800
Fax: (718) 416-7805
E-mail: sales@cfpeters-ny.com
Web site: www.cfpeters-ny.com

THEODORE PRESSER
(Elkan-Vogel, Durand, Peermusic)
Phone: (610) 592-1222
Fax: (610) 592-1229
E-mail: sales@presser.com
Web site: www.presser.com

SHAWNEE PRESS
(Distributed by Schirmer)
Phone: (800) 962-8584
Fax: 800-971-4310
E-mail: sales@shawneepress.com
Web site: www.shawneepress.com

G. SCHIRMER
(AMP, Chester, Music Sales Corp.,
Novello)
Phone: (212) 254-2100 (N.Y. office)
Fax: (212) 254-2013 (N.Y. office)
Phone: (845) 469-4699 (rental office)
Fax: (845) 469-7544 (rental office)
E-mail: rental@schirmer.com
Web site: www.schirmer.com

SUBITO MUSIC
Phone: (973) 857-3440
Fax: (973) 857-3442
E-mail: mail@subitomusic.com
Web site: www.subitomusic.com

POPS MUSIC PUBLISHERS

ALLSUN MUSIC
Bruce Healey, composer/arranger
Phone: (818) 905-9498
Fax: (818) 986-6336
E-mail: bahealey@pacbell.net

JAMES BECKEL, ARRANGER
(Symphonic pops, family, gospel)
Phone: (317) 842-3662
E-mail: lbeckelguard-music@yahoo.com
Web site: www.jimbeckelmusic.com

BECKENHORST PRESS
Craig Courtney, Arranger
(Christmas, chorus, and orchestra)
Phone: (614) 451-6461
Fax: (614) 451-6627
Web site: www.beckenhorstpress.com

BOURNE MUSIC PUBLISHERS
(Disney, Hermann, Chaplin, film
music)
Phone: (212) 391-4300
Fax: (212) 391-4306
E-mail: Bourne@bournemusic.com
Web site: www.bournemusic.com

DCI MUSIC
(Americana, holiday, classical pops)
Phone: (501) 374-7167
Fax: (501) 374-7167
E-mail: dcimusic@yahoo.com
Web site: www.dcimusic.com

DISNEY CONCERT LIBRARY
(Disney film music)
Phone: (818) 567-5033
Fax: (818) 567-5178
E-mail: concert.library@disney.com
Web site: www.disneyconcertlibrary.com

DRAGON MUSIC COMPANY
(Carmen Dragon arrangements)
Phone: (310) 567-5033
Fax: (310) 567-5178
E-mail: dragon.music@verizon.net
Web site: www.carmendragon.com

**EUROPEAN AMERICAN MUSIC DISTRIBUTORS
(EAMD LLC)**
(Warner Bros., Chappell, Belwin Mills)
Phone: (212) 461-6940
Fax: (212) 810-4565
E-mail: info@eamdllc.com or
rental@eamdllc.com
Web site: www.eamdllc.com

FIDELIO MUSIC PUBLISHING COMPANY
(Film and concert music by Franz
Waxman)
Phone: (203) 259-0401
Fax: (203) 259–0405
E-mail: tnv@tnv.net
Web site: www.franzwaxman.com

SAMUEL FRENCH
(Musical theater)
Phone: (212) 206-8990
Fax: (212) 206-1429
E-mail: info@samuelfrench.com
Web site: www.samuelfrench.com

ROBERT KING MUSIC
(Brass and orchestra arrangements)
Fax: (508) 238-2571
E-mail: commerce@rkingmusic.com
Web site: www.rkingmusic.com

KOZINSKI MUSICAL ARCHIVES
(Pops and jazz arrangements)
Phone: (610) 558-4855
Fax: (610) 558-4738
E-mail: kozinski@earthlink.net
web site: www.operareductions.com

LIBEN MUSIC PUBLISHERS
Frank Proto, composer/arranger
Phone: (513) 232-6920
Fax: (513) 232 1866
E-mail: info@Liben.com
Web site: www.Liben.com

LUCK'S MUSIC LIBRARY
(Symphonic pops catalogue)
Phone: (800) 348-8749
Fax: (248) 583-1114
E-mail: sales@lucksmusic.net
Web site: www.lucksmusic.net

MANCINI CONCERT LIBRARY
(Janen Music)
Phone: (877) 775-2636
Fax: (818) 450-0368
E-mail: rentals@janenmusic.com
Web site: janenrentals.com

MUSIC THEATER INTERNATIONAL
(Stage musicals—Sondheim, Lloyd
Webber)
Phone: (212) 541-4684
Fax: (212) 397-4684
E-mail: Licensing@MTIshows.com
Web site: www.mtishows.com

MUSICIAN'S PUBLICATIONS
Bill Holcombe, arranger
(Big band, pops, medleys)
Phone: (609) 882-8139
Fax: (609) 882-3182
E-mail: bhmuspub@aol.com
Web site: billholcombe.com

PARAMOUNT THEATRE MUSIC LIBRARY
(1950's, big band, silent film)
Phone: (510) 893-2300 ext. 810
Fax: (510) 893-1894
E-mail:
info@paramounttheatremusiclibrary.com
Web site:
www.paramounttheatremusiclibrary.com

PARTITUR MUSIC
Fred Morden, arranger
Bruce Broughton, arranger
Phone: 563-355-1572
E-mail: partiturmusic@music.com
Web site: www.partiturmusic.com

PECKTACULAR MUSIC
Russell Peck, composer
(Compositions for pops and educational
concerts)
Phone: (336) 288-7034
Fax: (336) 286-2940
E-mail: peckmusic@RussellPeck.com
Web site: www.RussellPeck.com

THEODORE PRESSER
(Belwin, Beatles, Grofe, Rosza)
Phone: (610) 592-1222
Fax: (610) 592-1229
E-mail: sales@presser.com
Web site: www.presser.com

ROBINSDALE MUSIC
Lee Norris, arranger (Christmas pops)
Phone: (212) 799-7169
Phone: (800) 655-8022
Fax: (212) 799-1674
E-mail: Robinsdale@juno.com
Web site: www.Robinsdalemusic.com

RODGERS & HAMMERSTEIN
CONCERT LIBRARY
(Musical theater)
Phone: 212-268-9300
Fax: (212) 268-1245
E-mail: concert@rnh.com
Web site: www.rnh.com

G. SCHIRMER RENTAL LIBRARY
(Chappell, Gershwin, Ellington, John
Williams)
Phone: (845) 469-4699 (rental office)
Fax: (845) 469-7544 (rental office)
E-mail: schirmer@schirmer.com
Web site: www.schirmer.com

TAMS-WITMARK MUSIC LIBRARY
(Musical theater)
Phone: 800-221-7196
Fax: (212) 688-5656
Web site: www.tams-witmark.com

JOHN TATGENHORST MUSIC
(Film music, theater music, Christmas
medleys)
Phone: (847) 251-3000
Fax: (847) 251-1199
E-mail: info@johntatgenhorst.com
Web site: www.johntagenhorstmusic.net

THEMES & VARIATIONS
(Film and television music)
Phone: (203) 259-0401
Fax: (203) 227-0405
E-mail: tnv@tnv.net
Web site: www.tnv.net

ROBERT WENDEL MUSIC
Robert Wendel, arranger
Phone: (212) 928-9094
Fax: (212) 928-9094
E-mail: bobwen@pipeline.com
Web site: www.wendelmusic.com

WOLKING MUSIC PUBLICATIONS
Henry Wolking (jazz arrangements)
Phone: (801) 532-1918
Fax: (801) 581-5683
E-mail: henry.wolking@utah.edu
Web site: www.music.utah.edu/faculty

LIBRARY SPECIAL COLLECTIONS

Many libraries around the country house fabulous collections that can be valuable resources for research, programming, and score study. A few of these even allow you to borrow scores and parts at a very reasonable fee. Access to these special collections seems to vary between each organization. Some collections are completely accessible at a moment's notice or can be studied online. Others will require you to make an appointment and to specify exactly what you are interested in. Make sure that you contact the library or music source in advance so that you can make the proper arrangements. I have tried to give you the most accurate Web address to facilitate locating the information quickly. If the link is not working, track backward in the path to the main Web site, or use the phone number to contact a librarian in person for more details.

Classical Composers

ANTHEIL

GEORGE ANTHEIL COLLECTION

Correspondence (including correspondence between Antheil and Mary Louise Curtis Bok), manuscripts, and holographs of Antheil's compositions:
The Library of Congress, Performing Arts Reading Room, Music Division
101 Independence Avenue SE, Room LM 113
James Madison Memorial Building
Washington, D.C. 20540–4710
Phone: (202) 707-5507
Fax: (202) 707-0621
Web site: www.loc.gov

GEORGE ANTHEIL MANUSCRIPTS

Manuscripts and manuscript sketches of major works:
The New York Public Library for the Performing Arts, Music Division
40 Lincoln Center Plaza, Third Floor, New York, N.Y. 10023–7498
Phone: (212) 870-1650
Fax: (212) 870-1794
Web site: www.nypl.org/research/lpa

GEORGE ANTHEIL PAPERS

Correspondence, manuscripts, music scores, and printed materials:
Columbia University, Rare Book and Manuscript Library
Butler Library, 6th Floor East, 535 West 114th Street, New York, N.Y. 10027
Phone: (212) 854-5153
Fax: (212) 854-1365
E-mail: rbml@libraries.cul.columbia.edu
Web site: www.columbia.edu/cu/libraries/indiv/rare/guides/Antheil

BACH

RIEMENSCHNEIDER BACH LIBRARY

The collection includes J.S. Bach-oriented books, archival materials, manuscripts, and
  scores:
Baldwin-Wallace College, Riemenschneider Bach Institute
275 Eastland Road, Berea, OH 44017–2088
Phone: (440) 826-2207
E-mail: bachinst@bw.edu
Web site: www.bw.edu/academics/libraries/bach/library

BACH/BEETHOVEN

SCHEIDE LIBRARY

Included in the collection are music manuscripts of J. S. Bach and Beethoven:
Princeton University Library, Department of Rare Books and Special Collections
One Washington Road, Princeton, N.J. 08544
Phone: (609) 258-3241
Fax: (609) 258-2324
E-mail: rbsc@princeton.edu
Web site: www.princeton.edu/~rbsc/department/scheide

BARTÓK

BÉLA BARTÓK PAPERS

Correspondence regarding Bartók's association with Columbia University (1940–1943),
    with manuscripts on Rumanian, Turkish, and Serbo-Croatian folk music:
Columbia University, Rare Book and Manuscript Library
Butler Library, 6th Floor East, 535 West 114th Street, New York, N.Y. 10027
Phone: (212) 854-5153
Fax: (212) 854-1365
E-mail: rbml@libraries.cul.columbia.edu
Web site: www.columbia.edu/cu/libraries/indiv/rare/guides/Bartok

BENJAMIN SUCHOFF COLLECTION OF BARTÓKIANA

Works by Bartók, and Suchoff's research materials:
University of South Florida Tampa Library, Department of Special Collections
4202 E. Fowler Avenue, LIB122, Tampa, FL 33620–5400
Phone: (813) 974-2731
Fax: (813) 396-9006
E-mail: mgreenbe@lib.usf.edu
Web site: www.lib.usf.edu

BEACH

AMY BEACH

Sets of orchestral parts in manuscript:
New England Conservatory, Spaulding Library
290 Huntington Avenue, Boston, MA 02115
Phone: (617) 585-1247
Fax: (617) 585-1245
E-mail: jmorrow@newenglandconservatory.edu
Web site: www.newenglandconservatory.edu/libraries/about.html

BERLIOZ

JACQUES BARZUN COLLECTION OF HECTOR BERLIOZ PAPERS

Correspondence, manuscripts, research notes, and printed and audiovisual materials on
Berlioz:
Columbia University, Rare Book and Manuscript Library
Butler Library, 6th Floor East, 535 West 114th Street, New York, N.Y. 10027
Phone: (212) 854-5153
Fax: (212) 854-1365
E-mail: rbml@libraries.cul.columbia.edu
Web site: www.columbia.edu/cu/libraries/indiv/rare/guides/Berlioz

BERNSTEIN

LEONARD BERNSTEIN COLLECTION

Correspondence, writings, photographs, programs, and date books:
The Library of Congress, Performing Arts Reading Room, Music Division
101 Independence Avenue SE, Room LM 113
James Madison Memorial Building
Washington, D.C. 20540–4710
Phone: (202) 707-5507
Fax: (202) 707-0621
Web site: www.loc.gov

BLOCH

ERNEST BLOCH COLLECTION (UNIVERSITY OF CALIFORNIA)

Music manuscripts and printed music by Bloch, correspondence, newspaper articles,
program notes, photographs, and lecture tapes:
University of California, Jean Gray Hargrove Music Library
Berkeley, CA 94720–6000
Phone: (510) 642-2624
Fax: (510) 642-8237
E-mail: merviti@library.berkeley.edu
Web site: www.oac.cdlib.org

ERNEST BLOCH COLLECTION (LIBRARY OF CONGRESS)

Manuscripts (music and lecture), correspondence, personal papers, photographs, and
programs:
The Library of Congress, Performing Arts Reading Room, Music Division
101 Independence Avenue SE, Room LM 113
James Madison Memorial Building
Washington, D.C. 20540–4710
Phone: (202) 707-5507
Fax: (202) 707-0621
Web site: www.loc.gov

BUSONI see Galston-Busoni

CADMAN

CHARLES WAKEFIELD CADMAN COLLECTION

Scores (some handwritten manuscripts), clippings, photographs, scrapbooks,
  correspondence, recordings, publications, and films:
Pennsylvania State University, University Libraries, Special Collections Library
104 Paterno Library, University Park, PA 16802
Phone: (814) 865-7931
Fax: (814) 863-5318
E-mail: jxe2@psulias.psu.edu
Web site: www.libraries.psu.edu/speccolls

CAGE

JOHN CAGE COLLECTION

Donated by John Cage, the collection includes correspondence and unsolicited material
  sent to Cage; recorded interviews, lectures, concerts, and Cage's Notations project:
Music Library, Northwestern University
1970 Campus Drive, Evanston, IL 60208–2300
Phone: (847) 491-3434
Fax: (847) 467-7574
E-mail: musiclib@northwestern.edu
Web site: www.library.northwestern.edu/music

JOHN CAGE MUSIC MANUSCRIPT COLLECTION

Autograph manuscripts, sketches and other pre-compositional materials:
The New York Public Library for the Performing Arts, Music Division
40 Lincoln Center Plaza, Third Floor, New York, NY 10023–7498
Phone: (212) 870-1650
Fax: (212) 870-1794
Web site: www.nypl.org/research/lpa/mus/mus.majcoll.html

CHADWICK

GEORGE WHITEFIELD CHADWICK

Sets of orchestral parts in manuscript:
New England Conservatory, Spaulding Library
290 Huntington Avenue, Boston, MA 02115
Phone: 617-585-1247
Fax: 617-585-1245
E-mail: jmorrow@newenglandconservatory.edu
Web site: www.newenglandconservatory.edu/libraries/about.html

CHÁVEZ

Carlos Chávez Collection

Autograph manuscripts of major works, memorabilia, and correspondence with
  contemporary composers:
The New York Public Library for the Performing Arts, Music Division
40 Lincoln Center Plaza, Third Floor, New York, N.Y. 10023–7498
Phone: (212) 870-1650
Fax: (212) 870-1794
Web site: www.nypl.org/research/lpa/mus/mus.majcoll.html

CONVERSE

Frederick Converse

Sets of orchestral parts in manuscript:
New England Conservatory, Spaulding Library
290 Huntington Avenue, Boston, MA 02115
Phone: (617) 585-1247
Fax: (617) 585-1245
E-mail: jmorrow@newenglandconservatory.edu
Web site: www.newenglandconservatory.edu/libraries/about.html

COPLAND

Aaron Copland Collection

Published and unpublished music by Copland and other composers; correspondence,
  writings, date books, journals, professional papers, photographs, awards, art work,
  and books:
The Library of Congress, Performing Arts Reading Room, Music Division
101 Independence Avenue SE, Room LM 113
James Madison Memorial Building
Washington, DC 20540⁸4710
Phone: (202) 707-5507
Fax: (202) 707-0621
Web site: www.loc.gov

COWELL

Henry Cowell Collection (New York Public Library for the Performing Arts)

Personal papers, correspondence, and photographs:
The New York Public Library for the Performing Arts, Music Division
40 Lincoln Center Plaza, Third Floor, New York, NY 10023–7498
Phone: (212) 870-1650
Fax: (212) 870-1794
Web site: www.nypl.org/research/lpa/mus/mus.majcoll.html

Henry Cowell Collection (Stanford University)

Published scores and recordings of Cowell's music:
Stanford University, Stanford Music Library, Braun Music Center 541 Lasuen Mall,
    Stanford, CA 94305–3076
Phone: (650) 723-1211
Fax: (650) 725-1145
E-mail: muslibref@stanford.edu
Web site: www-sul.stanford.edu/depts/music/collections/musiccolls.html#cowell

CRESTON

Paul Creston Collection

The collection includes Creston's three hundred manuscript scores, published scores,
    correspondence, diaries, lectures, program notes, sound recordings, and scrapbooks:
University of Missouri-Kansas City,
Miller Nichols Library
5100 Rockhill Road, Kansas City, MO 64110
Phone: (816) 235-1532
Fax: (816) 333-5584
Web site: www.umkc.edu/lib/spec-col/Creston-col.htm

DRAGONETTI

Domenico Dragonetti

Collection of correspondence, located in the General Manuscript Collection:
Music Library, Northwestern University
1970 Campus Drive, Evanston, IL 60208–2300
Phone: (847) 491-3434
Fax: (847) 467-7574
E-mail: musiclib@northwestern.edu
Web site: www.library.northwestern.edu/music/gmc.html

GALSTON-BUSONI

Galston-Busoni Archive

The collection includes correspondence, photos, programs, and manuscripts:
Special Collections Library
Hoskins Library, University of Tennessee
1401 Cumberland Avenue, Knoxville, TN 37996–4000
Phone: (865) 974-4480
Fax: (865) 974-0560
E-mail: special@aztec.lib.utk.edu
Web site: http://www.lib.utk.edu/music/special.html#galston

GRIFFES

CHARLES GRIFFES COLLECTION

100 manuscripts of Griffes' symphonic and chamber music:
The New York Public Library for the Performing Arts, Music Division
40 Lincoln Center Plaza, Third Floor, New York, NY 10023–7498
Phone: (212) 870-1650
Fax: (212) 870-1794
Web site: www.nypl.org/research/lpa/mus/mus.majcoll.html

HANDEL

JAMES S. HALL COLLECTION OF GEORGE FRIDERIC HANDEL

Works by Handel and his contemporaries in manuscript, as well as correspondence:
Princeton University Library
Department of Rare Books and Special Collections, Manuscripts Division
One Washington Road, Princeton, NJ 08540
Phone: (609) 258-3184
Fax: (609) 258-2324
E-mail: rbsc@princeton.edu
Web site: www.libweb.princeton.edu/libraries/firestone/rbsc/aids/handel/#coll

HANSON

HOWARD HANSON AUTOGRAPH MANUSCRIPT SCORES

Autograph manuscript scores, printed music by Hanson and other twentieth-century
    composers, books from Hanson's personal library, and personal papers:
Eastman School of Music
Sibley Music Library, Ruth T. Watanabe Special Collections
27 Gibbs Street, Rochester, NY 14604
Phone: (585) 274-1335
Fax: (585) 274-1380
E-mail: dcoppen@esm.rochester.edu
Web site: www.rochester.edu/Eastman/sibley/specialc/findaids

HARRIS

ROY HARRIS ARCHIVE

Personal papers, recordings, sketches, and original manuscripts, published and
    unpublished works, and correspondence:
California State University, John F. Kennedy Memorial Library
5151 State University Drive, Los Angeles, CA 90032
Phone: (323) 343-3958
Fax: (323) 343-5600
E-mail: dsigler@calstatela.edu
Web site: www.calstatela.edu/library/sc6.htm

HINDEMITH

PAUL HINDEMITH COLLECTION

Autograph manuscripts, programs, reviews, correspondence, and photographs:
Yale University Library, Irving S. Gilmore Music Library
120 High Street, PO Box 208240, New Haven, CT 06520–8240
Phone: (203) 432-0492
Fax: (203) 432-7339
E-mail: musiclibrary@yale.edu
Web site: html://webtext.library.yale.edu/xml2html/music.Hindemith.nav.html

IVES

CHARLES IVES PAPERS

Music sketches, manuscripts, and published works, as well as diaries, scrapbooks,
    and photographs:
Yale University Library, Irving S. Gilmore Music Library
120 High Street, PO Box 208240, New Haven, CT 06520–8240
Phone: (203) 432-0492
Fax: (203) 432-7339
E-mail: musiclibrary@yale.edu
Web site: html://webtext.library.yale.edu/xml2html/music.ives-sinclair.nav.html
Web site: html://webtext.library.yale.edu/xml2html/music.ives.nav.html

MAHLER-WERFEL

ALMA MAHLER AND FRANZ WERFEL PAPERS

Correspondence, manuscripts, diaries, memorabilia and photographs (which are
    available online):
University of Pennsylvania
Walter H. and Leonore Annenberg Rare Book & Manuscript Library
Van Pelt—Dietrich Library Center
3420 Walnut Street, Philadelphia, PA 19104–6206
Phone: (215) 898-7552
E-mail: shawcros@pobox.upenn.edu
Web site: www.library.upenn.edu/collections/rbm/mss/mss.html#mas-musichistory

MILHAUD

DARIUS MILHAUD COLLECTION

Published scores, autograph scores, recordings, books and articles by and about
    Milhaud, videos, programs, and photographs:
Mills College, F. W. Olin Library, Special Collections and Archives, Oakland, CA 94613
Phone: (510) 430-2047
Fax: (510) 430-2278
E-mail: jbraun@mills.edu
Web site: www.mills.edu/academics/library/special_collections/sc_milhaud.php

PARKER

Horatio Parker Papers

Music manuscripts, correspondence, programs, clippings, and writings:
Yale University Library, Irving S. Gilmore Music Library
120 High Street, PO Box 208240, New Haven, CT 06520–8240
Phone: (203) 432-0492
Fax: (203) 432-7339
E-mail: musiclibrary@yale.edu
Web site: http://webtext.library.yale.edu/xml2html/music.parker.nav.html

PARTCH

Harry Partch Instrumentarium

A collection of instruments designed and built by Partch for the performance of his
    compositions:
Harry Partch Institute, Kasser Theater 105, Montclair State University
Montclair, NJ 07043
Phone: (973) 655-6984
E-mail: drummondd@mail.montclair.edu
Web site: www.harrypartch.com

PERSICHETTI

Vincent Persichetti Papers

Holograph scores, sketches, personal and professional papers:
The New York Public Library for the Performing Arts, Music Division
40 Lincoln Center Plaza, Third Floor, New York, NY 10023–7498
Phone: (212) 870-1650
Fax: (212) 870-1794
Web site: www.nypl.org/research/lpa/mus/mus.majcoll.html

PISTON

Walter Piston Collection

Scores, books, personal items, and antique musical instruments, as well as the Piston
    Room—a recreation of Piston's home library:
Boston Public Library, Music Department, McKim Building, 3rd Floor
700 Boylston Street, Copley Square, Boston, MA 02116
Phone: (617) 536-5400 ext. 2285
E-mail: music@bpl.org
Web site: www.bpl.org/research/music/spmusic.htm

RUGGLES

CARL RUGGLES PAPERS

Music sketches, correspondence, programs, clippings, and photographs:
Yale University Library, Irving S. Gilmore Music Library
120 High Street, PO Box 208240, New Haven, CT 06520–8240
Phone: (203) 432-0492
Fax: (203) 432-7339
E-mail: musiclibrary@yale.edu
Web site: http://webtext.library.yale.edu/xml2html/music.ruggles.nav.html

SAINT-SAËNS

CAMILLE SAINT-SAËNS

Collection of correspondence located in the General Manuscript Collection:
Music Library, Northwestern University
1970 Campus Drive, Evanston, IL 60208–2300
Phone: (847) 491-3434
Fax: (847) 467-7574
E-mail: musiclib@northwestern.edu
Web site: www.library.northwestern.edu/music/gmc.html

SCHÖNBERG

ARNOLD SCHÖNBERG CENTER

The archive and library house Schönberg's music and writing manuscripts, paintings,
    drawings, photographs, programs, historical clippings, and correspondence:
Palais Fanto
Schwarzenbergplatz 6
A—1030 Vienna
Phone: 43-1-7121888
Fax: 43-1-7121888-88
E-mail: office@schoenberg.at
Web site: www.schoenberg.at

SCHÖNBERG-NACHOD COLLECTION

Music manuscripts, including early songs and arrangements, as well as correspondence
    between Schönberg and his cousin Hans Nachod, for whom Schönberg created the
    role of Waldemar in *Gurre-Lieder:*
University of North Texas, Music Library
PO Box 305190, Denton, TX 76203–5190
Phone: (940) 565-2860
Fax: (940) 565-2599
E-mail: darnold@library.unt.edu
Web site: www.library.unt.edu/music/speccol.htm

SCHUMAN

William Schuman Papers

Complete documentation of Schuman's work as composer, educator, and administrator.
The New York Public Library for the Performing Arts, Music Division
40 Lincoln Center Plaza, Third Floor, New York, NY 10023–7498
Phone: (212) 870-1650
Fax: (212) 870-1794
Web site: www.nypl.org/research/lpa/mus/mus.majcoll.html

STILL

William Grant Still Music

Books, recordings, and other resources on William Grant Still, as well as his sheet music
and music by other minority composers:
1109 S. University Plaza Way, Suite 109, Flagstaff, AZ 86001–6317
Phone: (928) 526-9355
Fax: (925) 526-0321
E-mail: wgsmusic@bigplanet.com
Web site: www.williamgrantstill.com

THOMPSON

Randall Thompson Papers

Materials related to Thompson's *Testament of Freedom*: drafts, printed copies,
correspondence, and clippings:
University of Virginia, Albert & Shirley Small Special Collections Library
PO Box 400110, Charlottesville, VA 22904–41190
Phone: (434) 924-1776
Email: mssbks@virginia.edu
Web site: www.lib.virginia.edu/MusicLib/collections/cannon.html

THOMSON

Virgil Thomson Papers

Music manuscripts, correspondence, financial records, and photographs:
Yale University Library, Irving S. Gilmore Music Library
120 High Street, PO Box 208240, New Haven, CT 06520–8240
Phone: (203) 432-0492
Fax: (203) 432-7339
E-mail: musiclibrary@yale.edu
Web site: http://webtext.library.yale.edu/xml2html/music.Thomson.nav.html

TOCH

ERNST TOCH ARCHIVE

Manuscripts, printed scores, published writings, photographs, correspondence, and
    recordings:
University of California, Los Angeles, Music Library Special Collections
Box 951490, Los Angeles, CA 90095–1490
Phone: (310) 825-1665
Fax: (310) 206-7322
E-mail: music-spec@library.ucla.edu
Web site: www.library.ucla.edu/libraries/music/mlsc/toch/index.htm

Musical Theater, Pops, and Jazz

LEROY ANDERSON PAPERS

Manuscripts and published music, scrapbooks, recordings, and photographs:
Yale University Library, Irving S. Gilmore Music Library
120 High Street, PO Box 208240, New Haven, CT 06520–8240
Phone: (203) 432-0492
Fax: (203) 432-7339
E-mail: musiclibrary@yale.edu
Web site: http://webtext.library.yale.edu/xml2html/music.anderson.nav.html

BELL TELEPHONE HOUR MUSIC COLLECTION

Manuscripts, orchestral parts, scripts, and musical interludes from the *Bell Telephone
    Hour* radio and television programs:
Allentown Symphony
23 North 6th Street, Allentown, PA 18101
Phone: (610) 432-6175
Fax: (610) 432-6735
E-mail: info@allentownsymphony.org
Web site: www.allentownsymphony.org

BUDDY BAKER DISNEY SCORE COLLECTION

Sketches and conductor's scores for Baker's Disney compositions:
Fales Library and Special Collections
New York University, Elmer Holmes Bobst Library
70 Washington Square South, 3rd Floor, New York, NY 10012
Phone: (212) 998-2596
Fax: (212) 995-3835
E-mail: fales.library@nyu.edu
Web site: www.nyu.edu/library/bobst/research/fales

George M. Cohan Collection

A collection of twenty-seven boxes of materials plus files on each of his shows that played in New York:

Museum of the City of New York

1220 Fifth Avenue, New York, NY 10029

Phone: (212) 534-1672 ext.3380

Fax: (212) 423-0759

E-mail: research@mcny.org

Web site: www.mcny.org

George and Ira Gershwin Collection

A collection of prints, articles, programs, and files on all of their shows that played New York.

Museum of the City of New York

1220 Fifth Avenue, New York, NY 10029

Phone: (212) 534-1672 ext.3380

Fax: (212) 423-0759

E-mail: research@mcny.org

Web site: www.mcny.org

Benny Goodman Papers

Arrangements, photographs, master tapes, scrapbooks, clippings, and programs:

Yale University Library, Irving S. Gilmore Music Library

120 High Street, PO Box 208240, New Haven, CT 06520–8240

Phone: (203) 432-0492

Fax: (203) 432-7339

E-mail: musiclibrary@yale.edu

Web site: http://webtext.library.yale.edu/xml2html/music.Goodman.nav.html

Ferde Grofé Collection

Music scores composed or arranged by the composer:

Southern Methodist University, The Jake & Nancy Hamon Arts Library

Dallas, TX 75275–0356

Phone: (214) 768-2303

Fax: (214) 768-1800

E-mail: sratclif@smu.edu

Web site: www.smu.edu/cul/hamon/collections/collinv.html

Scott Joplin Collection

A collection of correspondence, newspaper clippings, photographs, and sheet music:

Fisk University, Franklin Library, Special Collections

1000 Seventeenth Avenue, Nashville, TN 37208

Phone: (615) 329-8646

Fax: (615) 329-8761

E-mail: bhowse@fisk.edu

Web site: www.fisk.edu

The William Ransom Hogan Archive of New Orleans Jazz

A collection of oral histories, clippings, photographs and film, manuscripts, recorded
    music, sheet music, and orchestrations:
Tulane University, 304 Jones Hall
6801 Freret Street, New Orleans, LA 70118–5682
Phone: (504) 865-5688
Fax: (504) 865-5761
E-mail: raeburn@tulane.edu
Web site: www.tulane.edu/~lmiller/JazzHome.html

Nelson Riddle Collection

Awards, photographs, correspondence, and Riddle's personal collection of
    arrangements:
Nelson Riddle Library
University of Arizona Music Building
School of Music, Room 109, Tucson, AZ 85721
Phone: (520) 621-1655
Fax: (520) 621-8118
E-mail: keithp@email.arizona.edu
Web site: www.arts.arizona.edu/riddle

Paul Whiteman Collection

Manuscripts of orchestral arrangements, recordings, clippings, photographs, and
    artifacts:
Williams College Archives and Special Collections
Stetson Hall, Williamstown, MA 01267
Phone: (413) 597-2568
Fax: (413) 597-3931
E-mail: archives@williams.edu
Web site: www.williams.edu/library/archives/pwc/pwc1.html

Conductors

Leonard Bernstein Collection

Bernstein's personal conducting scores:
New York Philharmonic Archives, Avery Fisher Hall
10 Lincoln Center Plaza, New York, NY 10023–6990
Phone: (212) 875-5900 ext. 8
Fax: (212) 875-5933
E-mail: hawsb@nyphil.org
Web site: www.nyphil.org

OTTO KLEMPERER COLLECTION OF MUSICAL SCORES

Over two hundred scores from Klemperer's personal collection, many annotated by the
conductor:
California State University, John F. Kennedy Memorial Library
5151 State University Drive, Los Angeles, CA 90032
Phone: (323) 343-3958
Fax: (323) 343-5600
E-mail: dsigler@calstatela.edu
Web site: www.calstatela.edu/library/sc6.htm

THE SERGE KOUSSEVITZKY ARCHIVE

Correspondence, photographs, personal and business papers:
The Library of Congress, Performing Arts Reading Room, Music Division
101 Independence Avenue SE, Room LM 113
James Madison Memorial Building
Washington, DC 20540–4710
Phone: (202) 707-5507
Fax: (202) 707-0621
Web site: www.loc.gov

SERGE KOUSSEVITZKY COLLECTION

A collection of photographs, scrapbooks, and scores, some annotated by Koussevitzky.
Boston Public Library, Music Department, McKim Building, 3rd Floor
700 Boylston Street, Copley Square, Boston, MA 02116
Phone: (617) 536-5400 ext. 2285
E-mail: music@bpl.org
Web site: www.bpl.org/research/music/spmusic.htm

EUGENE ORMANDY

Collection of Photographs; Collection of Scores; Commercial Sound Recordings;
Oral History Collection; Papers:
"Eugene Ormandy: A Centennial Celebration" (available online)
University of Pennsylvania
Walter H. and Leonore Annenberg Rare Book & Manuscript Library
Van Pelt—Dietrich Library Center
3420 Walnut Street, Philadelphia, PA 19104–6206
Phone: (215) 898-7552
E-mail: shawcros@pobox.upenn.edu
Web site: www.library.upenn.edu/collections/rbm/mss/mss.html#mas-musichistory

Fritz Reiner Library

Over seven hundred of the conductor's marked scores, correspondence, memorabilia, and books, as well as furnishings from his study:
Music Library, Northwestern University
1970 Campus Drive, Evanston, IL 60208–2300
Phone: (847) 491-3434
Fax: (847) 467-7574
E-mail: musiclib@northwestern.edu
Web site: www.library.northwestern.edu/music/gmc.html

Robert Shaw Papers

Yale University Library, Irving S. Gilmore Music Library
120 High Street, PO Box 208240, New Haven, CT 06520–8240
Phone: (203) 432-0492
Fax: (203) 432-7339
E-mail: musiclibrary@yale.edu
Web site: www.library.yale.edu/musiclib/archival.htm#shaw

Leopold Stokowski

Collection of Orchestral Transcriptions; Collection of Scores; Papers:
Oliver Daniel Research Collection on Leopold Stokowski
"Leopold Stokowski: Making Music Matter" (available online)
University of Pennsylvania
Walter H. and Leonore Annenberg Rare Book & Manuscript Library
Van Pelt—Dietrich Library Center
3420 Walnut Street, Philadelphia, Penn. 19104–6206
Phone: (215) 898-7552
E-mail: shawcros@pobox.upenn.edu
Web site: www.library.upenn.edu/collections/rbm/mss/mss.html#mas-musichistory

Toscanini Legacy

The conductor's annotated scores and parts, correspondence, photographs, biographical material, and memorabilia:
The New York Public Library for the Performing Arts, Music Division
40 Lincoln Center Plaza, Third Floor, New York, NY 10023–7498
Phone: (212) 870-1650
Fax: (212) 870-1794
Web site: www.nypl.org/research/lpa/mus/mus.majcoll.html

Bruno Walter Papers

Materials documenting Walter's career, including letters and music manuscripts of Mahler, such as a complete draft of the first movement of Mahler's 7th Symphony:
The New York Public Library for the Performing Arts, Music Division
40 Lincoln Center Plaza, Third Floor, New York, NY 10023–7498
Phone: (212) 870-1650
Fax: (212) 870-1794
Web site: www.nypl.org/research/lpa/mus/mus.majcoll.html

General Collections

GUIDO ADLER COLLECTION

Programs, clippings, correspondence (includes Brahms, Mahler, Bartok, others), and
    published works from the 1870s to the 1930s:
Hargrett Rare Book and Manuscript Library, Main Library
University of Georgia
Athens, GA 30602–1641
Phone: (706) 542-7123
Fax: (706) 542-0672
E-mail: hargrett@uga.edu
Web site: www.libs.uga.edu/hargrett/manuscrip/guidoadler.html

THE AMERICAN MUSIC CENTER COLLECTION

Fifty thousand music scores, representing over sixty years of American concert music
    and jazz:
The New York Public Library for the Performing Arts, Music Division
40 Lincoln Center Plaza, Third Floor, New York, NY 10023–7498
Phone: (212) 870-1650
Fax: (212) 870-1794
Web site: www.nypl.org/research/lpa/mus/mus.majcoll.html

BOSTON SYMPHONY ORCHESTRA ARCHIVE

Scores including those commissioned for the orchestra's fiftieth anniversary, most signed
    by the composers:
Boston University, Howard Gotlieb Archival Research Center
771 Commonwealth Avenue, Boston, MA 02215
Phone: (617) 353-3696
Fax: (617) 353-2838
E-mail: archives@bu.edu
Web site: www.bu.edu/archives/bossym.htm

CALIFORNIA ARTS COMMISSION COLLECTION
OF ORCHESTRAL SCORES AND PARTS

One hundred seventy orchestral scores and parts, including works by Beethoven,
    Brahms, Mozart, and Wagner:
California State University, John F. Kennedy Memorial Library
5151 State University Drive, Los Angeles, CA 90032
Phone: (323) 343-3958
Fax: (323) 343-5600
E-mail: dsigler@calstatela.edu
Web site: www.calstatela.edu/library/sc6.htm#b

CONDUCTORS GUILD NEW MUSIC PROJECT

Scores, recording, and biographical information regarding new music (past 1985)
   presented at conferences of the Conductors Guild:
Old Dominion University, Perry Library, Diehn Composers Room
4427 Hampton Boulevard, Norfolk, VA 23529
Phone: (757) 683-4178
Fax: (757) 683-1475
Web site: www.lib.odu.edu/musiclib/index.htm

CONTEMPORARY MUSIC RESEARCH COLLECTION

Scores in manuscript, recordings of performances, and papers of composers, focusing
   on the twentieth-century postwar period:
Old Dominion University Libraries
Diehn Composers Room, Diehn Fine and Performing Arts Building, Room 189
4427 Hampton Boulevard, Norfolk, VA 23529–0256
Phone: (757) 683-4173
Fax: (757) 683-4175
Web site: www.lib.odu.edu/musiclib/index.htm

OLIN DOWNES COLLECTION

Collection of papers from 1900 to 1964, including manuscripts, correspondence, lectures,
   photographs, articles, and scrapbooks:
Hargrett Rare Book and Manuscript Library, Main Library
University of Georgia
Athens, GA 30602–1641
Phone: (706) 542-7123
Fax: (706) 542-0672
E-mail: hargrett@uga.edu
Web site: www.libs.uga.edu/hargrett/manuscrip/index.html

EDWIN A. FLEISHER COLLECTION OF ORCHESTRAL MUSIC

Lending library of orchestral performance materials, with titles numbering over twenty-
   one thousand:
The Free Library of Philadelphia
1901 Vine Street, Philadelphia, PA 19103
Phone: (215) 686-5313
E-mail: smithk@library.phila.gov
Web site: http://www.library.phila.gov/research/research.taf

GRAWEMEYER COLLECTION OF CONTEMPORARY MUSIC

Scores and recordings for all compositions submitted to the Grawemeyer Award for
   Music Composition competition:
University of Louisville, University Libraries, Music Library
2301 S. Third Street, Louisville, KY 40292
Phone: (502) 852-5659
Fax: (502) 852-7701
E-mail: klittle@louisville.edu
Web site: http://library.louisville.edu/music/coll/grawemeyer.html

GENERAL MANUSCRIPT COLLECTION

Manuscripts, scores, parts, sketches, and correspondence from the seventeenth century
to the present:
Music Library, Northwestern University
1970 Campus Drive, Evanston, IL 602018–2300
Phone: (847) 491-3434
Fax: (847) 467-7574
E-mail: www.musiclib@northwestern.edu
Web site: www.library.northwestern.edu/music/gmc.html

GEORGE GERSHWIN MEMORIAL COLLECTION
OF MUSIC AND MUSICAL LITERATURE

Named in honor of George Gershwin, the collection includes sheet music representing
composers such as W. C. Handy and William Grant Still, correspondence,
photographs, books, and recordings:
Fisk University, Franklin Library, Special Collections
1000 Seventeenth Avenue, Nashville, TN 37208
Phone: (615) 329-8646
Fax: (615) 329-8761
E-mail: bhowse@fisk.edu
Web site: www.fisk.edu

LATIN AMERICAN MUSIC CENTER

Manuscripts, published scores, recordings, books, photographs, periodicals, and colonial
music anthologies:
Indiana University, School of Music
Bloomington, IN 47405
Phone: (812) 855-2991
Fax: (812) 855-4936
Email: lamc@indiana.edu
Web site: www.music.indiana.edu/som/lamc

LESTER S. LEVY COLLECTION

Twenty-nine thousand pieces of popular American sheet music from 1780 to 1960:
Special Collections and Archives
Johns Hopkins University, The Milton S. Eisenhower Library
3400 North Charles Street, Baltimore, MD 21218
Phone: (410) 516-8348
Fax: (410) 516-7202
E-mail: mburri@jhu.edu
Web site: http://levysheetmusic.mse.jhu.edu

Los Angeles Public Library—Orchestral Scores

Classical orchestral scores and parts available for checkout to community orchestras:
Los Angeles Public Library, Art, Music, and Recreation Department
630 W. 5th Street, Los Angeles, CA 90071
Phone: (213) 228-7231
Fax: (213) 228-7239
Web site: www.lapl.org/resources/indexes/oraps.html

NBC Symphony Orchestra

Collection of scores and parts from the NBC Symphony Orchestra:
Buffalo and Erie County Public Library, Music Department
1 Lafayette Square, Buffalo, NY 14203
Phone: (716) 858-8900
Fax: (716) 858-6211
Web site: www.buffalolib.org/libraries/collections

New American Music for Young Audiences

An online catalog of works for educational programming:
American Music Center
30 West 26th Street, Suite 1001
New York, NY 10010
Phone: (212) 366-5260 ext. 11
Fax: (212) 366-5265
Web site: www.amc.net/resources/library/mfya.html

NewMusicJukeBox

An online library and listening room for music by contemporary American composers:
American Music Center
30 West 26th Street, Suite 1001
New York, NY 10010
Phone: (212) 366-5260 x11
Fax: (212) 366-5265
Web site: www.newmusicjukebox.org

Orchestra Collection

Scores and parts for two thousand works in the orchestral repertoire:
The New York Public Library for the Performing Arts
40 Lincoln Center Plaza, New York, NY 10023–7498
Phone: (212) 870-1624
E-mail: orchlib@nypl.org
Web site: www.nypl.org/research/lpa/circ/orchestra.html

Ricordi Collection

A collection of printed music and correspondence (including letters from composers
  dating from the nineteenth century) from the Ricordi publishing company:
Music Library, Northwestern University
1970 Campus Drive, Evanston, IL 60208–2300
Phone: (847) 491-3434
Fax: (847) 467-7574
E-mail: musiclib@northwestern.edu
Web site: www.library.northwestern.edu/music/gmc.html

Rodgers and Hammerstein Archives of Recorded Sound

Five hundred thousand recordings and ten thousand printed items, including recorded
  music in practically every format, spoken word recordings, and videos of
  performances:
The New York Public Library for the Performing Arts
40 Lincoln Center Plaza, New York, NY 10023–7498
Phone: (212) 870-1663
E-mail: rha@nypl.org
Web site: www.nypl.org/research/lpa/rha/rha.html

Schreiber Jewish Music Library

Over twenty thousand recordings, books, and scores ranging from Jewish liturgy to
  popular music:
Gratz College
7605 Old York Road, Melrose Park, PA 19027
Phone: (800) 475-4635
Fax: (215) 635-7320
Web site: www.gratzcollege.edu

Toscanini Memorial Archives

Over three thousand autographed music manuscripts on microfilm from eighteenth-
  through twentieth-century composers:
The New York Public Library for the Performing Arts, Music Division
40 Lincoln Center Plaza, Third Floor, New York, NY 10023–7498
Phone: (212) 870-1650
Fax: (212) 870-1794
Web site: www.nypl.org/research/lpa/mus/mus.majcoll.html

Training and Personal Development

SUMMER FESTIVALS AND WORKSHOPS

ASPEN MUSIC FESTIVAL (THE AMERICAN ACADEMY OF CONDUCTING AT ASPEN)
Length: 9 weeks (mid-June to mid-August)
Location: Aspen, CO
Phone: (970) 925 3254
Fax: (970) 925-5708
E-mail: studentservices@aspenmusic.org
Web site: www.aspenmusicfestival.com

BEYOND THE BATON CONDUCTING SEMINAR AND WORKSHOPS
Length: 4 days
Location: Norwalk, CT
Phone: 908-432-5188
E-mail: info@beyondthebaton.com
Web site: www.beyondthebaton.com

BLUE DANUBE MUSIK IMPRESARIO
(Assorted conducting workshops)
Length: 1–2 weeks
Location: Various locations in Europe
Phone: 43-1-405-40-30
E-mail: office@bluedanubeviolins.com
(Productions)
Web site: www.bluedanubeviolins.com

CALIFORNIA CONDUCTING WORKSHOP
Length: 4 days (May)
Location: Bakersfield, CA
Phone: (661) 323-7928
Fax: (661) 323-7331
E-mail: music@bakersfieldsymphony.org
Web site: bakersfieldsymphony.org

CONDUCTOR'S GUILD CONDUCTING WORKSHOPS
Length: 3–5 days
Location: various cities, USA
Phone: (804) 553-1378
Fax: (804) 553-1876
E-mail: guild@conductorsguild.org
Web site: www.conductorsguild.org

CONDUCTOR INSTITUTE AT BARD COLLEGE
Length: 4 weeks (July)
Location: Annandale-on-Hudson, NY
Phone: (845) 758-7425
Fax: (845) 758-0815
E-mail: ci@bard.edu
Web site: www.bard.edu/ci

CONDUCTORS INSTITUTE OF SOUTH CAROLINA
Length: 1–2 weeks (June)
Location: Columbia, SC
Phone: (803) 777-7500
Fax: (803) 777-9774
E-mail: charl@mailbox.sc.edu
Web site: www.conductorsinstitute.com

CONDUCTOR RETREAT AT MEDOMAK
Length: 18 days (July)
Location: Washington, ME
Phone: 734-332-0869 (fall and spring)
Phone: (207) 845-3219 (Maine, July)
Fax: 734-332-0869
E-mail: info@conductorsretreat.org
Web site: www.conductorsretreat.org

DONALD THULEAN
CONDUCTING WORKSHOPS
League of American Orchestras
Length: 4 days
Location: various cities, USA
Phone: (212) 262-5161
Fax: (212) 262-5198
E-mail: league@americanorchestras.org
Web site: www.americanorchestras.org

EASTMAN SCHOOL OF MUSIC
SUMMER CONDUCTING INSTITUTE
Length: 1 week, (July)
Location: Rochester, N.Y.
Phone: (585) 274-1403
E-mail: summer@esm.rochestr.edu
Web site:
www.rochester.edu/Eastman/summer

INTERNATIONAL ACADEMY
OF ADVANCED CONDUCTING
Length: 3 weeks (July–August)
Location: Macon, GA, and St. Petersburg,
Russia
Phone: (478) 301 2748
E-mail: advancedconducting_musin
@hotmail.com
Web site:
www.advancedconducting.spb.ru

INTERNATIONAL CONDUCTING
MASTERCLASSES
Length: 1 week
Location: TBA, Germany
Phone: +49 (0) 30 720–111-0
Fax: +49 (0) 30 720-111-29
E-mail: info@philharmonie.com
Web site: www.philharmonie.com

INTERNATIONAL CONDUCTING
WORKSHOPS AND FESTIVAL
Length: 10 days
Location: Sofia, Bulgaria
Phone: (915) 525-4033
Fax: (915) 875-0231
E-mail: info@conductingworkshop.org
Web site: www.conductingworkshop.org

INTERNATIONAL INSTITUTE FOR CONDUCTORS
Length: 2 weeks (July)
Location: Bacau, Romania
Phone: 336-643-8730
E-mail: rconductors@triad.rr.us
Web site: www.rconductors.com

PIERRE MONTEUX SCHOOL FOR CONDUCTORS
AND ORCHESTRA MUSICIANS
Length: six weeks (mid-June to late July)
Location: Hancock, ME
Phone: 207-422-3286
Fax: 207-422-3280
(September through May)
E-mail: www.admin@monteuxschool.org
Web site: www.monteuxschool.org

ARS MUSICA CONDUCTING ACADEMY
Length: 1 week
Location: Vidin, Bulgaria
Phone: +49 (0) 179 750 82 55
Fax: + 49 (0) 941 5992 00 863
E-mail: academy@ars-musica.org
Web site: www.ars-musica.org

NATIONAL ARTS CENTRE
CONDUCTORS PROGRAMME
Length: 10 days (June)
Location: Ottawa, Ontario, Canada
Phone: (613) 947-7000 ext. 568
Fax: (613) 992-5225
E-mail: info@nac-cna.ca
Web site: www.nac-cna.ca

OREGON BACH FESTIVAL MASTER CLASS
IN CONDUCTING
Length: 3 weeks
Location: Eugene, OR
Phone: (800) 457-1486
E-mail: bachfest@uoregon.edu

SYMPHONIC WORKSHOPS
(Assorted workshops for conductors)
Location: Toronto, Ontario, Canada
Phone: 705-887-4094
E-mail: info@symphonicworkshops.com
Web site: www.symphonicworkshops.com

TANGLEWOOD MUSIC CENTER
The Boston Symphony Orchestra's
Academy for Advanced Musical Study
Length: 8 weeks (mid-June to
mid-August)
Location: Lenox, MA
Phone: (617) 638-9230
(September–mid-June)
Phone: (413) 637-5240 (Summer)
E-mail: tmc@bso.org
Web site: www.bso.org

TRANS-ATLANTIC CONCERT CONNECTIONS,
NEW YORK
(Guest conducting opportunities for
a fee)
Length: 1 week (TBA)
Location: Central Europe and Russia
Phone: (718) 445-5923
Fax: (718) 445-5923
E-mail: taccinfo@nyc.rr.com

CONDUCTING COMPETITIONS

ANSBACHER FELLOWSHIP FOR YOUNG CONDUCTORS

Purpose: To provide young and promising conductors from the United States with
the opportunity to attend rehearsals at the Salzburg Festival and to visit
the Herbert von Karajan Centrum in Vienna.

Awards: Fellowship covers airfare, accommodation in a furnished studio
apartment in Salzburg, and a small stipend (€290).

Phone: (212) 856-1075
Fax: (212) 856-1226
E-mail:ansbacher@americanaustrianfoundation.org
Web site: www.aaf-online.org

BAD HOMBURGER CONDUCTING COMPETITION

Dates/How often: July, Biennial
Application fee: None
Age restrictions: under 35
Location of Comp: Friedrichsdorf, Germany
Awards/Prizes: 1st Prize 10,000 and concert performances

Phone: 49 0 60 07 93 00 76
Fax: 49 0 60 07 93 00 78
E-mail: infor@kulturkommunikation.de
Web site: www.kulturkommunikation.de

BAMBERGER SYMPHONIKER CONDUCTORS' COMPETITION

Dates/How often: May, Biennial
Age restrictions: under 35
Location of Comp: Bamberg, Germany
Awards/Prizes: 1st Prize 20,000, 2nd Prize 10,000, 3rd Prize 5,000
    Phone: (951) 96 47 100
    Fax: (951) 96 47 123
    E-mail: intendanz@bamberger-symphoniker.de
    Web site: www.bambergsymphony.com

BESANCON INTERNATIONAL COMPETITION FOR YOUNG CONDUCTORS

Dates/How often: September, Biennial (odd years)
Application fee: €230
Age restrictions: under 35
Location of Comp: Besancon, France
Awards/Prizes: €12,000 and numerous engagements
    Phone: (+33) 381 25 05 85
    Fax: (+33) 381 81 52 15
    E-mail: contact@festival-besancon.com
    Web site: www.festival-besancon.com

BLUE DANUBE OPERA CONDUCTING COMPETITION

Dates/How often: June, Biennial
Application fee: €50; Participation fee: €650
Age restrictions: None
Location: Cluj-Napoca, Romania
Awards/Prizes: 1st Prize €3,500 and 2 opera engagements, 2nd Prize €2,000
     and 1 opera engagement, 3rd Prize 1000 and gala performance
    Phone: 431 405-4030
    Fax: 431 405-4030
    E-mail: office@bluedanubeviolins.com
    Web site: www.bluedanubeviolins.com/competition.html

CADAQUES INTERNATIONAL CONDUCTING COMPETITION

Dates/How often: July, Biennial (even years)
Application fee: €360
Age restrictions: under 35
Location of Comp: Barcelona, Spain
Orchestra: the Orquestra de Cadaqués
Awards/Prizes: 1st Prize €6,000 and guest conducting, 2nd Prize €1,500
    Phone: (34) 93 317 42 89
    Fax: (34) 93 302 26 70
    E-mail: odc@orquestradecadaques.com
    Web site: www.orquestradecadaques.com

DONATELLA FLICK CONDUCTING COMPETITION

Dates/How often: October, Biennial (even years)
Application fee: £30; Participation fee: £40
Age restrictions: under 35; must be a citizen of the European Union
Location: London, United Kingdom
Orchestra: London Symphony Orchestra
       Awards/Prizes: £15,000
       Fax: +44 0 20 7267 0068
       Web site: www.conducting.org

GRZEGORZ FITELBERG INTERNATIONAL COMPETITION FOR CONDUCTORS

Dates/How often: November, Quadrennial
Application fee: $50; Competition fee: $200
Age restrictions: under 35
Location of Comp: Katowice, Poland
Prizes: 1st Prize $10,000, 2nd Prize $8,000, 3rd Prize $5,000
Awards: $4,000, $3,000, $2,000
       Phone: (48) 32 351 17 09
       Fax: (48) 32 351 17 14
       E-mail: konkurs@fiharmoniaslaska.art.pl
       Web site: www.konkursfitelberg.art.pl

HUNGARIAN TELEVISION CONDUCTORS COMPETITION

Dates/How often: May, Triennial
Application fee: $250
Age restrictions: under 35
Location: Budapest, Hungary
Awards/Prizes: 1st Prize $5,000, 2nd Prize $3,000, 3rd Prize $2,000
       Phone: 36 1 317 9838
       Fax: 36 1 317 9910

INTERNATIONAL PROKOFIEV COMPETITION

Dates/How often: April, Triennial
Application fee: $100
Age restrictions: under 40
Location: St. Petersburg, Russia
Orchestra: St. Petersburg Academic Philharmonic Orchestra
Awards/Prizes: 1st Prize $10,000, 2nd Prize $7,000, 3rd Prize $3,000,
                   4th Prize $1,000
       Phone: (812) 279-64-86
       Fax: (812) 279-64-86
       E-mail: musicomp@online.ru
       Web site: www.prokofiev.org

KIRILL KONDRASHIN COMPETITION FOR YOUNG CONDUCTORS

Dates/How often: June, Quadrennial
Application fee: 150 Dutch Florin
Age restrictions: up to 30
Location of Comp: Amsterdam, Holland
Orchestra: Concertgebouw
Awards/Prizes: Guest conducting with leading European orchestras
    Phone: (35) 677 54 53
    Fax: (35) 677 43 11
    E-mail: kondrashin@gsd.nos.ni

MAAZEL/VILAR CONDUCTORS COMPETITION

Dates/How often: September, Triennial
Application fee: None
Age restrictions: under 30
Location: New York, N.Y.
Orchestra: Orchestra of St. Luke's
Awards/Prizes: 1st Prize $45,000 and guest conducting
    Phone: (212) 418-2589
    Fax: (212) 832-5272
    E-mail: info@maazel-vilar.org
    Web site: www.maazel-vilar.org

NICOLAI MALKO INTERNATIONAL COMPETITION FOR YOUNG CONDUCTORS

Dates/How often: April, Triennial
Application fee: None
Age restrictions: 20–32 years old
Location: Copenhagen, Denmark
Orchestra: Danish National Symphony Orchestra
Awards/Prizes: 1st Prize 100,000 Danish Kroner, 2nd Prize 50,000 Danish
    Kroner, 3rd Prize 40,000 Danish Kroner, 4th Prize 30,000
    Danish Kroner, 5th Prize 25,000 Danish Kroner
    Phone: +45 35 20 63 71
    Fax: +45 35 20 63 21
    E-mail: malko@dr.dk
    Web site: www.malko.dk

EDUARDO MATA INTERNATIONAL CONDUCTING COMPETITION

Dates/How often: November, Biennial
Application fee: $300
Age restrictions: under 35
Location: Mexico City, Mexico
Awards/Prizes: 1st Prize $10,000
    Phone: 52 55 5286 4295
    E-mail: premiointernacionalemata@instrumenta.org
    Web site: www.instrumenta.org

Lovro von Matačić International Competition for Young Conductors
Dates/How often: September, Quadrennial
Application fee: €200
Age restrictions: under 35
Location of Comp: Zagreb, Croatia
Awards/Prizes: 1st Prize €5,000, 2nd Prize €3,000, 3rd Prize €1,500
    Phone: +385 1 61 21 184
    Fax: +385 1 61 11 267
    E-mail: fond-matacic@zg.htnet.hr
    Web site: www.fond-matacic.t-com.hr

Dimitris Mitropoulos Conducting Competition
Dates/How often: November, Biennial (even years)
Application fee: None
Age restrictions: under 40
Location: Athens, Greece
Orchestra: The Orchestra of Colours
Awards/Prizes: 1st Prize €10,000, 2nd Prize €7,000, 3rd Prize €5,000
    Phone: (+30) (210) 36 27 412
    Fax: (+30) (210) 36 21 477
    E-mail: info@mitropouloscompetition.gr
    Web site: www.mitropouloscompetition.gr

Antonio Pedrotti International Competition for Orchestra Conductors
Dates/How often: September, Biennial (even years)
Application fee: €220
Age restrictions: 18 to 35
Location: Trento, Italy
Awards/Prizes: 1st Prize €7000 and 15 concerts, 2nd Prize €5000,
                    3rd Prize €3500
    Phone: +39 0461 23 12 23
    Fax: +39 0461 18 20 531
    E-mail: a.pedrotti.competition@tn.nettuno.it
    Web site: concorsopedrotti.it/info_e.htm

Sibelius International Conductors' Competition
Dates/How often: September, Quinquennial (0 and 5)
Application fee: None
Age restrictions: under 35
Location: Helsinki, Finland
Awards/Prizes: 1st Prize $15.000, 2nd Prize $12,000, 3rd Prize $10,000
    Phone: +358 40 5030 997
    Fax: +358 9 497 597
    E-mail: elina.siltanen@hel.fi
    Web site: www.sibeliusconductorscompetition.org

Sir Georg Solti International Conductors' Competition

Dates/How often: September, Biennial (even years)
Application fee: €75
Age restrictions: ages 22–37
Location: Frankfurt (am Main), Germany
Orchestra: Frankfurter Museumsorchester
Awards/Prizes: 1st Prize €15,000, 2nd Prize €10,000, 3rd Prize €5,000
        Phone: (+49) (0) 18 03 16 17 19
        Fax: (+49) (0) 69 28 94 43
        E-mail: info@dirigentenwettbewerb-solti.de
        Web site: www.dirigentenwettbewerb-solti.de

Arturo Toscanini International Conducting Competition

Dates/How often: September, Biennial
Age restrictions: under 35
Location: Parma, Italy
Orchestra: Arturo Toscanini Philharmonic Orchestra
Awards/Prizes: 1st Prize €15,000, 2nd Prize €10,000, 3rd Prize €5,000
        Phone: +39 0521 39 13 20
        Fax: +39 0521 39 13 12
        E-mail: concorsi@fondazione-toscanini.it
        Web site: www.fondazione-toscanini.it

Vakhtang Jordania International Conducting Competition

Dates/How often: September, Annual
Application fee: $50
Age restrictions: None
Location: Kharkov, Ukraine
Orchestra: Kharkov Philharmonic Symphony Orchestra
Awards/Prizes: 1st prize and guest conducting engagements
        Phone: (516) 586-3433
        Fax: (516) 797-9166
        E-mail: jamesarts@catt.net
        Web site: www.jamesarts.com

Grants and Residencies

Foundations and Scholarships

The American Conducting Fellows Program—League of American Orchestras

Purpose: This program supports the musical and leadership development of exceptionally talented conductors in the early stages of their professional careers.
Award: Placement with a major American orchestra for a 2–3 year residency
        Phone: (212) 262-5161
        Fax: (212) 262-5198
        E-mail: league@americanorchestras.org
        Web site: www.americanorchestras.org

AMERICAN MUSICOLOGICAL SOCIETY—AWARDS, GRANTS, FELLOWSHIPS

Purpose: To provide support to further the talents of performers involved with music.

Awards: Awards and grants of undisclosed amounts

> Phone: 207-798-4243
> Fax: 207-798-4254
> E-mail: ams@ams.net.org
> Web site: www.ams-net.org/awards

FRANK HUNTINGTON BEEBE FUND FOR MUSICIANS

Purpose: To provide fellowships for gifted young musicians to pursue advanced music study/performance abroad.

Awards: about $16,000

> Phone: (617) 585-1267
> Fax: (617) 585-1270
> Email: admin@beebefund.org
> Web site: www.beebefund.org

AARON COPLAND FUND FOR MUSIC PERFORMING ENSEMBLES PROGRAM

Purpose: To support organizations whose performances encourage and improve public knowledge and appreciation of serious contemporary American music.

Eligibility: Funds are available for general operating support or project support, to professional performing ensembles with histories of substantial commitment to contemporary American music, and with plans to continue that commitment.

Awards: $1,000–$20,000

> Phone: (212) 461-6956
> E-mail: ensembles@copelandfund.org
> Web site: www.grants.copelandfund.org

AARON COPLAND FUND FOR MUSIC RECORDING PROGRAM

Purpose: To document and provide wider exposure for the music of contemporary American composers.

Eligibility: Proposals may be submitted by nonprofit professional performance ensembles, presenting institutions and nonprofit or commercial recording companies. Performance ensembles and presenting institutions must include a letter of intent from a recording company.

Awards: $2,000–$20,000. Grants for the recording of orchestral works may cover up to a maximum of 50 percent of the total project costs.

> Phone: (212) 461-6956
> E-mail: recording@copelandfund.org
> Web site: www.grants.copelandfund.org

JOHN SIMON GUGGENHEIM MEMORIAL FOUNDATION

Purpose: To further the development of scholars and artists by assisting them to engage in research in any field of knowledge and creation in any of the arts.

Awards: The amounts of the grants will be adjusted to the needs of the applicant, considering their other resources and the purpose and scope of their project.

> Phone: (212) 687-4470
> Fax: (212) 697-3248
> E-mail: fellowships@gf.org
> Web site: www.gf.org

INTERNATIONAL EÖTVÖS INSTITUTE FOUNDATION FOR YOUNG CONDUCTORS & COMPOSERS

Purpose: Provides postgraduate instruction in theoretical and practical training prior to the individual becoming a professional conductor.

Awards: Scholarship to attend a workshop.

Location: Budapest, Hungary

> Phone: (35) 533 59 40
> Fax: (35) 531 32 65
> E-mail: eotvosp@hotmail.com
> Web site: www.eotvospeter.com

MUSICIANS FOUNDATION

Purpose: To provide support for professional musicians who need help in meeting current expenses.

Awards: Grants of undisclosed amounts.

> Phone: (212) 239-9137
> Fax: (212) 239-9138
> E-mail: info@musiciansfoundation.org
> Web site: www.musiciansfoundation.org

NEA—ACCESS TO ARTISTIC EXCELLENCE—GRANTS TO ORGANIZATIONS AND INDIVIDUALS

Purpose: To promote and support artistic excellence in the arts including professional artistic development and training programs for musicians, such as conducting, mentorship, and career development.

Awards: $5,000 to $150,000

> Phone: (202) 682-5400
> E-mail: webmgr@arts.gov
> Web site: www.arts.endow.gov

RECORDING ASSISTANCE PROGRAM

Purpose: To aid composers and performer/ensembles in the publication and dissemination of contemporary music.

Eligibility: Must be a member of the American Composers Forum.

Prize: $2,500–$6,000 loan, repaid through CD sales

> Phone: (651) 228-1407
> Fax: (651) 291-7978
> E-mail: jwalters@composersforum.org
> Web site: www.composersforum.org

THE WILLIAM SCHUMAN MUSIC TRUST

Purpose: To encourage performances and new recordings of music by
William Schuman.

Prize: Gifts of tapes, recordings, and modest grants.
> Phone: (212) 769-6433
> Fax: (631) 324-0627
> E-mail: sasha9bh@gmail.com
> Web site: Williamschuman.org

THE SINFONIA FOUNDATION

Purpose: Provides annual research grants for scholarly research on music in
America or American music.

Awards: $1,000 maximum
> Phone: (812) 867-2433 or (800) 473-2649
> Fax: (812) 867-0633
> E-mail: lyrecrest@sinfonia.org
> Web site: www.sinfonia.org

THE BRUNO WALTER MEMORIAL FOUNDATION

Purpose: The Bruno Walter Memorial Foundation undertakes projects that help
the career development of orchestral conductors.

Awards: $10,000 grants to United States–based orchestras or opera companies in
support of their assistant/associate conductor positions. Each award will
be split into two components, with $7,500 being granted to the
institution and $2,500 to its assistant conductor.
> E-mail: info@brunowalter.org
> Web site: www.brunowalter.org

Residencies

ATLANTIC CENTER FOR THE ARTS

Purpose: To provide artists from all artistic disciplines spaces to live, work, and
collaborate.

Eligibility: Literary, visual, and performing artists

Awards: Three-week residencies (fee of $850)

Location: New Smyrna Beach, FL
> Phone: (386) 427-6975
> Fax: (386) 427-5669
> E-mail: program@atlanticcenterforthearts.org
> Web site: www.atlanticcenterforthearts.org

Banff—Leighton Artist Colony Residencies

Purpose: To provide a concentrated, retreat environment to professional artists engaged in the creation of new work.

Awards: Artists' studios are available for a fee.

Fees: Studio fee per day: $53.00, Single room per day: $51.00, Flex meal plan per day: $14.00 or $19.25

Location: Banff, Alberta, Canada

> Phone: (800) 565-9989
> Fax: (403) 762-6345
> E-mail: arts_info@banffcentre.ca
> Web site: www.banffcentre.ca

Bellagio—Residential Program for Scholars and Artists— The Rockerfeller Foundation.

Purpose: To provide a contemplative environment in which scholars, scientists, artists, writers, policymakers, and practitioners from all over the world may pursue their creative and scholarly work.

Awards: Residencies of one month. The Foundation provides room and board without charge for all residents and workshop/team participants. Some travel assistance is available.

Location: Lake Como, Italy

> Phone: (212) 764-3468
> E-mail: bellagio_res@iie.org
> Web site: www.rockfound.org

Blue Mountain Center

Purpose: The Center exists to provide a peaceful and comfortable environment in which writers, artists, and musicians are able to work, free from the distractions and demands of normal daily life.

Awards: Four-week residencies including room, board, and all meals.

Location: Blue Mountain Lake, New York

> Phone: 518-352-7391
> Fax: 518-352-7700
> E-mail: bmc@bluemountaincenter.org
> Web site: www.bluemountaincenter.org

Djerassi Resident Artists Program

Purpose: The mission of the Djerassi Resident Artists Program is to support and enhance the creativity of artists by providing uninterrupted time for work, reflection, and collegial interaction in a beautiful setting.

Awards: Residency grants of one month. Room, board, and studios are provided.

Location: Woodside, CA

> Phone: (650) 747-1250
> Fax: (650) 747-0105
> E-mail: drap@djerassi.org
> Web site: www.djerassi.org

MacDowell Colony

Purpose: To serve as a working retreat for creative artists and musicians.

Awards: Average residency of six weeks includes room, board, and the exclusive use of a studio. Travel grants are also available.

Location: Peterborough, NH

Phone: (603) 924-3886
Fax: (603) 924-9142
E-mail: info@macdowellcolony.org
Web site: www.macdowellcolony.org

Millay Colony for the Arts

Purpose: To promote the vitality of the arts and the development of writers, visual artists, and composers by providing a retreat for creative work.

Awards: Residencies of one month, including housing, studio space, and food, are available to visual artists, writers, and composers.

Location: Austerlitz, NY

Phone: (518) 392-3103
E-mail: apply@millaycolony.org
Web site: www.millaycolony.org

Ragdale Foundation Artist Residencies

Purpose: To provide a place where writers and artists of all disciplines can work uninterrupted in a peaceful setting.

Awards: Residencies of two weeks to two months. Residents pay $25 per day. Some fee waivers are available.

Location: Lake Forest, IL

Phone: (847) 234-1063
Fax: (847) 234-1063
E-mail: info@ragdale.org
Web site: www.ragdale.org

Helene Wurlitzer Foundation of New Mexico

Purpose: To provide residency grants to stimulate creative work in music and other creative fields.

Awards: Three-month residencies (housing and utilities) between April and September.

Location: Taos, NM

Phone: (505) 758-2413
Fax: (505) 758-2559
E-mail: hwf@taosnet.com
Web site: www.wurlitzerfoundation.org

YADDO

Purpose: To provide professional creative artists uninterrupted time to work in a supportive community.

Awards: Residencies from two weeks to two months. Room, board, and studio provided.

Location: Saratoga Springs, NY

> Phone: (518) 584-0746
> Fax: (518) 584-1312
> E-mail: yaddo@yaddo.org
> Web site: www.yaddo.org

Programming Resources

Thematic Programming Lists

As a music director, you will want to program concerts based on specific themes. The following lists should help you in identifying new pieces or movements of pieces that might fit in a specific spot on a program. Further information about these pieces can be obtained by contacting the publisher listed or their American distributor.

Table R.1 Music Publishers, American Distributors for Following Publishers

B&H	BOOSEY & HAWKES*		ECS	ECS PUBLISHING*	
	B&B	Bote & Bock		ECS	E. C. Schirmer
	BA	Barry Ed.		GAL	Galaxy Music Corp.
	CAR	Carisch		HG	Highgate Press
	DUR	Durand			
	ESC	Eschig	P	C. F. PETERS*	
	FAB	Faber Music			
	FUER	Fuerstner		BELA	Belaieff, M. P.
	RIC	G. Ricordi & Co.		MWV	Musikwissenschaftlicher
	SAL	Salabert (Editions)			Verlag
	SIM	Simrock	PR	PRESSER*	
EAMD	EAMD LLC*			AME	American Music Edition
				B	Billaudot (Editions)
	BEL	Belwin Publishing		BA	Bazelon
	EAMD	European American		BS	Boccaccini & Spada
		Music			Editori
	HEL	Helicon Music		CF	Carl Fischer
	M	Mills		EBM	E. B. Marks
	SCH	Schott & Co., Ltd.		EFM	Editions Françaises de
	UNI	Universal Edition			Musique
	WB	Warner Brothers		EV	Elkan-Vogel

* American distributors for each publisher subject to change.

Table R.1 (continued)

PR	**PRESSER* (continued)**		GM	GunMar Music
	HAM	Hamelle	GS	G. Schirmer, Inc.
	HEU	Heugel & Cie.	GSR	Russian Music
	IMI	Israel Music Institute	LEN	Alfred Lengnick & Co Ltd
	JO	Jobert, Societé des	NOV	Novello & Co
		Editions	PAT	Patersons
	LED	Leduc	SHA	Shawnee Press
	LIN	Lindsay Music	SIK	Musikverlage Hans
	MER	Merion Music		Sikorski
	MERC	Mercury Music	TPL	Templeton
	ONTS	Ongaku No Tomo Sha	TPO	Tempo Music
	PEER	Peermusic Classical	UME	Unión Musical Ediciones
	PEM	Pembroke			
	PIED	Piedmont	**FS**	**FOR SALE***
	PR	Theodore Presser	BAR	Bärenreiter
		Company	BREIT	Breitkopf and Härtel
	PWM	Polskie Wydawnictwo	DOB	Doblinger Music
		Muzyczne	EUL	Eulenburg Miniature
	SF	Sam Fox		Scores
	TT	Tritone Tenuto	KAL	Edwin F. Kalmus
	UMP	United Music Publishers	LUCK	Luck's Music Library
	WM	Woodbury Music	RIC	G. Ricordi & Co.
GS	**SCHIRMER***		**OP**	**OTHER PUBLISHERS***
	AMP	Associated Music	ACA	American Composers
		Publishers		Alliance
	BREIT	Breitkopf & Härtel	BR	Broude Bros.
	CH	Chester Music	FC	Fleischer Collection
	CHA	Chappell & Co.	GR	Ed. Green Music
	CMC	Carlanita Music	LI	Liben Music
	CUR	J. Curwen & Sons	MTI	Music Theatre
	EMI	EMI Music Publishing		International
	EWM	Weintraub Music	OX	Oxford
	G&C	G & C Music	ST	Stangland
		Corporation	WGS	William Grant Still

* American distributors for each publisher subject to change.

Table R.2 Thematic Programming Table

Full name	Title	Publisher	Timing
Afro-American			
Beveridge, Thomas	Once (Tribute to Martin Luther King)	SHA (GS)	
Dawson, William	Negro Folk Symphony	SHA (GS)	35′
Ellington, Duke	Black, Brown and Beige	GS	35′
Ellington, Duke	Harlem	GS	19′
Gould, Morton	Spirituals for Orchestra	BEL	20′
Gould, Morton	Symphony of Spirituals	GS	27′
Gruenberg, Louis	The Creation: A Negro Sermon	GM (GS)	22′
McDonald, Harl	Suite for Strings on American Negro Themes	EV (PR)	9′
Mechem, Kirke	Songs of the Slave	GS	34′
Robinson, Walter H.	Harriet Tubman	SHA (GS)	5′
Schuman, William	On Freedom's Ground	MER (PR)	40′
Still, William Grant	Afro-American Symphony	NOV (GS)	23′
Still, William Grant	Darker America	CF (PR)	9′
Still, William Grant	From the Black Belt	CF (PR)	12′
Still, William Grant	Pages from Negro History	CF (PR)	12′
Still, William Grant	Symphony No. 2 (Songs of a New Race)	CF (PR)	25′
Still, William Grant	Troubled Island Opera	PEER (PR)	120′
Villa-Lobos, Heitor	Danses Africaines	B&H	14′
Animals			
Bach, J.S.	Sheep May Safely Graze (Cantata No. 208)	BAR; BREIT; KAL	38′
Catán, Daniel	Obsidian Butterfly	GS	26′
Creston, Paul	Kangaroo Kaper	SHA (GS)	4′
Debussy, Claude	Le Coin des Enfants (Children's Corner), mvt 2, Jumbo's Lullaby	DUR (B&H); KAL	3′
Friml, Rudolf	Medley from "The Firefly"	GS	7′
Fučik, Julius	Der alte Brummbär, Op. 210 (The Old Grumbling Bear)	LUCK	5′
Grieg, Edvard	Two Norwegian Airs, Op. 63, Cow Keeper's Tune	KAL; LUCK	5′
Haydn, Franz Joseph	Symphony No. 82, (L'Ours) (The Bear)	UNI (EAMD)	27′
Hovhaness, Alan	And God Created Great Whales	P	12′
Mamlok, Ursula	Grasshoppers: Six Humoresques for Orchestra	ACA	5′

continued

Table R.2 (continued)

Full name	Title	Publisher	Timing
Animals (continued)			
Milhaud, Darius	Le Boeuf sur le Toit, Op.58	ESC (B&H)	15′
Mussorgsky, Modest	The Songs of the Flea	CH (GS)	3′
Poulenc, Francis	Animaux Modèles	B&H	21′
Poulenc, Francis	The Story of Babar the Little Elephant	CHA (GS)	23′
Prokofiev, Serge	Peter and the Wolf	B&H; GSR (GS); KAL	25′
Purcell, Henry	The Fairy Queen: Suite No. 2	EUL	15′
Rawsthorne, Alan	Practical Cats	OX	24′
Rimsky-Korsakov, Nicolai	Tsar Saltan: Flight of the Bumblebee	BREIT; GSR (GS); KAL	3′
Rorem, Ned	Lions	B&H	14′
Roussel, Albert	Le Festin de l'araignée, Op. 17, (The Spider's Feast)	DUR (B&H); KAL	16′
Saint-Saëns, Camille	Carnival of the Animals	DUR (B&H); LUCK	23′
Schickele, Peter	A Zoo Called Earth	PR	15′
Schubert, Franz	"The Trout"	B&H	4′
Shchedrin, Rodion	The Little Humpbacked Horse	KAL; GSR (GS)	25′
Shostakovich, Dmitri	The Gadfly: Suite, Op. 97a	KAL; GSR (GS)	44′
Strauss, Jr., Johann	Feldermaus: Overture and Suite	B&H; KAL; LUCK	9′
Tavener, John	The Lamb	GS	4′
Tavener, John	The Whale: A Biblical Fantasy	CHA (GS)	35′
Vaughan Williams, Ralph	The Wasps: Overture and Suite	CUR (GS); KAL	9′
Birds			
Adams, John	Chamber Symphony, mvt. 3, Roadrunner	B&H	6′
Berg, Alban	Seven Early Songs, mvt. 3, The Nightingale	UNI (EAMD)	2′
Bond, Victoria	Urban Bird	PR	24′
Burrell, Diana	Scene With Birds	UMP (PR)	12′
Chatman, Stephen	Grouse Mountain Lullaby	EBM (PR)	4′
Davis, Carl	A Duck's Diary	B&H	16′
Dvořák, Antonín	Wood Dove, Op. 110	BAR; SIM (B&H)	19′
Elgar, Edward	Cockaigne, Op. 40	B&H; KAL	13′
Griffes, Charles	The White Peacock	GS	6′
Haydn, Franz Joseph	Symphony No. 83, (La Poule)	UNI (EAMD)	24′

Full name	Title	Publisher	Timing
Birds (continued)			
Jones, Samuel	Eudora's Fable: The Shoebird	CF (PR)	48'
Kats-Chernin, Elena	Wild Swans Ballet	B&H	90'
Kodály, Zoltán	Variations on a Hungarian Folksong, (The Peacock)	B&H	25'
La Montaine, John	Birds of Paradise	CF (PR)	13'
Lees, Benjamin	The Trumpet of the Swan	B&H	17'
Liadov, Anatol	Eight Russian Folk Songs, Op. 58, mvt. 5, Legend of the Birds	BELA; KAL	2'
MacMillan, James	The Birds of Rhiannon	B&H	24'
Mecham, Kirke	The Jayhawk: Magic Bird Overture, Op. 43	GS	9'
Messager, André	Les Deux Pigeons	LED (PR)	
Messiaen, Olivier	Reveil des oiseaux	B&H	22'
Milhaud, Darius	La Branche des oiseaux	HEU (PR)	30'
Nielsen, Carl	Maskarade: Hanedans (Dance of Cocks)	WH (GS); KAL	5'
Nigg, Serge	Million d'oiseaux d'or	JO (PR)	14'
Respighi, Ottorino	Gli Uccelli (The Birds), mvt. 2, Dove/ mvt. 3, Hen/ mvt. 4, Nightingale/ mvt. 5, Cuckoo	RIC	5'/3'/ 4'/4'
Richter, Marga	Bird of Yearning	CF (PR)	30'
Rimsky-Korsakov, Nicolai	Le Coq d'or (The Golden Cockerel): Suite	KAL; GSR (GS)	25'
Rimsky-Korsakov, Nicolai	Snegourotchka: The Snow Maiden Suite, mvt. 2, Dance of the Birds	UNI (EAMD); BREIT; KAL	3'
Rogers, Bernard	The Song of the Nightingale	EV (PR)	19'
Rorem, Ned	Eagles	B&H	9'
Rossini, Gioacchino	La gazza ladra (The Thieving Magpie)	KAL; RIC	10'
Sculthorpe, Peter	Kakadu	FAB (B&H)	15'
Shchedrin, Rodion	The Seagull: Suite	GS	20'
Sibelius, Jean	Legends Op. 22: The Swan of Tuonela	BREIT; KAL	10'
Slatkin, Leonard	The Raven	GS	18'
Strauss, Josef	Dorfschwalben aus Österreich, Op. 164, (Village Swallows)	KAL; LUCK	8'
Stravinsky, Igor	L'Oiseau de feu (Firebird) Suite	SCH (EAMD); CHA (GS); KAL	22'

continued

Table R.2 (continued)

Full name	Title	Publisher	Timing
Birds (continued)			
Stravinsky, Igor	Le Chant du Rossignol, (Song of the Nightingale)	B&H	19'
Takemitsu, Toru	A Flock Descends into the Pentagonal Garden	B&H	13'
Tann, Hilary	With the Heather and Small Birds	OX	10'
Tchaikovsky, Piotr Ilyich	Swan Lake: Suite, Op. 20a, mvt. 3, Danse of the Swans	KAL 2'	
Thomson, Virgil	Sea Piece with Birds	GS	5'
Vaughan Williams, Ralph	The Lark Ascending	OX	14'
Villa-Lobos, Heitor	Uirapurú (The Magic Bird)	AMP (GS)	18'
Circus			
Bamert, Matthias	Circus Parade	EAMD	12'
Berezowsky, Nicolai	Circus Music from "Barbar the Elephant"	CF (PR)	2'
Fučik, Julius	March of the Gladiators	LUCK	5'
Hamilton, Iain	Circus	PR	17'
Maggio, Robert	Big Top for Orchestra	PR	12'
Moore, Douglas	The Pageant of P.T. Barnum	CF (PR)	16'
Piston, Walter	The Incredible Flutist	AMP (GS)	17'
Respighi, Ottorino	Feste Romane (Roman Festivals), mvt. 1, Circus Games	RIC	5'
Stravinsky, Igor	Circus Polka	SCH (EAMD)	4'
Toch, Ernst	Circus Overture	KAL; M (EAMD)	6'
William, Schuman	Circus Overture (Sideshow)	AMP (GS)	7'
Fairy Tales/Stories			
Amos, Keith	The Steadfast Tin Soldier	CF (PR)	30'
Antheil, George	Tom Sawyer Overture (California Overture)	GS	7'
Arlen, Harold	The Wizard of Oz, Munchkin-land/ Yellow Brick Road	EMI (GS)	8'/5'
Bartók, Béla	The Wooden Prince	B&H	30'
Beethoven, Ludwig van	Creatures of Prometheus	BREIT; KAL	5'
Bergsma, William	Paul Bunyan Suite	CF (PR)	8'
Berlioz, Hector	La Damnation de Faust, Op.24	BREIT; KAL; GS	120'
Berlioz, Hector	La Mort de Cleopatre	BR; LUCK	22'
Bernstein, Leonard	West Side Story: Symphonic Dances	B&H	22'

Full name	Title	Publisher	Timing
Fairy Tales/Stories (continued)			
Britten, Benjamin	King Arthur	OX	24'
Britten, Benjamin	Paul Bunyan: Overture	FAB (B&H)	5'
Britten, Benjamin	The Sword in the Stone	FAB (B&H)	10'
Caltabiano, Ronald	Pegasus Fanfare for Chamber Orchestra	MER (PR)	4'
Carter, Elliot	Pocahontas: Suite	AMP (GS)	20'
Chadwick, George Whitefield	Rip Van Winkle: Overture	CF (PR)	10'
Cherubini, Luigi	Ali Baba: Overture	BAR; BREIT; KAL	7'
Coombes, Douglas	The Elves and the Shoemaker	LIN (PR)	45'
Copland, Aaron	Billy the Kid: Suite	B&H	5'
Corigliano, John	Pied Piper Fantasy	GS	38'
Dankworth, John	The Diamond and the Goose	CH (GS)	33'
Daugherty, Michael	Metropolis Symphony (Superman)	PEER (PR)	41'
Deak, Jon	Heidi—A Symphonic Narrative	CF (PR)	25'
Deak, Jon	Jack and the Beanstalk	CF (PR)	12'/22'
Deak, Jon	The Snow Queen	CF (PR)	14'
Deak, Jon	The Wind in the Willows, Scene 7	CF (PR)	15'
Dorff, Daniel	Billy and the Carnival, A Children's Guide to the Instruments	PR	14'
Dorff, Daniel	Goldilocks and the Three Bears	PR	8'
Dukas, Paul	L'Apprenti Sorcier (The Sorcerer's Apprentice)	DUR (B&H); KAL	12'
Foss, Lukas	Elegy for Anne Frank	CF (PR)	5'
Gerhard, Roberto	Don Quixote: Dances	B&H	16'
Gershwin, George	Porgy and Bess	CHA (GS)	24'
Gillis, Don	The Night Before Christmas for Narrator and Orchestra	PR	4'
Ginastera, Alberto	Overture to the Creole Faust	BA	9'
Gould, Morton	Jekyll and Hyde Variations	G&C (GS)	22'
Gounod, Charles	Faust: Ballet Music	KAL	15'
Granados, Enrique	Dante, Op.21	GS	15'
Gruber, Heinz Karl	Frankenstein	B&H	28'
Handel, George Frideric	The Choice of Hercules	BAR; NOV (GS)	55'
Harbison, John	Remembering Gatsby: Foxtrot	AMP (GS)	7'
Harsányi, Tibor	L'Histoire du Petite Tailleur (The Story of the Little Tailor)	ESC (B&H)	30'

continued

Table R.2 (continued)

Full name	Title	Publisher	Timing
Fairy Tales/Stories (continued)			
Herschel, Lee	How the Camel Got His Hump	SF (PR)	9'
Herschel, Lee	How the Whale Got His Tiny Throat	SF (PR)	9'
Humperdinck, Engelbert	Hansel und Gretel: Prelude/ Three Excerpts	SCH (EAMD); KAL	8'/13'
Humperdinck, Engelbert	Sleeping Beauty: Suite	FC	19'
Jones, Samuel	Eudora's Fable: The Shoebird	CF (PR)	48'
Kapilow, Robert	Dr. Seuss's Green Eggs and Ham	GS	17'
Kasschau, Howard	The Legend of Sleepy Hollow	GS	10'
Khachaturian, Aram	Spartacus: Suite No. 1/ Suite No. 2/ Suite No. 3	KAL; GSR (GS)	26'/ 21'/16'
Kleinsinger, George	Tubby the Tuba	MTI	13'
Kodály, Zoltán	Háry János: Suite	UNI (EAMD)	25'
Koechlin, Charles	Les Bandar-log (The Jungle Book)	ESC (B&H)	15'
Liadov, Antol	Baba-Yaga, Op. 56	BELA; KAL	4'
Liszt, Franz	A Faust Symphony	BREIT; KAL	65'
Liszt, Franz	Dante Symphony	BREIT; KAL	52'
Liszt, Franz	Orpheus (Symphonic Poem No. 4)	BREIT; KAL	13'
Liszt, Franz	Prometheus (Symphonic Poem No. 5)	BREIT; KAL	12'
Lombardo, Mario	Drakestail: A Symphonic Fairy Tale	CHA (GS)	18'
MacDowell, Edward	Lancelot and Elaine, Op. 25 (Symphonic Poem No. 2)	KAL; GS	20'
McBride, Robert	Pumpkin-Eater's Little Fugue for Orchestra	AMP (GS)	4'
McCabe, John	The Lion, the Witch and the Wardrobe: Suite	NOV (GS)	15'
McDonald, Harl	Legend of the Arkansas Traveler	EV (PR)	4'
Mennin, Peter	Concertato: Moby Dick	CF (PR)	11'
Monteverdi, Claudio	Orfeo: Overture	KAL	5'
Nielsen, Carl	Aladdin: 7 Pieces, Op. 34	WH (GS); KAL	23'
Nordoff, Paul	The Frog Prince	PR	15'
Offenbach, Jacques	La Belle Hélène: Overture	KAL; LUCK	8'
Offenbach, Jacques	Orpheus in the Underworld: Overture	KAL	11'
Ohki, Masao	Five Fairy Tales	EV (PR)	12'

Full name	Title	Publisher	Timing
Fairy Tales/Stories (continued)			
Patterson, Paul	Little Red Riding Hood	B&H	33'
Patterson, Paul	The Three Little Pigs	B&H	21'
Persichetti, Vincent	Fairy Tale	CF (PR)	4'
Pierné, Gabriel	March of the Lead Soldiers, Op. 14, No. 6	KAL; LED (PR)	4'
Poulenc, Francis	The Story of Babar the Little Elephant	CHA (GS)	22'
Prokofiev, Serge	Alexander Nevsky	KAL; GSR (GS)	36'
Prokofiev, Serge	Cinderella: Suite No. 1/ Suite No. 2/ Suite No. 3	KAL; GSR (GS)	29'/ 20'/26'
Prokofiev, Serge	Lieutenant Kijé, Op. 60, Suite	B&H	21'
Prokofiev, Serge	Peter and the Wolf	B&H; GSR (GS); KAL	25'
Proto, Frank	Casey at Bat	LI	13'
Purcell, Henry	The Fairy Queen: Suite No. 1	EUL	6'
Rachmaninoff, Sergei	Cinq Études-tableaux, mvt. 4, Little Red Riding Hood and the Wolf	B&H	5'
Ran, Shulamit	Legends	PR	22'
Ranjbaran, Behzad	The Blood of Seyavash	PR	40'
Ravel, Maurice	Ma Mère l'Oye (Mother Goose), mvt. 1, Sleeping Beauty/ mvt. 2, Tom Thumb/ mvt. 4, Beauty and the Beast	DUR (B&H); KAL	2'/3'/4'
Ravel, Maurice	Shéhérazade	DUR (B&H); CF (PR); KAL	17'
Rimsky-Korsakov, Nicolai	Schéhérazade, Op. 35	BELA; KAL	42'
Rimsky-Korsakov, Nicolai	Skazka, Op. 29 (Russian Fairy Tale)	BELA; KAL	13'
Rodríquez, Robert Xavier	Scrooge	GS	20'
Rogers, Bernard	Once Upon a Time: 5 Fairy Tales for Orchestra	KAL	12'
Rogers, Bernard	The Musicians of Bremen	PR	22'
Rogers, Bernard	The Nightingale	PEER (PR)	65'
Rossini, Gioacchino	Guillaume Tell (William Tell)	BREIT; KAL; RIC	12'
Rossini, Gioacchino	La Cenerentola (Cinderella) Overture	KAL; RIC	8'
Saint-Saëns, Camille	La Jeunesse d'Hercule	DUR (B&H); KAL	16'
Satie, Erik	Jack in the box	UNI (EAMD)	7'

continued

Table R.2 (continued)

Full name	Title	Publisher	Timing
Fairy Tales/Stories (continued)			
Schickele, Peter	Sneaky Pete and the Wolf, Narr. For Prokofiev's Peter and the Wolf	EV (PR)	26′
Schmitt, Florent	La Tragédie de Salomé, Op. 50	KAL	28′
Schuman, William	A Song of Orpheus	MER (PR)	20′
Schumann, Robert	Faust: Overture	FC	6′
Shchedrin, Rodion	Anna Karenina	GSR (GS)	27′
Shchedrin, Rodion	The Little Humpbacked Horse: Suite No. 1	KAL; GSR (GS)	25′
Strauss, Richard	Don Juan, Op. 20	KAL; P	17′
Strauss, Richard	Don Quixote, Op. 35	KAL; P	38′
Strauss, Richard	Salome, Op. 54: Salome's Dance	B&H; KAL	12′
Strauss, Richard	Till Eulenspiegels Lustige Streiche, Op. 28	KAL; P	15′
Stravinsky, Igor	Abraham and Isaac	B&H	12′
Stravinsky, Igor	L'Histoire du Soldat (The Soldier's Tale)	CHA (GS); KAL	27′
Stravinsky, Igor	L'Oiseau de feu (Firebird) Suite	SCH (EAMD); CHA (GS); KAL	22′
Stravinsky, Igor	Oedipus Rex	B&H	51′
Stravinsky, Igor	Orpheus	B&H	30′
Stravinsky, Igor	Persephone	B&H	48′
Stravinsky, Igor	Petrouchka	B&H	34′
Stravinsky, Igor	The Fairy's Kiss	B&H	45′
Suk, Josef	Pohadka, Op 16 (Ein Marche; Fairy Tale)	KAL; SIM (B&H)	31′
Tchaikovsky, Piotr Ilyich	Sleeping Beauty: Suite, Op. 66	KAL; GSR (GS)	23′
Tchaikovsky, Piotr Ilyich	Swan Lake, Op. 20/ Suite Op. 20a	KAL	130′/24′
Tchaikovsky, Piotr Ilyich	The Nutcracker	KAL	85′
Telemann, Georg Philipp	Don Quichotte	KAL	16′
Toch, Ernst	Pinocchio, a Merry Overture	AMP (GS)	6′
Tredici, David Del	An Alice Symphony (Alice in Wonderland)	B&H	24′
Tredici, David Del	Dracula	B&H	20′
Turrin, Joseph	The Steadfast Tin Soldier	PR	15′
Verdi, Giuseppe	Aïda: Prelude, Triumphal March, Ballet	KAL; LED (PR); RIC	6′

Full name	Title	Publisher	Timing
Fairy Tales/Stories (continued)			
Wagner, Richard	Eine Faust: Overture	BREIT; KAL	12'
Wagner, Richard	The Flying Dutchman: Overture	BREIT; KAL	11'
Weber, Carl Maria	Abu Hassan: Overture	BREIT; KAL	4'
Weber, Carl Maria	Der Freischütz: Overture	BREIT; KAL	10'
Weinberger, Jaromir	Shvanda the Bagpiper	AMP (GS); LUCK	8'
Welcher, Dan	Haleakala (How Maui Snared the Sun)	EV (PR)	21'
Welcher, Dan	The Visions of Merlin	EV (PR)	21'
Fire			
Adler, Samuel	Show An Affirming Flame A Poem for Orchestra	PR	5'
Berkeley, Michael	Flames	OX	12'
Cowell, Henry	Saturday Night at the Firehouse	AMP (GS)	12'
Deak, Jon	New York, 1842: A City on Fire	CF (PR)	23'
Falla, Manuel de	El Amor brujo: Ritual Fire Dance	CHA (GS)	5'
Friml, Rudolf	Medley from "The Firefly"	GS	7'
Gould, Morton	Hosedown: A Firefighter Fable	GS	18'
Handel, George Frideric	Royal Fireworks Music	BAR; BREIT; P	19'
Haydn, Franz Joseph	SymphonyNo. 59, Feuersymphonie	UNI (EAMD)	17'
Ives, Charles	Firemen's Parade on Main Street (The Gong on the Hook and Ladder)	PEER (PR)	3' /
Khachaturian, Aram	Gayne: Suite No. 2, mvt. 7, Fire	KAL; GSR (GS)	7'
Larsen, Libby	Ring of Fire	OX	12'
Leef, Yinam	A Place of Fire	IMI (PR)	17'
Levinson, Gerald	Five Fires	MER (PR)	9'
Lieberson, Peter	Fire	GS	5'
McChesney, Kevin	Ring of Fire Concerto for Handbell Choir and Orchestra	PR	25'
Meyer, Krzysztof	Fireballs for Orchestra, op. 37	PWM (PR)	16'
Natra, Sergiu	Voices of Fire (Leshonot ha'esh) for Orchestra	IMI (PR)	35'
Nielsen, Carl	Symphony No. 4, Op. 29 (Inextinguishable)	WH (GS); KAL	36'
Primosch, James	Fire-Memory/River Memory	MER (PR)	21'

continued

Table R.2 (continued)

Full name	Title	Publisher	Timing
Fire (continued)			
Rodríguez, Robert Xavier	Forbidden Fire, Cantata	GS	22′
Scriabin, Alexander	Prométhée, le poème du feu, Op. 60 (Prometheus, Poem of Fire (Symphony No 5))	B&H; KAL	24′
Stravinsky, Igor	Fireworks	SCH (EAMD); KAL	5′
Stravinsky, Igor	L'Oiseau de feu (Firebird) Suite	SCH (EAMD); CHA (GS); KAL	22′
Tan Dun	Death and Fire: Dialogue with Paul Klee	GS	27′
Tan Dun	Intercourse of Fire and Water (Yi)***	GS	25′
Vangelis	Chariots of Fire Suite	EMI (GS)	7′
Wagner, Richard	Die Walküre: Magic Fire Music	SCH (EAMD); KAL	18′
Zhou, Long	The Future of Fire	OX	6′
Flowers			
Albert, Stephen	Flower of the Mountain	GS	16′
Anderson, Leroy	To a Wild Rose	WM (PR)	1′
Bartók, Béla	Two Pictures, mvt. 1, Virágzás (In Full Flower)	B&H; KAL	8′
Berkeley, Michael	The Romance of the Rose	OX	12′
Britten, Benjamin	Now Sleeps the Crimson Petal	B&H	5′
Chou, Wen-chung	And the Fallen Petals	P	10′
Délibes, Léo	Le Corsair-Valse du pas des fleurs	HEU (PR)	6′
Geminiani, Francesco	Concerto Grosso No. 12 (La Follia)	SCH (EAMD); RIC	12′
Glière, Reinhold	The Red Poppy: Suite	GSR (GS)	27′
Henze, Hans Werner	Aria de la Folía Española	SCH (EAMD)	21′
Holloway, Robin	Scenes from Schumann, Op. 13, mvt. 2, Flowering Lotus	B&H	3′
Khachaturian, Aram	Gayane: Three Pieces, mvt. 3, Dance of the Young Rose Maidens	KAL; GSR (GS)	2′
La Montaine, John	Birds of Paradise	CF (PR)	13′
La Montaine, John	Songs of the Rose of Sharon	BR	15′

Full name	Title	Publisher	Timing
Flowers (continued)			
Persichetti, Vincent	Flower Songs (Cantata No. 6)	EV (PR)	21'
Puccini, Giacomo	I Crisantemi (The Chrysanthemums)	KAL; LUCK; RIC	6'
Strauss, Jr., Johann	Roses from the South	BREIT; KAL; LUCK	7'
Strauss, Richard	Der Rosenkavalier: Suite	B&H	22'
Halloween			
Berlioz, Hector	Symphonie Fantastique, Op. 14, mvt. 5, Witches Sabbath	BAR; BREIT; KAL	10'
Bremer, Carolyn	Dracula's Guide to the Orchestra	CF (PR)	
Chadwick, George Whitefield	Symphonic Sketches, mvt. 4, Hobgoblin	GS 30'	
Corigliano, John	The Ghosts of Versailles	GS	170'
Dvořák, Antonín	Midday Witch, Op. 108	BAR; LUCK	14'
Edwards, Ross	White Ghost Dancing	B&H	9'
Gould, Morton	Holiday Music:, mvt. 1, Halloween	G&C (GS)	3'
Grantham, Donald	El Album de los duendecitos (A Goblin's Album)	PR	16'
Heudebert, Lionel	Ghost-Town Cemetery	SF (PR)	
Humperdinck, Engelbert	Hansel und Gretel: Witch's Ride	KAL	4'
Kernis, Jay Aaron	Goblin Market	AMP (GS)	45'
Liadov, Antol	Baba-Yaga, Op. 56	BELA; KAL	4'
Maggio, Robert	The Hand-Prints of Sorcerers	PR	12'
Mussorgsky, Modest	A Night on Bald Mountain	BREIT (GS)	12'
Puccini, Giacomo	Le Villi; Intermezzo (La tregenda-The Witches' Sabbath)	BS (PR)	15'
Purcell, Henry	Dido and Aeneas Suite, mvt. 7, Dance of the Witches and Sailors	OX	2'
Saint-Saëns, Camille	Danse Macabre, Op. 40	DUR (B&H); KAL	8'
Salzedo, Leonard	The Witch Boy: Square Dance	CH (GS)	4'
Schmitt, Florent	Étude, Op. 49 (The Haunted Palace)	KAL	15'
Shostakovich, Dmitri	Hamlet: Film Suite (1964) Op. 116, mvt. 3, The Ghost	KAL; GSR (GS) 5'	

continued

Table R.2 (continued)

Full name	Title	Publisher	Timing
Holidays/Carnivals/Festivals			
Bennett, Richard Rodney	Celebration	NOV (GS)	5′
Berlioz, Hector	Roman Carnival Overture	BREIT; KAL	8′
Britten, Benjamin	Canadian Carnival, Op. 19	B&H	14′
Carter, Elliott	Holiday Overture	AMP (GS)	10′
Copland, Aaron	From Rodeo: Four Dance Episodes, mvt. 1, Buckaroo Holiday	B&H	7′
Debussy, Claude	Images: Ibéria, mvt. 3, Matin d'un jour de fete (Morning of the Festival Day)	DUR (B&H); CF (PR); KAL	5′
Dvořák, Antonín	Carnival Overture, Op. 92	BAR; KAL	10′
Floyd, Carlisle	In Celebration	BEL	10′
Gould, Morton	Cheers!—A Celebration March	GS	5′
Gould, Morton	Festive Fanfare	GS	2′
Ippolitov-Ivanov, Mikhail	Turkish Fragments, Op. 62, mvt. 4, At the Festival	KAL; GSR (GS)	3′
Ives, Charles	Holidays Symphony: Decoration Day/ Thanksgiving Day	PEER (PR)	10′/15′
Ives, Charles	Holidays Symphony: Washington's Birthday The Fourth of July	AMP (GS)	9′/7′
Mathias, William	Carnival of Wales	OX	26′
Mathias, William	Festival Overture	OX	8′
Mathias, William	Holiday Overture	OX	16′
Milhaud, Darius	Le Carnaval d'Aix	HEU (PR)	19′
Milhaud, Darius	Le Carnaval de Londres	B&H	30′
Respighi, Ottorino	Feste Romane (Roman Festivals), mvt. 2, The jubilee/ mvt. 3, Harvest Festivals in October	RIC	7′/7′
Roldan, Amadeo	La Rebambaramba (Carnival Ballet)	CF (PR)	11′
Satie, Erik	Parade	SAL (B&H)	14′
Shchedrin, Rodion	Symphonic Fanfares (Festive Overture)	KAL; GSR (GS)	5′
Shostakovich, Dmitri	Festive Overture, Op. 96	KAL; GSR (GS)	7′
Still, William Grant	Festive Overture	WGS	10′
Stravinsky, Igor	Petrouchka, mvt.1/ mvt. 4, The Shrove-tide Fair	B&H	10′/13′
Svoboda, Tomas	Festive Overture Op. 103	ST	9′
Ward, Robert	Jubilation—An Overture	HG (ECS)	7′
Zwilich, Ellen Taaffe	Celebration for Orchestra	MER (PR)	10′

Full name	Title	Publisher	Timing
Irish/Scottish			
Anderson, Leroy	Irish Suite	EMI (GS)	20'
Argento, Dominick	Four Irish Dances, Op. 126	B&H	11'
Arnold, Malcolm	Four Scottish Dances, Op. 59	PAT (GS)	9'
Arnold, Malcom	Tam O'Shanter Overture, Op. 51	PAT (GS)	8'
Barry, Gerald	The Conquest of Ireland	OX	20'
Britten, Benjamin	Scottish Ballade, Op. 26 (2 Solo Pianos)	B&H	13'
Bruch, Max	Scottish fantasy, Op. 46 (Violin and Orch)	KAL; SIM (B&H)	30'
Butterworth, George	A Shropshire Lad: Rhapsody for Orchestra	KAL	11'
Chadwick, George Whitefield	Tam O' Shanter	LUCK	18'
Cowell, Henry	Four Irish Tales (Tales of Our Countryside)	AMP (GS)	13'
Duff, Arthur	Irish Suite	NOV (GS)	10'
Esposito, Michele	Irish Suite	NOV (GS)	21'
Field, John	Irish Concerto for Piano and Orchestra	SIK (GS)	18'
Foote, Arthur	Irish Folk Song	LUCK	4'
Gardner, John	A Scots Overture	OX	6'
Grainger, Percy	Irish Tune from County Derry	SCH (EAMD); KAL	3'
Grainger, Percy	Molly on the Shore	SCH (EAMD); KAL	3'
Harty, Hamilton	In Ireland	B&H	7'
Herbert, Victor	Irish Rhapsody	GS	14'
Holst, Gustav	A Somerset Rhapsody	B&H	10'
Leighton, Kenneth	Dance Suite No. 3 (Scottish Dances), Op. 89	NOV (GS)	15'
Loeffler, Charles Martin	Five Irish Fantasies	GS	30'
Mathias, William	Celtic Dances	OX	14'
Roussel, Albert	Irish Rhapsody No. 6	B&H	12'
Scott, Cyril	Irish Serenade	NOV (GS)	
Sowerby, Leo	Irish Washerwoman: Country Dance Tune	PR	4'
Stanford, Charles Villiers	Irish Rhapsody No. 1, Op. 78	BREIT (GS)	14'
Strommen, Carl	Irish Song	CF (PR)	5'

continued

Table R.2 (continued)

Full name	Title	Publisher	Timing
Irish/Scottish (continued)			
Tavener, John	Celtic Requiem	CHA (GS); WH (GS)	23′
William, Alwyn	Suite of Scottish Dances	EMI (GS)	7′
Machines			
Adams, John	Short Ride in a Fast Machine	B&H	4′
Antheil, George	Ballet Mécanique	GS	18′
Arnold, Malcolm	Symphonic Study 'Machines'	B&H	6′
Barber, Samuel	Night Flight, Op. 19a (plane)	GS	8′
Copland, Aaron	Music for a Great City, mvt. 3, Subway Jam	B&H	3′
Copland, Aaron	Music for Movies, mvt. 4, Threshing Machines	B&H	3′
Corigliano, John	The Mannheim Rocket	GS	11′
Grofé, Ferde	Symphony in Steel	EMI (GS)	15′
Hindson, Matthew	Boom-Box	B&H	4′
Honegger, Arthur	Pacific 231(train)	B&H	7′
Jones, Samuel	Roundings, mvt. 2, Windmills/ mvt. 3, Oil Well/ mvt. 4, Locomotive/ mvt. 5, Plow	CF (PR)	8′/6′/ 7′/6′
Lumbye, H.C.	Copenhagen Steam Railway Gallop	WH (GS)	4′
Matthews, Colin	Machines and Dreams	B&H	15′
Matthews, Colin	Three Machines	B&H	10′
Mosolov, Alexander	The Iron Foundry, Op. 19	GSR (GS)	3′
Rouse, Christopher	The Infernal Machine	HEL (EAMD)	5′
Torke, Michael	Adjustable Wrench	B&H	11′
Villa-Lobos, Heitor	Bachianas Brasileiras No. 2, mvt. 4, The Little Train of Caipira	RIC	4′
Walton, William	Prelude and Fugue ("The Spitfire") (plane)	OX	8′
Whitthorne, Emerson	The Aeroplane, Op. 38, No. 2	CF (PR)	5′
Magic			
Coombes, Douglas	Merlin, Magician of the Universe	LIN (PR)	50′
Dukas, Paul	L'Apprenti Sorcier (The Sorcerer's Apprentice)	DUR (B&H); KAL	13′
Falla, Manuel de	El Amor brujo: Ballet Suite (Love the Magician)	CHA (GS)	24′

Full name	Title	Publisher	Timing
Magic (continued)			
Gruenberg, Louis	Enchanted Isle Symphonic Poem	PR	20'
Laderman, Ezra	Magic Prison	OX	25'
Maggio, Robert	The Hand-Prints of Sorcerers	PR	12'
Mahler, Gustav	Lieder aus Des Knaben Wunderhorn	UNI (EAMD)	42'
Mecham, Kirke	The Jayhawk: Magic Bird Overture, Op. 43	GS	8'
Mozart, Wolfgang Amadeus	The Magic Flute: Overture	BAR; KAL; RIC	7'
Prokofiev, Serge	Love for Three Oranges: Suite, mvt. 2, Le Magicien Tchelio et Fata Morgana jouent aux cartes	B&H; KAL	3'
Rochberg, George	Music for the Magic Theater	PR	30'
Schwartz, Elliott	Magic Music	CF (PR)	12'
Surinach, Carlos	Feria Mágica (Magic Fair), Overture	AMP (GS)	6'
Villa-Lobos, Heitor	Uirapurú (The Magic Bird)	AMP (GS)	18'
Wagner, Richard	Die Walküre: Magic Fire Music	SCH (EAMD); KAL	18'
Welcher, Dan	The Visions of Merlin for Orchestra	EV (PR)	21'
Williams, John	Harry Potter: Suite	GS	
Wuorinen, Charles	The Magic Art	P	75'
Mountains			
Becker, John	Two Pieces for Orchestra, mvt. 2, The Mountains	FC	3'
d'Indy, Vincent	Symphony on a French Mountain Air	HAM (PR); KAL	24'
Grieg, Edvard	Lyric Pieces, Op. 68, mvt. 1, Evening in the Mountains	LUCK; P	6'
Grieg, Edvard	Peer Gynt: Suite No. 1, mvt. 4, Hall of the Mountain King	KAL; P	3'
Hovhaness, Alan	Mysterious Mountain (Symphony No. 2)	AMP (GS)	16'
Ippolitov-Ivanov, Mikhail	Caucasian Sketches, mvt. 1, In the Mountain Pass	KAL; GSR (GS)	8'
Ives, Charles	Symphony No. 4: Fugue, (From Greenland's Icy Mountains)	AMP (GS)	8'

continued

Table R.2 (continued)

Full name	Title	Publisher	Timing
Mountains (continued)			
Khachaturian, Aram	Gayne: Suite No. 1, mvt. 4, Mountaineers' Dance	KAL; GSR (GS)	5'
Liszt, Franz	Ce Qu'on Entend Sur La Montagne, (Berg Symphonie)	BREIT; KAL	38'
Mussorgsky, Modest	Night on Bald Mountain	UNI (EAMD); GSR (GS); KAL	12'
Ruggles, Carl	Men and Mountains	AME (PR)	15'
Strauss, Richard	Alpine Symphony	KAL	47'
Music inspired by art			
Bliss, Arthur	A Colour Symphony	B&H	32'
Diamond, David	The World of Paul Klee	PEER (PR)	12'
Francesconi, Luca	Cobalt, Scarlet: Two Colors of Dawn	B&H	17'
Goossens, Eugene	Fanfare for the Artists	CH (GS)	4'
Grant, Stewart	Sam Black Sketches	PR	20'
Griffes, Charles	Three Tone Pictures	GS	5'
Husa, Karel	Two Sonnets by Michelangelo	AMP (GS)	16'
Larsen, Libby	Mary Cassatt: Seven Songs	OX	29'
Lees, Benjamin	Portrait of Rodin	B&H	17'
Martinu, Bohuslav	The Frescos of Piero della Francesca	UNI (EAMD)	18'
Maxwell Davies, Peter	Five Klee Pictures	B&H	10'
Mussorgsky, Modest	Pictures at an Exhibition	B&H	25'
Respighi, Ottorino	Trittico Botticelliano	B&H	16'
Reynolds, Roger	Graffiti	P	9'
Schuller, Gunther	Seven Studies on Themes of Paul Klee	UNI (EAMD)	23'
Schurmann, Gerard	Six Studies of Francis Bacon	NOV (GS)	30'
Shchedrin, Rodion	Self-Portrait	UNI (EAMD); GSR (GS)	19'
Siegmeister, Elie	Fantasies in Line and Color (5 American Paintings)	CF (PR)	21'
Stucky, Steven	Pinturas de Tamayo	MER (PR)	18'
Tan Dun	Death and Fire: Dialogue with Paul Klee	GS	27'
Thomson, Virgil	Bugles and Birds—a Portrait of Pablo Picasso	GS	2'
Thomson, Virgil	Eight Portraits, mvt. 1, Bugles and Birds (Picasso)	GS	2'

Full name	Title	Publisher	Timing
Music inspired by art (continued)			
Torke, Michael	Black & White	B&H	24'
Torke, Michael	Bright Blue Music	B&H	9'
Torke, Michael	Ecstatic Orange	B&H	11'
Torke, Michael	Green	B&H	12'
Torke, Michael	Purple	B&H	7'
Vaughan Williams, Ralph	Three Portraits from "The England of Elizabeth"	OX	16'
Welcher, Dan	Prairie Light: Three Texas Water Colors of Georgia O'Keeffe	EV (PR)	14'
Nature			
Arnold, Malcolm	Larch Trees	B&H	9'
Beethoven, Ludwig	Symphony No. 6, Op. 68 (Pastorale)	BREIT; KAL	39'
Berkeley, Michael	Secret Garden	OX	12'
Berkeley, Michael	The Garden of Earthly Delights	OX	21'
Berkeley, Michael	The Wild Winds	OX	12'
Berlioz, Hector	Symphonie Fantastique, Op. 14, mvt. 3, Scene in the Country	BAR; BREIT; KAL	15'
Borodin, Alexander	In the Steppes of Central Asia	KAL; GSR (GS); RIC	9'
Copland, Aaron	Eight Poems of Emily Dickinson, mvt. 1, Nature, the Gentlest Mother	B&H	4'
Copland, Aaron	Music for the Movies, mvt.1, New England Countryside	B&H	5'
Copland, Aaron	Prairie Journal	B&H	13'
Corigliano, John	Fern Hill	GS	16'
Delius, Frederick	The Walk to Paradise Garden	B&H	8'
Dvořák, Antonín	In Nature's Realm, Op. 91	BAR; KAL	14'
Finney, Ross Lee	Landscapes Remembered	P	14'
Finzi, Gerald	The Fall of the Leaf, Op. 20	B&H	9'
Goldmark, Karl	Rustic Wedding Symphony, Op. 26, mvt. 4, Im Garten	SCH (EAMD); KAL	10'
Griffes, Charles	Clouds	GS	5'
Grofé, Ferde	The Grand Canyon Suite	LUCK; PR	33'
Henze, Hans Werner	Ode an den Westwind	SCH (EAMD)	22'
Hindemith, Paul	The Four Temperaments	SCH (EAMD)	29'
Hoddinott, Alun	Landscapes	OX	20'

continued

Table R.2 (continued)

Full name	Title	Publisher	Timing
Nature (continued)			
Holloway, Robin	Scenes from Schumann, Op. 13, mvt. 4, Enchanted Forest	B&H	3'
Jones, Samuel	Symphony No. 3 (Palo Duro Canyon)	CF (PR)	23'
Lambert, Constant	Rio Grande	OX	15'
Larsen, Libby	Sky Concerto	OX	15'
Ligeti, György	Atmosphères	UNI (EAMD)	9'
Martin, Frank	The Four Elements	UNI (EAMD)	20'
Massenet, Jules	Scènes alsaciennes (Suite No. 7), mvt. 3, Under the Linden Trees	HEU (PR); KAL	5'
Menotti, Gian Carlo	Landscapes and Remembrances	GS	45'
Milhaud, Darius	Pastorale	UNI (EAMD)	4'
Milhaud, Darius	Symphony No. 12 (Rurale)	HEU (PR)	17'
Musgrave, Thea	Rainbow	NOV (GS)	12'
Nielsen, Carl	Symphony No. 2, Op. 16 (The Four Temperaments)	WH (GS); KAL	32'
Noskowski, Sigismund	The Steppe	PWM	18'
Piston, Walter	Pine Tree Fantasy	AMP (GS)	10'
Piston, Walter	Three New England Sketches	AMP (GS)	17'
Reich, Steve	The Desert Music	B&H	46'
Respighi, Ottorino	Pini di Roma (Pines of Rome)	RIC	23'
Reynolds, Roger	Fiery Wind	P	15'
Schubert, Franz	Rosamunde, D797, mvt. 6, Pastoral Music	BREIT	2'
Schwantner, Joseph	A Sudden Rainbow	HEL (EAMD)	15'
Schwertsik, Kurt	Fünf Naturstücke (Five Nature Pieces)	B&H	16'
Shostakovich, Dmitri	Hamlet: Film Suite (1964) Op. 116, mvt. 4, In the Garden	KAL; GSR (GS)	5'
Shostakovich, Dmitri	Song of the Forests, Op. 81	GSR (GS)	37'
Singleton, Alvin	Shadows	EAMD	20'
Smetana, Bedrich	From Bohemia's Meadows and Forests	BREIT; KAL	12'
Sowerby, Leo	Prairie, a Poem for Orchestra	CF (PR)	17'
Strauss, Jr., Johann	Tales from the Vienna Woods	BREIT; KAL; LUCK	11'
Svoboda, Tomas	Nocturne, Op. 100 (Cosmic Sunset)	ST	20'
Svoboda, Tomas	Symphony No. 1, Op. 20 (Of Nature)	ST	36'

Full name	Title	Publisher	Timing
Nature (continued)			
Takemitsu, Toru	Music of the Tree	P	17'
Takemitsu, Toru	Tree Line	SCH (EAMD)	14'
Tann, Hilary	Here, the Cliffs	OX	17'
Tann, Hilary	Through the Echoing Timber	OX	4'
Tann, Hilary	With the Heather and Small Birds	OX	10'
Tavener, John	Eternity's Sunrise	GS	15'
Thomson, Virgil	The Plow that Broke the Plains: Suite	GS	14'
Thomson, Virgil	Wheat Field at Noon	GS	6'
Tower, Joan	Sequoia	AMP (GS)	16'
Varèse, Edgard	Déserts	RIC	24'
Varèse, Edgard	In the Fen Country	OX	14'
Vaughan Williams, Ralph	Symphony No. 3 (Pastoral)	CUR (GS)	34'
Vaughan Williams, Ralph	Symphony No. 7 (Antarctica)	OX	41'
Villa-Lobos, Heitor	Bachianas Brasileiras No. 2, mvt. 3, Dansa: Memory of the Desert	RIC	5'
Wagner, Richard	Siegfried: Forest Murmurs (Waldweben)	SCH (EAMD); KAL	9'
Walton, William	As you like it, mvt. 3, Under the Greenwood Tree	OX	2'
Weinberger, Jaromir	Under the Spreading Chestnut Tree	AMP (GS)	12'
Zwilich, Ellen Taaffe	Symphony No. 4 ("The Gardens")	MER (PR)	28'
Night			
Barber, Samuel	Die Natali: Silent Night	GS	3'
Barber, Samuel	Night Flight, Op. 19a	GS	8'
Bennett, Richard Rodney	Nocturnes—for Chamber Orchestra	EMI (GS)	12'
Berg, Alban	Seven Early Songs (Sieben Fruhe Lieder), mvt. 1, Night	UNI (EAMD)	4'
Bernstein, Leonard	Arias and barcaroles, mvt. 8, Nachspiel	B&H	4'
Bizet, Georges	Carmen Suite No. 2, mvt. 3, Nocturne	BREIT; KAL	4'

continued

Table R.2 (continued)

Full name	Title	Publisher	Timing
Night (continued)			
Bizet, Jean	Les Chants de la Nuit	EFM (PR)	21′
Borodin, Alexander	Nocturne	KAL	9′
Britten, Benjamin	Nocturen, Op. 60	B&H	25′
Carlson, David	Twilight Night	CF (PR)	7′
Chopin, Frédéric	Les Sylphides (arr Glazunov), mvt. 2, Nocturne Op. 32	KAL	5′
Copland, Aaron	Music for a Great City, mvt. 2, Night Thoughts	B&H	7′
Copland, Aaron	Rodeo: Four Dances Episode, mvt.2, Corral Nocturne	B&H	4′
Dallapiccola, Luigi	Piccola Musica Notturna	SCH (EAMD)	7′
Danielpour, Richard	Celestial Night	GS	20′
Danielpour, Richard	First Light	AMP (GS)	13′
Debussy, Claude	Images: Ibéria, mvt. 2, The Fragrance of the Night	DUR (B&H); CF (PR); KAL	8′
Debussy, Claude	Nocturnes	JO (PR)	25′
Delius, Frederick	Two Pieces for Small Orchestra: mvt. 2, Summer Night on the River	OX	5′
Ellington, Duke	Night Creature	GS	17′
Ellison, Michael	Twilight	EBM (PR)	11′
Falla, Manuel de	Nights in the Gardens of Spain	ESC (B&H); CHA (GS)	23′
Fauré, Gabriel	Shylock, Op. 57, mvt. 5, Nocturne	KAL	5′
Finzi, Gerald	Dies Natalis, Op. 8	B&H	25′
Finzi, Gerald	Nocturne (New Year Music)	B&H	9′
Foss, Lucas	Night Music for John Lennon	PEM (PR)	15′
Glinka, Mikhail	Summer Night in Madrid	KAL; GS	10′
Gottschalk, Louis Moreau	Night in the Tropics (Symphony No. 1)	B&H	19′
Gould, Morton	Night Music from "Audubon"	GS	5′
Gould, Morton	Windjammer: Night Watch	G&C (GS)	3′
Hartway, James	Cityscapes, mvt. 3, Saturday Night	LUCK	8′
Hoddinott, Alun	Nocturnes and Cadenzas	OX	23′
Holloway, Robin	Scenes from Schumann, Op. 13, mvt. 6, Moonlit Night	B&H	3′
Ippolitov-Ivanov, Mikhail	Turkish Fragments, Op. 62, mvt. 3, In the Night	KAL; GSR (GS)	2′
Kennan, Kent	Night Soliloquy	CF (PR)	4′

Full name	Title	Publisher	Timing
Night (continued)			
Khachaturian, Aram	Masquerade Suite, mvt. 2, Nocturne	KAL; GSR (GS)	5′
Liszt, Franz	Nocturnal Procession	KAL	15′
Lully, Jean Baptiste	Ballet Suite: mvt. 2, Nocturno	KAL; P	4′
Massenet, Jules	Suite No. 1, Op. 13, mvt. 3, Nocturne	DUR (B&H)	6′
McPhee, Colin	Tabuh-Tabuhan: mvt. 2, Nocturne	AMP (GS)	6′
Mendelssohn, Felix	Midsummernight's Dream	CF (PR); KAL	62′
Mozart, Wolfgang Amadeus	Eine Kleine Nachmusik	BAR; KAL; P	16′
Mozart, Wolfgang Amadeus	Serenade No. 8, K.286 (Notturno)	BREIT; KAL	19′
Mozart, Wolfgang Amadeus	Serenade No. 6, K. 239 (Serenata Notturna)	BAR; BREIT; KAL	13′
Mumford, Jeffrey	As the Air Softens in Dusklight for Orchestra	PR	10′
Musgrave, Thea	Night Music for Chamber Orchestra	CHA (GS)	18′
Mussorgsky, Modest	Night on Bald Mountain	KAL	12′
Persichetti, Vincent	Night Dances, Op. 114	EV (PR)	19′
Prokofiev, Serge	A Summer's Day, mvt. 6, Evening	B&H; GSR (GS); KAL	2′
Prokofiev, Serge	Cinderella, Suite No. 1: mvt. 8, Midnight	KAL; GSR (GS)	2′
Prokofiev, Serge	Scythian Suite, Op. 20: mvt. 3, Night	B&H	5′
Rabaud, Henri	La Procession Nocturne, Op. 6	DUR (B&H); KAL	16′
Ravel, Maurice	Daphnis et Chloé: Suite No. 1, mvt. 1, Nocturne	DUR (B&H); KAL	5′
Ravel, Maurice	Gaspard de la nuit	DUR (B&H)	22′
Ravel, Maurice	Rapsodie espagnole, mvt. 1, Prélude à la nuit	DUR (B&H); CF (PR); KAL	4′
Read, Gardner	Night flight, Op. 44	P	7′
Respighi, Ottorino	Impressioni Brasiliane (Brazilian Impressions), mvt. 1, Tropical Night	RIC	10′
Respighi, Ottorino	La Boutique Fantasque: Suite, mvt. 7, Nocturne	CHA (GS); KAL	4′

continued

Table R.2 (continued)

Full name	Title	Publisher	Timing
Night (continued)			
Rimsky-Korsakov, Nicolai	May Night: Overture	BELA; KAL	8'
Rochberg, George	Night Music	PR	12'
Rorem, Ned	String Symphony, mvt. 4, Nocturne	B&H	8'
Saint-Saëns, Camille	La Nuit, Op. 114	DUR (B&H)	10'
Satie, Erik	Cinq Grimances pour un Songe d'une nuit d'été	UNI (EAMD)	3'
Schumann, Robert	Evening Song, "Abendlied"	EV (PR)	4'
Sibelius, Jean	Night Ride and Sunrise, Op. 55	KAL	16'
Strauss, Johann	Thousand and One Nights Waltz, Op. 346	NOV (GS)	5'
Strauss, Richard	Sechs Lieder, Op. 68, mvt. 1, An die Nacht	FUER (B&H)	3'
Svoboda, Tomas	Nocturne, Op. 100 (Cosmic Sunset)	ST	20'
Swanson, Howard	Night Music	EWM (GS)	9'
Szymanowski, Karol	Symphony No. 3, Op. 27 (Song of the Night)	UNI (EAMD)	25'
Templeton, Alec	Night Pieces	TPL (GS)	
Thomas, Augusta Read	In My Sky at Twilight	GS	22'
Thomson, Virgil	The Seine at Night	GS	8'
Varèse, Edgard	Nocturnal	RIC	7'
Wagner, Richard	Tristan und Isolde: Nachgesang	BREIT; CF (PR); KAL	10'
Walton, William	As You Like It, mvt. 2, Moonlight	OX	3'
Welcher, Dan	Night Watchers (Symphony No. 2)	PR	29'
Zaninelli, Luigi	Night Voices	SHA (GS)	11'
Patriotic/Americana			
Bagley, Edwin Eugene	National Emblem	PR	5'
Bazelon, Irwin	Early American Suite	BA (PR)	15'
Benjamin, Arthur	North American Square Dance	B&H	11'
Binder, Abraham W.	Poem of Freedom	EMI (GS)	6'
Bliss, Arthur	Christopher Columbus	NOV (GS)	5'
Bloch, Ernest	America: An Epic Rhapsody in Three Parts	BR	42'
Brubeck, Dave	They All Sang Yankee Doodle	AMP (GS)	20'
Buck, Dudley	Festival Overture on the American National Air, The Star-spangled Banner	FC	7'

Full name	Title	Publisher	Timing
Patriotic/Americana (continued)			
Cadman, Charles	American Suite	LUCK	10'
Copland, Aaron	Canticle of Freedom	B&H	13'
Copland, Aaron	Lincoln Portrait	B&H	14'
Copland, Aaron	Old American Songs: First Set, Second Set	B&H	13'
Dahl, Ingolf	Quodlibet on American Folk Tunes and Folk Dances	P	5'
Danielpour, Richard	An American Requiem	GS	62'
Dvořák, Antonín	Symphony No. 9, Op 95 (New World)	BAR; BREIT; KAL	22'
Effinger, Cecil	An American Hymn (A Setting of "America the Beautiful")	GS	5'
Foss, Lukas	American Fanfare	CF (PR)	4'
Foss, Lukas	Three American Pieces	CF (PR)	13'
Gershwin, George	American in Paris	WB (EAMD); LUCK	16'
Gottschalk, Louis Moreau	L'Union: Paraphrase de Concert sur les Airs Nationaux	GS	8'
Gould, Morton	A Song of Freedom	EMI (GS)	10'
Gould, Morton	Amber Waves—on "America the Beautiful"	GS	7'
Gould, Morton	American Caprice	EMI (GS)	5'
Gould, Morton	American Salute	EMI (GS)	5'
Gould, Morton	American Sing: Settings of Folk Songs	GS	16'
Gould, Morton	Declaration	G&C (GS)	30'
Gould, Morton	Holiday Music:, mvt. 5, Fourth of July	G&C (GS)	2'
Gould, Morton	Lincoln Legend	GS	18'
Gould, Morton	Memorials—on "Taps"	GS	6'
Gould, Morton	Star-Spangled Overture	GS	5'
Gould, Morton	Symphonette No. 2 (Second American Symphonette)	EMI (GS)	9'
Gould, Morton	Yankee Doodle	EMI (GS)	3'
Grainger, Percy	Marching Song of Democracy	GS	12'
Hagen, Daron	Postcards from America	CF (PR)	20'
Hailstork, Adolphus	American Fanfare	PR	4'
Harris, Roy	American Creed	AMP (GS)	18'
Harris, Roy	Epilogue to Profiles in Courage: JFK	AMP (GS)	10'
Harris, Roy	Freedom's Land	AMP (GS)	3'
Harris, Roy	When Johnny Comes Marching Home, Overture	AMP (GS)	8'

continued

Table R.2 (continued)

Full name	Title	Publisher	Timing
Patriotic/Americana (continued)			
Ives, Charles	Holiday Symphony: Decoration Day/ Thanksgiving Day	PEER (PR)	10'/15'
Ives, Charles	Holiday Symphony: Washington's Birthday Fourth of July	AMP (GS)	9'/7'
Ives, Charles	Lincoln the Great Commoner	KAL; PR	4'
Ives, Charles	Three Places in New England	MERC (PR)	18'
Ives, Charles	Variations on America	MER (PR)	8'
Jones, Samuel	Let Us Now Praise Famous Men	CF (PR)	16'
Kay, Ulysses	Presidential Suite	CF (PR)	12'
Kleinsinger, George	I Hear America Singing	PIED (PR)	20'
Kraft, William	A Kennedy Portrait (Contextures III)	PR	18'
Persichetti, Vincent	A Lincoln Address for Narrator and Orchestra	EV (PR)	11'
Piston, Walter	Bicentennial Fanfare	AMP (GS)	2'
Prokofiev, Serge	Overture in B-flat major, Op. 42 (American)	B&H	8'
Ranjbaran, Behzad	Thomas Jefferson	PR	16'
Ringwald, Roy	Battle Hymn of the Republic	SHA (GS)	
Ringwald, Roy	The Song of America	SHA (GS)	34'
Rodríguez, Robert Xavier	Jargon: The Story of the American Constitution	GS	15'
Rogers, Bernard	Elegy (to the Memory of Franklin D. Roosevelt)	EV (PR)	8'
Schuller, Gunther	American Triptych	AMP (GS)	14'
Schuller, Gunther	Music for a Celebration	AMP (GS)	6'
Schuman, William	American Festival Overture	GS	9'
Schuman, William	American Hymn	MER (PR)	27'
Schuman, William	On Freedom's Ground: An American Cantata	MER (PR)	40'
Schuman, William	Symphony No. 10, The American Muse	PR	30'
Schwantner, Joseph	New Morning for the World (Daybreak of Freedom)	HEL (EAMD)	27'
Sousa, John Philip	The Liberty Bell March	NOV (GS)	3'
Sousa, John Philip	The Stars and Stripes Forever	NOV (GS)	3'
Sousa, John Philip	Washington Post March	NOV (GS)	3'
Sowerby, Leo	Song for America	PR	9'
Strauss, Johann	Greetings to America: Waltz	OX	

Full name	Title	Publisher	Timing
Patriotic/Americana (continued)			
Strilko, Anthony	March and Funeral Music (In Memoriam John F. Kennedy)	PR	5'
Thomson, Virgil	Fugue and Chorale on Yankee Doodle	GS	5'
Turok, Paul	Variations on an American Song	CF (PR)	8'
Turrin, Joseph	Civil War Suite	PR	20'
Tyzik, Jeff	Fantasy on American Themes	GS	10'
Vaughan Williams, Ralph	Amériques	RIC	26'
Wagner, Richard	Christoph Columbus: Overture	BREIT; KAL	8'
Wagner, Richard	Grosser Festmarsch (American Centennial March)	SCH (EAMD); LUCK; KAL	12'
Walton, William	Christopher Columbus: Suite	OX	10'
Weiss, Adolph	American Life (Scherzo Jazzoso)	FC	6'
Welcher, Dan	JFK: The Voice of Peace	EV (PR)	54'
Zwilich, Ellen Taaffe	American Concerto for Trumpet and Orchestra	MER (PR)	16'
Zwilich, Ellen Taaffe	One Nation (Reflections on the Pledge of Allegiance)	MER (PR)	5'
Planets			
Converse, Frederick S.	The Answer of the Stars	PR	
Debussy, Claude	Clair de lune	JO (PR)	4'
Erb, Donald	Solstice for Chamber Orchestra	MER (PR)	12'
Hamilton, Iain	The Transit of Jupiter	PR	17'
Haydn, Franz Joseph	Symphony No. 43, (Mercury)	DOB	25'
Holst, Gustav	The Planets	GS	51'
Lamb, Marvin	The Eagle has Landed (The Moon)	CF (PR)	10'
Mozart, Wolfgang Amadeus	Symphony No. 41, K. 551 (Jupiter)	BAR; KAL; P29'	
Roxburge, Edwin	Saturn	UMP (PR)	29'
Ruggles, Carl	Sun-Treader	PR	14'
Satie, Erik	Les Aventures de Mercure	UNI (EAMD)	20'
Strauss, Josef	Sphärenklänge, Op. 235 (Music of the Spheres)	KAL; LUCK	9'
Wagner, Richard	Tannhäuser: Venusberg Music	KAL	12'

continued

Table R.2 (continued)

Full name	Title	Publisher	Timing
Planets (continued)			
Warren, Elinor Remick	Singing Earth	PR	18′
Williams, John	Star Wars: Suite	GS	30′
Romance/love			
Barber, Samuel	The Lovers, Op. 43	GS	31′
Berkeley, Michael	Songs of Awakening Love	OX	26′
Berlioz, Hector	Roméo et Julliette: Love Scene	KAL	19′
Bernstein, Leonard	Arias and Barcaroles: mvt. 2, Love duet/ mvt. 4, The Love of my Live	B&H	4′/4′
Bruckner, Anton	Symphony No. 4, (Romantic)	MWV (P)	70′
Busoni, Ferruccio	Lustspiel Overture, Op. 38	BREIT	8′
Chadwick, George Whitefield	Aphrodite	KAL	20′
Chávez, Carlos	Symphony No. 4 (Sinfonia Romantica)	B&H	22′
Coleridge-Taylor, Samuel	Petite Suite de concert, Op. 77, Sonnet d'amour (mvt 3)	B&H	4′
Dorff, Daniel	The Kiss	PR	14′
Dvořák, Antonín	Romance, Violin and Orchestra Op. 11	BAR; KAL	8′
Elgar, Edward	Salut d'amour (Love's Greeting)	KAL	4′
Falla, Manuel de	El Amor brujo: Ballet Suite	CHA (GS)	24′
Gottschalk, Louis Moreau	Symphony No. 2, (Romantique)	BEL	16′
Grainger, Percy	The Power of Love	GS	
Hanson, Howard	Merry Mount Suite, mvt. 3, Love Duet	WB (EAMD)	4′
Hanson, Howard	Symphony No. 2, Romantic	CF (PR)	28′
Kernis, Jay Aaron	Valentines	AMP (GS)	25′
Khachaturian, Aram	Masquerade: Suite, mvt. 4, Romance	KAL; GSR (GS)	3′
Kreisler, Fritz	Liebesfreud	CF (PR)	4′
Kreisler, Fritz	Liebesleid	CF (PR)	4′
Lully, Jean Baptiste	Le Triomphe de l'amour: Ballet Suite	DOB	20′
Milhaud, Darius	Symphony No. 11 (Romantique)	HEU (PR)	18′
Newson, George	Valentine	LEN (GS)	35′
Nøgård, Per	Three Love Songs	WH (GS)	10′
Nono, Luigi	Canti di vita e d'amore	SCH (EAMD)	18′

Full name	Title	Publisher	Timing
Romance/love (continued)			
Orff, Carl	Trionfo di Afrodite	SCH (EAMD)	45'
Paisiello, Giovanni	Nina (La pazza per amore) Overture	CAR (B&H)	5'
Ravel, Maurice	Don Quichotte à Dulcinée, mvt. 1, Chanson Romanesque	DUR (B&H)	2'
Rózsa, Miklós	Love Scene from "El Cid"	EMI (GS)	5'
Rózsa, Miklós	Love Theme from "Ben Hur"	EMI (GS)	3'
Saint-Saëns, Camille	Romance, Op. 36 and Op. 37	DUR (B&H); KAL	5'
Sibelius, Jean	Rakastava, Op. 14, mvt. 1, The Lover/ mvt. 2, The Lover's Path/ mvt.3, Farewell	BREIT; KAL	4'/2'/ 5'
Sibelius, Jean	Romance, Op. 42	BREIT; KAL	5'
Sowerby, Leo	Two Romantic Pieces	PR	15'
Strauss, Josef	Mein Lebenslauf ist Lieb' und Lust, Op. 263	KAL; LUCK	7'
Strauss, Richard	Romanze	SCH (EAMD)	12'
Strauss, Richard	Sechs Lieder, Op. 68, mvt. 5, Amor	FUER (B&H)	3'
Wagner, Richard	Tristan und Isolde: Prelude and Liebestod	BREIT; KAL	17'
Walton, William	Anon in Love	OX	10'
Warlock, Peter	Aspects of Love and Contentment	CH (GS)	16'
Wolf-Ferrari, Ermanno	L'amore medico (Doctor Cupid), Intermezzo	KAL	3'
Royalty			
Adam, Adolph-Charles	Si J'Étais Roi (If I Were King): Overture	BREIT; LED (PR); KAL	8'
Bach, P.D.Q.	Royal Firewater Musick	PR	16'
Balakirev, Mily	King Lear: Incidental Music	FC	35'
Barbirolli, John	An Elizabethan Suite: The King's Hunt	OX	12'
Bartók, Béla	The Wooden Prince:Suite	B&H	30'
Beethoven, Ludwig	Cantata on the Death of Emperor Joseph II	BREIT; KAL; GS	33'
Beethoven, Ludwig	King Stephan, Op 117: Overture	BREIT; KAL	8'
Beethoven, Ludwig	Piano Concerto No. 5, Op. 73 (Emperor)	BREIT; KAL	38'

continued

Table R.2 (continued)

Full name	Title	Publisher	Timing
Royalty (continued)			
Berlioz, Hector	Le Roi Lear (King Lear)	BREIT; KAL	16′
Borodin, Alexander	Prince Igor: Overture	KAL	10′
Boyce, William	Overture (Ode to his Majesty's Birthday-1769)	GAL (ECS)	7′
Britten, Benjamin	The Prince of the Pagodas: Pas de six	B&H	11′
Chabrier, Emmanuel	Le Roi malgré lui (The King in Spite of Himself)	KAL	10′
Clark, Jeremiah	The Prince of Denmark's March	LUCK	3′
Debussy, Claude	Musiques Pour le Roi Lear	JO (PR)	
Délibes, Leo	Le Roi l'a dit Overture	HEU (PR)	6′
Elgar, Edward	Pomp and Circumstance, Op. 39	B&H; KAL	22′
Elgar, Edward	The Kingdom, Op. 51	KAL; NOV (GS)	104′
Ellington, Duke	Les Trois Rois Noirs (Three Black Kings)	GS	15′
Glinka, Mikhail	A Life for the Tsar: Overture	KAL	10′
Grieg, Edvard	Peer Gynt: Suite No. 1, mvt. 4, In the Hall of the Mountain King	KAL; P	3′
Handel, George Frideric	Solomon: Entrance of the Queen of Sheba	KAL; LUCK 3′	
Haydn, Franz Joseph	Lord Nelson Mass	BREIT; P	42′
Haydn, Franz Joseph	March for the Royal Society of Musicians	DOB	4′
Haydn, Franz Joseph	Symphony No. 53, (L'imperiale)	UNI (EAMD)	24′
Haydn, Franz Joseph	Symphony No. 85, (La Reine)	UNI (EAMD)	20′
Honegger, Arthur	Le Roi David (King David)	EAMD	69′
Humperdinck, Engelbert	Königskinder: Prelude	KAL	8′
Ippolitov-Ivanov, Mikhail	Caucasian Sketches, mvt. 4, Procession of the Sardar	KAL; GSR (GS) 5′	
Kodály, Zoltán	Háry János: Suite, mvt. 4, Battle and Defeat of Napoleon/ mvt. 6, Entrance of the Emperor and His Court	UNI (EAMD)	4′/4′
Lalo, Edouard	Le Roi d'Ys Overture	HEU (PR)	10′
Mathias, William	Elegy for a Prince	OX	15′
Moniuszko, Stanislaw	The Countess: Overture	PWM	8′
Mozart, Wolfgang Amadeus	Mass, K. 317 (Coronation)	BAR; BREIT; KAL	24′
Mozart, Wolfgang Amadeus	Regina Coeli	BREIT; KAL	7′

Full name	Title	Publisher	Timing
Royalty (continued)			
Mozart, Wolfgang Amadeus	Thamos, König in Ägypten	BAR; KAL	19′
Parry, Hubert	Suite in F (Lady Radnor's Suite)	KAL	21′
Prokofiev, Serge	Ivan the Terrible	KAL	74′
Purcell, Henry	Indian Queen: Trumpet Overture	OX	3′
Purcell, Henry	The Fairy Queen: Suite No. 1	EUL	6′
Ravel, Maurice	Ma Mère l'Oye: Suite, mvt. 3, Empress of the Pagodas	DUR (B&H); KAL	3′
Ravel, Maurice	Pavane pour une infante défunte (Pavane for a Dead Princess)	ESC (B&H); KAL	6′
Rimsky-Korsakov, Nicolai	Le Coq d'or (The golden cockerel): Suite, mvt. 1, King Dodon at his Palace/ mvt. 2, On the Battle Field/ mvt. 3, With the Queen	KAL; GSR (GS)9′/4′/ 6′/6′	
Rimsky-Korsakov, Nicolai	Mlada: Suite, mvt. 5, Procession of the Nobles (Cortège)	BELA; KAL	5′
Rimsky-Korsakov, Nicolai	Scheherazade, Op. 35, mvt. 2, The Tale of Prince Kalendar/ mvt. 3, The Young Prince and the Princess	BELA; KAL 11′/10′	
Rimsky-Korsakov, Nicolai	Tsar Saltan: Suite, Op. 57	BREIT; KAL	17′
Roussel, Albert	Bacchus et Ariane, Op. 43: Suite No. 2, mvt. 8, Bacchanale and the Coronation of Ariadne	DUR (B&H)	3′
Saint-Saëns, Camille	Coronation March, Op. 117	KAL	8′
Saint-Saëns, Camille	La Princesse Jaune, Op. 30: Overture	DUR (B&H); KAL	6′
Schubert, Franz	Salve Regina D. 106, D. 223, D. 676	BREIT	8′
Smetana, Bedrich	Richard III	KAL	11′
Strauss, Jr., Johann	Emperor Waltzes (Kaiser-Walzer)	BREIT; KAL; LUCK	10′
Stravinsky, Igor	L'Oiseau de feu (Firebird) Suite (1919), mvt. 3, The Princesses and the Golden Apples/ mvt. 4, Round Dance of the Princesses	SCH (EAMD); CHA (GS); KAL	6′/5′
Stucky, Steven	Funeral Music for Queen Mary	MER (PR)	10′

continued

Table R.2 (continued)

Full name	Title	Publisher	Timing
Royalty (continued)			
Tchaikovsky, Piotr Ilyich	Marche solenelle du couronnement (Coronation March)	KAL	5′
Wagner, Richard	Das Rheingold: Entry of the Gods into Valhalla	SCH (EAMD); KAL	9′
Wagner, Richard	Die Walküre: Ride of the Valkyries	SCH (EAMD); LUCK; KAL	5′
Wagner, Richard	Kaisermarch	KAL; LUCK	9′
Walton, William	Crown Imperial March	OX	7′
Walton, William	Orb and Sceptre: Coronation March	OX	9′
Weber, Carl Maria	Ruler of the Spirits	BREIT; KAL	7′
Seasons			
Ashmore, Lawrence	Four Seasons	B&H	16′
Hadley, Henry	Symphony No. 2, Op. 30 (The Four Seasons)	FC	36′
Haydn, Franz Joseph	Die Jahreszeiten (The Seasons)	BREIT; KAL; P	134′
Svoboda, Tomas	Overture of the Season, Op. 89	ST	8′
Vivaldi, Antonio	Le Quattro Staggioni, Op. 8 (The Four Seasons)	CAR (B&H); KAL; RIC	43′
Seasons: Spring			
Adler, Samuel	In Just Spring: Overture for Symphony Orchestra	PR	8′
Argento, Dominick	Songs about Spring	B&H	12′
Avidom, Menahem	Spring (Aviv)	IMI (PR)	12′
Berkeley, Michael	Primavera	OX	6′
Bolcom, William	Spring Concertino for Oboe and Chamber Orchestra	EBM (PR)	10′
Britten, Benjamin	Spring Symphony, Op. 44	B&H	45′
Chou, Wen-chung	All in the Spring Wind	P	8′
Copland, Aaron	Appalachian Spring: Suite	B&H	23′
Debussy, Claude	Images: Rondes de printemps	DUR (B&H); KAL	9′
Debussy, Claude	Printemps	DUR (B&H); CF (PR); KAL	15′
Delius, Frederick	Two Pieces for Small Orchestra: mvt. 1, On Hearing the First Cuckoo in Spring	OX	4′
Goldmark, Karl	Im Frühling, Op. 36 (Springtime)	SCH (EAMD); KAL	10′

Full name	Title	Publisher	Timing
Seasons: Spring (continued)			
Grieg, Edvard	To Spring	GS	4′
Grieg, Edvard	Two Elegiac Melodies, Op. 34, mvt. 2, Last Spring	KAL; P	5′
Holloway, Robin	Scenes from Schumann, Op. 13, mvt. 7, Spring-night-rounds	B&H	3′
Ikebe, Shin-Ichiro	Haru no umi (The Sea in Springtime)	ONTS (PR)	7′
Ingelbrecht, Desire-Emile	Rapsodie de Printemps	SAL (B&H)	10′
Koechlin, Charles	La Course de Printemps, Op. 95	ESC (B&H)	28′
Kraft, Leo	To Spring	CF (PR)	8′
Lajtha, László	Symphony No. 4, Le Printemps	LED (PR)	25′
Milhaud, Darius	Concertino de Printemps, Op. 135	B&H	9′
Milhaud, Darius	Le Printemps	SAL (B&H)	9′
Paine, John Knowles	Symphony No. 2, Op. 34 (Im Frühling)	FC	51′
Respighi, Ottorino	Trittico Botticelliano, mvt. 1, La Primavera (Spring)	RIC	6′
Roussel, Albert	Pour Un Fête de Printemps, Op.22	DUR (B&H)	12′
Schumann, Robert	Symphony No. 1, Op. 38 (Spring)	BREIT; KAL	30′
Strauss, Jr., Johann	Fruhlingsstimmen, Op. 410, (Voices of Spring)	BREIT; KAL; LUCK	6′
Strauss, Richard	Vier Letzte Lieder (Four Last Songs), mvt. 1, Fruhling	B&H	5′
Stravinsky, Igor	Le Sacred du printemps (The Rite of Spring)	B&H; KAL	33′
Vivaldi, Antonio	Le Quattro Staggioni, Op. 8, No. 1, La Primavera (Spring)	CAR (B&H); KAL; RIC	11′
Seasons: Summer			
Anderson, Leroy	Summer Skies	EMI (GS)	2′
Berg, Alban	Seven Early Songs, mvt. 7, Sommertage	UNI (EAMD)	2′
Bliss, Arthur	Dance of Summer	GS	18′
Bolcom, William	A Summer Divertimento	EBM (PR)	25′
Corigliano, John	Summer Fanfare (Echoes of Forgotten Rites)	GS	6′
Delius, Frederick	A Song of Summer	B&H	10′

continued

Table R.2 (continued)

Full name	Title	Publisher	Timing
Seasons: Summer (continued)			
Delius, Frederick	Two Pieces for Small Orchestra: mvt. 2, Summer Night on the River	OX	5′
Druckman, Jacob	Summer Lightning	B&H	8′
Glinka, Mikhail	Summer Night in Madrid	KAL; GS	10′
Kodály, Zoltán	Summer Evening	UNI (EAMD)	16′
La Montaine, John	A Summer's Day	GS	5′
Mathias, William	Symphony No. 2 (Summer Music)	OX	28′
Muczynski, Robert	A Serenade for Summer	PR	
Prokofiev, Serge	A Summer Day, Op. 65	B&H; GSR (GS); KAL	13′
Saegusa, Shigeaki	Symphonic Suite "Tokyo," mvt. 2, Summer for Orchestra	ONTS (PR)	9′
Sowerby, Leo	All On a Summer's Day	PR	13′
Vivaldi, Antonio	Le Quattro Staggioni, Op. 8, No. 2, L'estate (Summer)	CAR (B&H); KAL; RIC	10′
Seasons: Fall			
Bax, Arnold	November Woods	CHA (GS)	15′
Erb, Donald	Autumn Music	MER (PR)	20′
Glazunov, Alexander	The Seasons: Autumn	BELA; KAL	11′
Gould, Morton	Harvest	G&C (GS)	12′
Grieg, Edvard	In Autumn, Op. 11	KAL; P	10′
Ingelbrecht, Desire-Emile	Automne	B&H	9′
Jaffe, Stephen	Autumnal	MER (PR)	23′
Kang, Sukhi	The Feast of Automne	B&H	10′
Panufnik, Andrzej	Autumn Music	B&H	16′
Sowerby, Leo	Comes Autumn Time	PR	6′
Strauss, Richard	Vier Letzte Lieder (Four Last Songs), mvt. 2, September	B&H	5′
Takemitsu, Toru	A String Around Autumn	SCH (EAMD)	17′
Takemitsu, Toru	Automne	B&H	18′
Vivaldi, Antonio	Le Quattro Staggioni, Op. 8, No. 3, L'autunno (Autumn)	CAR (B&H); KAL; RIC	9′
Seasons: Winter			
Debussy, Claude	Le Coin des enfants (Children's corner), mvt. 4, The Snow is Dancing	DUR (B&H); KAL	3′

Full name	Title	Publisher	Timing
Seasons: Winter (continued)			
Glazunov, Alexander	The Seasons: Winter	BELA; KAL	9'
Lieberson, Samuel	In a Winter Garden	PR	7'
Prokofiev, Sergei	Winter Bonfire, Suite, Op. 122	GSR (GS)	20'
Takemitsu, Toru	Winter	B&H	6'
Tchaikovsky, Piotr Ilyich	Symphony No. 1, Op. 13 (Winter Dreams)	UNI (EAMD); KAL	44'
Tsontakis, George	Winter Lightning	MER (PR)	15'
Vivaldi, Antonio	Le Quattro Staggioni, Op. 8, No. 4, L'inverno (Winter)	CAR (B&H); KAL; RIC	7'
Shakespeare			
Amram, David	Shakespearian Concerto	P	22'
Balakirev, Mily	King Lear: Incidental Music	FC	8'
Bazelon, Irwin	Overture to Shakespeare's "The Taming of The Shrew"	PR	10'
Bazelon, Irwin	Suite from Shakespeare's "The Merry Wives of Windsor"	PR	14'
Beethoven, Ludwig	Egmont: Overture and Incidental Music	BREIT; KAL	9'
Berlioz, Hector	Béatrice et Bénédict: Overture	B&B (B&H); BREIT; KAL	8'
Berlioz, Hector	King Lear	KAL; LUCK	
Berlioz, Hector	Roméo et Juliette	BREIT; KAL; GS	95'
Debussy, Claude	Musiques Pour le Roi Lear	JO (PR)	
Diamond, David	Music for Shakespeare's Romeo and Juliet	B&H	18'
Doyle, Patrick	Music from Henry V		
Dvořák, Antonín	Othello Overture, Op. 93	BAR; LUCK	15'
Elgar, Edward	Falstaff, Op. 68	KAL; NOV (GS)	30'
Ellison, Michael	Overture to "Henry V"	EBM (PR)	6'
German, Edward	Henry VIII: Three Dances	KAL; NOV (GS)	8'
Green, Edward	Music for Shakespeare	GR	14'/22'
Harbison, John	Incidental Music from The Merchant of Venice	AMP (GS)	
Harbison, John	Merchant of Venice: Incidental Music	AMP (GS)	12'
Honegger, Arthur	Prélude Pour "La Tempête" de Shakespeare	SAL (B&H)	
Lambert, Constant	Romeo and Juliet	OX	30'
Liszt, Franz	Hamlet (Symphonic Poem No. 10)	BREIT; KAL	10'

continued

Table R.2 (continued)

Full name	Title	Publisher	Timing
Shakespeare (continued)			
Locke, Matthew	Incidental Music: The Tempest	OX	24'
MacDowell, Edward	Hamlet & Ophelia, Op. 22	KAL	17'
Mendelssohn, Felix	Midsummernight's Dream	CF (PR); KAL	62'
Nicolai, Otto	Overture to The Merry Wives of Windsor	B&B (B&H); BREIT; KAL	8'
Paine, John Knowles	As You Like it: Overture,Op. 28	KAL	8'
Paine, John Knowles	Shakespeare's Tempest	BREIT; KAL	25'
Porter, Cole	Brush Up Your Shakespeare from Kiss Me, Kate	MTI	5'
Prokofiev, Serge	Romeo and Juliet: Suite No. 1/ Suite No. 2/ Suite No.3	KAL; GSR (GS)	27'/ 30'/18'
Reed, Alfred	Hamlet A Symphonic Suite	PR	17'
Rodríguez, Robert Xavier	The Tempest	GS	34'
Sallinen, Aulis	A Solemn Overture (King Lear), Op. 75	GS	10'
Schickele, Peter	Songs from Shakespeare	EV (PR)	6'
Schumann, Robert	Julius Caesar, Op. 128: Overture	BREIT; KAL	9'
Shostakovich, Dmitri	Hamlet, Suite from the Film, Op. 116a	GSR (GS)	42'
Sibelius, Jean	The Tempest: Suite No. 1/ Suite No. 2	WH (GS)	20'/12'
Sørensen, Bent	The Echoing Garden (Romeo & Juliet)	GS	40'
Strauss, Richard	Macbeth, Op. 23	KAL; P	18'
Sullivan, Arthur	Overture to The Tempest/ Three Dances	NOV (GS); KAL	10'/11'
Tchaikovsky, Piotr Ilyich	Duo de Roméo et Juliette for Soprano and Tenor	B (PR)	12'
Tchaikovsky, Piotr Ilyich	Hamlet, Op. 67	UNI (EAMD); GSR (GS); KAL	18'
Tchaikovsky, Piotr Ilyich	Romeo and Juliet Fantasy Overture	B&B (B&H); KAL	19'
Tchaikovsky, Piotr Ilyich	The Tempest (Fantasy Overture) Op. 18	KAL	18'
Turok, Paul	Two Pieces for Orchestra from "Richard the Third"	CF (PR)	8'
Verdi, Giuseppe	Overture to Macbeth	KAL	
Walton, William	As You Like It: Poem for Orchestra	OX	10'
Walton, William	Funeral March from "Hamlet"	OX	5'

Full name	Title	Publisher	Timing
Shakespeare (continued)			
Walton, William	Hamlet and Ophelia	OX	14'
Walton, William	Hamlet: A Shakespeare Scenario	OX	50'
Walton, William	Henry V: Suite	OX	16'
Walton, William	Macbeth: Fanfare and March	OX	5'
Walton, William	Richard III: Shakespeare Suite	OX	11'
Weber, Carl Maria	Oberon:Overture	BREIT; KAL	9'
Spanish/Latin			
Albéniz, Isaac	Iberia	ESC (B&H)	28'
Albéniz, Isaac	Iberia (arr. Carlos Surinach)	AMP (GS)	50'
Albéniz, Isaac	Rapsodia Española	B&H	15'
Aubert, Louis	Habanera	B&H	11'
Basler, Paul	Mangulina (Overture on Dominican Rhythms)	CF (PR)	5'
Benjamin, Arthur	Caribbean Dance (A New Jamaican Rumba)	B&H	3'
Benjamin, Arthur	Two Jamaican Pieces	B&H	5'
Berio, Luciano	Ritirata notturna di Madrid	UNI (EAMD)	10'
Bizet, Georges	Carmen: Suite No. 1/ Suite No. 2	BREIT; KAL	12'/19'
Chabrier, Emmanuel	España	KAL	8'
Chabrier, Emmanuel	Habanera	KAL	4'
Chávez, Carlos	Cantos de Mexico	CMC (GS)	4'
Chávez, Carlos	Chapultepec (Three Famous Mexican Pieces)	EMI (GS)	7'
Chávez, Carlos	El Sol (The Sun)—A Mexican Ballad	EMI (GS)	36'
Chávez, Carlos	Sinfonía de Antígona (Symphony No. 1)	GS	11'
Chávez, Carlos	Sinfonia India (Symphony No. 2)	GS	11'
Collet, Henri	Concerto Flamenco No. 2, Op. 255	B&H	20'
Collet, Henri	Rapsodie Castillane Op. 73-2	B&H	8'
Copland, Aaron	Danzón Cubano	B&H	6'
Copland, Aaron	El Salón México	B&H	12'
Copland, Aaron	Three Latin-American Sketches	B&H	10'
Creston, Paul	Sunrise in Puerto Rico	SHA (GS)	4'
Daugherty, Michael	Flamingo	PEER (PR)	9'
Debussy, Claude	Images: Ibéria	DUR (B&H); CF (PR); KAL	20'
Elgar, Edward	Spanish Lady Suite	NOV (GS)	16'

continued

Table R.2 (continued)

Full name	Title	Publisher	Timing
Spanish/Latin (continued)			
Falla, Manuel de	El Sombrero de tre picos (Three cornered Hat)	CHA (GS)	30′
Falla, Manuel de	La vida breve: Spanish Dance No. 1	ESC (B&H)	4′
Falla, Manuel de	Nights in the Gardens of Spain	ESC (B&H); CHA (GS)	23′
Ferrero, Lorenzo	La Nueva España [Mexico]	B&H	72′
Frank, Gabriela Lena	Three Latin American Dances	GS	17′
Geehl, Henry	Suite Espagnole	NOV (GS)	18′
Ginastera, Alberto	Dances from Estancia	B&H	12′
Ginastera, Alberto	Overture to the Creole "Faust"	BA	10′
Ginastera, Alberto	Popol vuh, Op. 44, (Creation of the Maya World)	B&H	23′
Ginistera, Alberto	Estancia: Ballet Suite	BA	13′
Glinka, Mikhail	Jota Aragonesa (Spanish Overture No. 1)	UNI (EAMD); KAL	9′
Glinka, Mikhail	Summer Night in Madrid (Spanish Overture No. 2)	KAL; GS	10′
Goossens, Eugene	Flamenco: Ballet	CH (GS)	8′
Gould, Morton	Latin-American Symphonette	M (EAMD)	17′
Granados, Enrique	Tres Danzas Espanola	UME (GS)	13′
Kay, Ulysses	Danse Calinda (Ballet Suite)	CF (PR)	14′
Kreisler, Fritz	Malaguena	CF (PR)	5′
Larsen, Libby	Sonnets from the Portuguese	OX	20′
Liszt, Franz	Rhapsodie espagnole	KAL	14′
Milhaud, Darius	Musique pour Lisbonne, Op. 420	B&H	21′
Milhaud, Darius	Saudades do Brazil, Op. 67 b	B&H	22′
Ravel, Maurice	Alborada del gracioso	ESC (B&H); KAL	9′
Ravel, Maurice	Rapsodie espagnole	DUR (B&H); CF (PR); KAL	15′
Reed, H. Owen	La fiesta mexicana	BEL	23′
Respighi, Ottorino	Impressioni Brasiliane (Brazilian Impressions)	B&H	20′
Rimsky-Korsakov, Nikolai	Capriccio espagnol, Op. 34	BELA; KAL	15′
Rodrigo, Joaqun	Concierto Andaluz	SCH (EAMD); SAL (B&H)	24′
Rodrigo, Joaqun	Concierto de Aranjuez	SCH (EAMD); UME (GS)	21′
Rodríguez, Robert Xavier	Adoración Ambulante— A Mexican Folk Celebration	GS	60′

Full name	Title	Publisher	Timing
Spanish/Latin (continued)			
Rodríguez, Robert Xavier	Piñata	GS	5'
Rodríguez, Robert Xavier	Sinfonia à la Mariachi	GS	24'
Rossini, Gioacchino	Il Barbiere di Siviglia (The Barber of Seville)	RIC	8'
Roussel, Albert	Sones de Castilla	B&H	23'
Saint-Saëns, Camille	Havanaise, Op. 83	CF (PR); KAL	11'
Sarasate, Pablo de	Carmen Fantasie on Themes of Bizet, Op. 25	KAL	12'
Still, William Grant	Los Alnados de Espana	CF (PR)	12'
Surinach, Carlos	Fandango	AMP (GS)	8'
Tchaikovsky, Piotr Ilyich	Swan Lake: Suite, Op. 20a, mvt. 6, Danse Espagnole	KAL 3'	
Turina, Joaquin	Canto a Sevilla	UME (GS)	40'
Turina, Joaquin	Danzas Fantasticas	UME (GS)	17'
Turina, Joaquin	Sinfonia Sevillana	UME (GS)	22'
Storms			
Beethoven, Ludwig	Symphony No. 6, Op. 68, mvt. 4, The Storm	BREIT; KAL	4'
Berlioz, Hector	Les Troyens: Royal Hunt and Storm	KAL	7'
Druckman, Jacob	Summer Lightning	B&H	8'
Larsen, Libby	Roll Out the Thunder	OX	6'
Martinů, Bohuslav	Thunderbolt P-47	B&H	9'
Mumford, Jeffrey	Within a Cloudburst of Echoing Brightness	PR	4'
Strauss, Jr., Johann	Thunder and Lightning Polka	DOB; KAL; LUCK	3'
Strauss, Richard	Wanderers Sturmlied, Op. 14	UNI (EAMD); KAL	16'
Suderburg, Robert	Winds/Vents	PR	20'
Tsontakis, George	Winter Lightning	MER (PR)	15'
Welcher, Dan	Venti di Mare (Sea Winds) Fantasy: Concerto for Oboe and Small Orchestra	EV (PR)	23'
War			
Adams, John	The Wound-Dresser	B&H	19'
Britten, Benjamin	Ballad of Heroes	B&H	15'
Britten, Benjamin	War Requiem	B&H	85'

continued

Table R.2 (continued)

Full name	Title	Publisher	Timing
War (continued)			
Finzi, Gerald	Farewell to Arms	B&H	8'
Harris, Roy	Concert Overture—March in Time of War	AMP (GS)	4'
Harris, Roy	Epilogue to Profiles in Courage: JFK	GS	10'
Jenkins, Karl	The Armed Man: A Mass for Peace	B&H	68'
McDonald, Harl	My Country at War (Symphonic Suite)	EV (PR)	26'
Mendelssohn, Felix	Athalia: War March of the Priests	KAL; LUCK	5'
Panufnik, Andrzej	Heroic Overture	B&H	6'
Penderecki, Krzysztof	To the Victims of Hiroshima (Threnody)	BEL; PWM	9'
Pierné, Gabriel	March of the Lead Soldiers, Op. 14, No. 6	KAL; LED (PR)	4'
Prokofiev, Serge	Lieutenant Kijé, Op. 60, Suite	B&H; KAL	20'
Prokofiev, Serge	Ode to the End of War	GS	15'
Prokofiev, Serge	War and Peace: Overture	KAL	8'
Rogers, Bernard	The Colours of War	EV (PR)	6'
Rossini, Gioacchino	L'assedio di Corinto (The Siege of Corinth)	CAR (B&H); KAL; RIC	10'
Samuel, Gerhard	Requiem for Survivors	BEL	18'
Schubert, Franz	Marche Militaire, D. 733 (Op. 51)	LUCK; GS	5'
Schuman, William	On Freedom's Ground	MER (PR)	40'
Sheng, Bright	H'un (Lacerations): In Memoriam 1966–1976	GS	21'
Shostakovich, Dmitri	Symphony No. 2, Op. 14 (To the October Revolution)	KAL; GSR (GS)	20'
Shostakovich, Dmitri	Symphony No. 7, Op. 60 (Leningrad)	KAL; GSR (GS)	69'
Siegmeister, Elie	The Face of War	CF (PR)	27'
Suppé, Franz von	Light Cavalry: Overture	KAL; LUCK	8'
Tann, Hilary	The Open Field: In Memoriam Tiananmen Square (June 1989)	OX	11'
Tchaikovsky, Piotr Ilyich	1812 Overture, Op. 49	BREIT; KAL	16'
Turrin, Joseph	Civil War Suite	PR	20'
Walden, Stanley	After Auschwitz	PR	23'
Walton, William	A Wartime Sketchbook	OX	20'
Weill, Kurt	Das Berliner Requiem	UNI (EAMD)	25'

Full name	Title	Publisher	Timing
Water			
Albert, Stephen	RiverRun	GS	33'
Arnold, Malcolm	Suite from The Bridge on the River Kwai	GS	24'
Avni, Tzvi	By the Rivers of Babylon Prelude for Chamber Orchstra	IMI (PR)	15'
Bach, P.D.Q.	Royal Firewater Musick	PR	16'
Beethoven, Ludwig	Calm Sea and Prosperous Voyage	BREIT; KAL	10'
Beethoven, Ludwig	Symphony No. 6, Op 68, mvt. 2, Scene by the Brook	BREIT; KAL	12'
Borodin, Alexander	La Mer	KAL	8'
Britten, Benjamin	Peter Grimes: Four Sea Interludes	B&H	16'
Brouwer, Margaret	Symphony No. 1 (Lake Voices)	CF (PR)	16'
Carpenter, John Alden	Sea Drift	GS	17'
Chausson, Ernest	Poème de l'amour et de la mer	KAL; SAL (B&H)	27'
Cherubini, Luigi	Les Deux Journées: Overture, (The Water Carrier)	BREIT; KAL	8'
Copland, Aaron	Old American Songs: Second Set, mvt. 5, At the River	B&H	2'
Crumb, George	Echoes of Time and the River	BEL	20'
Debussy, Claude	La Mer	DUR (B&H); KAL	23'
Delius, Frederick	Sea Drift	B&H; KAL	30'
Delius, Frederick	Two Pieces for Small Orchestra: mvt. 2, Summer Night on the River	OX	5'
Dove, Jonathan	Seaside Postcards	B&H	15'
Dvořák, Antonín	Watersprite, Op.107	BAR; KAL	19'
Elgar, Edward	Sea Pictures	B&H; KAL	23'
Ellington, Duke	The River	TPO (GS)	30'
Grofé, Ferde	Hudson River Suite	EMI (GS)	19'
Grofé, Ferde	Mississippi (A Tone Journey)	EMI (GS)	13'
Grofé, Ferde	Niagara Falls Suite	EMI (GS)	20'
Guy, Barry	After the Rain	GS	21'
Handel, George Frideric	Water Music	BREIT; P	50'
Holloway, Robin	Seascape and Harvest	B&H	30'
Holloway, Robin	Sea-Surface Full of Clouds	B&H	35'
Holst, Gustav	Brook Green Suite	CUR (GS)	8'
Iannaccone, Anthony	Night Rivers (Symphony No. 3)	TT (PR)	18'
Ibert, Jacques	Escales (Ports of Call)	LED (PR)	5'

continued

Table R.2 (continued)

Full name	Title	Publisher	Timing
Water (continued)			
Ibert, Jacques	Symphonie Marine	LED (PR)	14'
Kernis, Jay Aaron	Symphony in Waves	GS	30'
Liadov, Anatol	The Enchanted Lake, Op. 62	BELA; KAL	6'
Mamlok, Ursula	Grasshoppers: mvt. 3, In the Rain	ACA	1'
Matthews, David	From Sea to Sky	B&H	4'
McDonald, Harl	The Sea for Chorus and String Orchestra	EV (PR)	5'
Mendelssohn, Felix	Calm Sea and Prosperous Voyage	BREIT; KAL	12'
Mendelssohn, Felix	The Hebrides, Op. 26 (Fingal's Cave)	BREIT; KAL	10'
Moeran, E. J.	Lonely Waters	NOV (GS)	9'
Nelson, Ron	Savannah River Holiday	CF (PR)	8'
Paine, John Knowles	Poseidon and Amphitrite: An Ocean Fantasy	KAL	10'
Picker, Tobias	Old and Lost Rivers	HEL (EAMD)	6'
Powers, Anthony	Stone, Water, Stars	OX	23'
Primosch, James	Fire-Memory/River Memory	MER (PR)	21'
Rachmaninoff, Sergei	Cinq Études-tableaux, mvt. 1, La Mer et les Mouettes (The Sea and the Seagulls)	B&H	5'
Respighi, Ottorino	Fontane di Roma (Fountains of Rome)	KAL; RIC	15'
Rimsky-Korsakov, Nicolai	Scheherazade, Op. 35, mvt. 1, The Sea and Sindbad's Ship/ mvt. 4, The Ship Goes to Pieces on the Rocks	BELA; KAL	10'/11'
Rorem, Ned	Water Music	B&H	17'
Saint-Saëns, Camille	Le Déluge, Op. 45 (The Flood)	DUR (B&H)	45'
Schuman, William	Undertow	GS	25'
Schumann, Robert	Symphony No. 3, Op. 97 (Rhenish)	BREIT; KAL	32'
Sheng, Bright	China Dreams, mvt. 3, The Stream Flows	GS	8'
Sibelius, Jean	The Oceanides, Op. 73	BREIT; KAL	17'
Smetana, Bedrich	Vltava (The Moldau)	BREIT; KAL	12'
Strauss, Jr., Johann	On the Beautiful Blue Danube	BREIT; KAL; LUCK	9'
Takemitsu, Toru	Rain Coming	SCH (EAMD)	13'
Takemitsu, Toru	Riverrun	SCH (EAMD)	14'
Tan Dun	Intercourse of Fire and Water (Yi)***	GS	25'
Tan Dun	Water Concerto	GS	27'

Full name	Title	Publisher	Timing
Water (continued)			
Tann, Hilary	Fanfare for a River	OX	4'
Tann, Hilary	The Grey Tide and the Green	OX	11'
Tann, Hilary	Water's Edge	OX	9'
Thomson, Virgil	Sea Piece with Birds	GS	5'
Thomson, Virgil	Sea Piece with Birds	GS	5'
Thomson, Virgil	The River: Suite	PEER (PR)	23'
Vaughan Williams, Ralph	Symphony No. 1 (A Sea Symphony)	GAL (ECS); KAL	62'
Wagner, Richard	Götterdämmerung: Siegfried's Rhine Journey	SCH (EAMD); LUCK; KAL	10'
Wagner, Richard	Götterdämmerung: Song of the Rhinemaidens	SCH (EAMD); KAL	10'
Walton, William	As You Like it, mvt. 4, The Fountain	OX	3'
Walton, William	Portsmouth Point Overture	OX	6'
Welcher, Dan	Venti di Mare (Sea Winds) Fantasy	EV (PR)	23'
White, Paul	Lake Placid Scenes	EV (PR)	16'
White, Paul	Lake Spray	EV (PR)	8'
Williams, Grace	Sea Sketches	OX	17'
Xenakis, Iannis	Sea Change	B&H	10'
Weddings			
Bernstein, Leonard	Arias and Barcaroles, mvt. 6, At My Wedding	B&H	4'
Brouwer, Margaret	Wedding Song	CF (PR)	3'
Coleridge-Taylor, Samuel	The Song of Hiawatha, Op. 30, Hiawatha's Wedding Feast	KAL; LUCK	31'
Goldmark, Karl	Rustic Wedding Symphony, Op. 26	SCH (EAMD); 22KAL	43'
Grieg, Edvard	Wedding Day at Troldhaugen, Op. 65, No. 6	KAL; LUCK; P	6'
Maxwell Davies, Peter	An Orkney Wedding with Sunrise	B&H	13'
Mendelssohn, Felix	Camacho's Wedding: Overture	BREIT	6'
Mendelssohn, Felix	Midsummernight's Dream: mvt. 9, Wedding March	BREIT; KAL	5'
Mozart, Wolfgang Amadeus	The Marriage of Figaro: Overture	BAR; BREIT; KAL	4'
Prokofiev, Serge	Lieutenant Kijé, Op. 60, Suite, mvt. 3, Kijé's Wedding	B&H; KAL	3'

continued

Table R.2 (continued)

Full name	Title	Publisher	Timing
Weddings (continued)			
Purcell, Henry	The Married Beau: Suite	NOV (GS)	12′
Rimsky-Korsakov, Nicolai	Le Coq d'or (The Golden Cockerel), Introduction and Wedding March	KAL	9′
Rimsky-Korsakov, Nicolai	The Tsar's Bride: Overture	BREIT; KAL	7′
Smetana, Bedrich	The Bartered Bride: Overture and Three Dances	BREIT; KAL	7′
Tippett, Michael	The Midsummer Marriage: Ritual Dances	SCH (EAMD)	28′

Encore Lists

More and more conductors are adding planned "encores" to their concert per-formances. Here is a list of popular encore suggestions. Often, a composer will se-lect an encore that ties in with the theme, or composer of the evening. All encores should be short, and most are lively. You want your audience to leave the concert excited about the evening. A good encore is like a refreshing mint or candy after a satisfying meal.

Bach	Air on the G string (from Orchestral Suite #3)	3′
Bartók	Rumanian Folk Dances	6′
Beethoven	Turkish March	3′
Berlioz	"Dance of the Sylphs"(from *La Damnation de Faust*)	2′
Berlioz	"Rakoczy March" (from *La Damnation de Faust*)	4′
Bernstein	Times Square 1944 (from *On the Town*)	5′
Bizet	"Adagietto" (from *L'Arlésienne Suite No. 1*)	3′
Bizet	Carmen "Les Toréadors" (from *Suite No. 1*)	2′
Bizet	"Farandole" (from *L'Arlésienne Suite No. 2*)	5′
Brahms	Hungarian Dance No. 1	3′
Brahms	Hungarian Dance No. 5	3′
Chabrier	Joyeuse Marche	4′
Chopin	Polonaise (arr. Glazunov)	4′

Copland	"Hoedown" (from *Rodeo*)	4'
Copland	Variations on a Shaker Melody	4'
Debussy	Clair de Lune	5'
Delibes	"Czardas" (from *Coppelia Suite No. 1*)	4'
Dvořák	Slavonic Dance Op. 46, #8	3'
Dvořák	Slavonic Dance Op. 72, #1	4'
Dvořák	Slavonic Dance Op. 72, #2	6'
Elgar	"Nimrod" (from the *Enigma Variations*)	3'
Ellington	Sophisticated Lady	4'
De Falla	El amor brujo: Ritual Fire Dance	4'
De Falla	La vida breve: Spanish Dance No. 1	4'
Fuãik	March of the Gladiators	4'
Gershwin	Promenade (Walking the dog)	3'
Glaznov	Cortége solennel (No. 1)	6'
Glière	Russian Sailors' Dance (from *The Red Poppy*)	4'
Gluck	"Dance of the Blessed Spirits" (from *Orfeo et Euridice*)	6'
Gould	Yankee Doodle	4'
Grainger	Irish tune from County Derry (Londonderry Air)	3'
Grieg	"In the Hall of the Mountain King" (from *Peer Gynt*)	3'
Grieg	"March of the Dwarfs" (from *Lyric Suite*)	4'
Grieg	"Wedding Day at Troldhaugen"	6'
Handel	"Entrance of the Queen of Sheba" (from *Solomon*)	3'
Handel	"Hallelujah" (from *The Messiah*) (need chorus)	4'
Handel	"Largo" (from *Xerxes*)	3'
Ippolitov-Ivanov	"Procession of the Sardar" (from *Caucasian Sketches*) 4'	
Kabalevsky	"Gallop" (from *The Comedians*)	2'
Khachaturian	"Sabre Dance" (from *Gayane*)	2'
Leoncavallo	"Intermezzo" (from *I pagliacci*)	4'
Liadov	Dance of the Amazon	4'
Liszt	Hungarian March (Rákóczi March)	6'
Lutoslawski	"Polka"	4'
Mascagni	"Intermezzo" (from *Cavalleria Rusticana*)	3'
Meachan	American Patrol	4'
Mendelssohn	"Scherzo" (from *A Midsummer Night's Dream*)	4'
Mendelssohn	"Wedding March" (from *A Midsummer Night's Dream*)	5'
Mozart	*Ave Verum Corpus*	4'
Mussorgsky	"Gopak" (from the *Fair at Sorochinsk*)	3'
Neilsen	"Negro Dance" (from *Aladdin*)	4'
Offenbach	Barcarolle (from *The Tales of Hoffmann*)	3'
Offenbach	"The Can-Can" (excerpt from *Orpheus in the Underworld*)	3'

Prokofiev	"March" (from *The Love for Three Oranges*)	2'
Prokofiev	"Quarrel" (from *Cinderella, Suite No. 1*)	3'
Rachmaninoff	"Vocalise"	6'
Rimsky-Korsakov	"Chanson Russe" (Dubinushka)	4'
Rimsky-Korsakov	"Cortege March" (from *Mlada Suite*)	4'
Rimsky-Korsakov	"Flight of the Bumble Bee" (from the *Tsar Sultan*)	3'
Rossini	William Tell Overture (excerpt – Allegro to end)	4'
Saint Saëns	Marche Militaire (from *Suite Algérienne*)	4'
Schubert	Marche Militaire	5'
Schumann	Träumerei	4'
Shostakovich	"Polka" (from *The Golden Age*)	3'
Shostakovich	"Romance" (from *The Gadfly Suite*)	4'
Shostakovich	Tahiti Trot	3'
Sibelius	Andante Festivo	5'
Sibelius	Valse Triste	6'
Smetana	"Dance of the Comedians" (from *The Bartered Bride*)	4'
Smetana	"Polka" (from Three Dances from *The Bartered Bride*)	4'
Sousa	Liberty Bell March	4'
Sousa	*Semper Fidelis* March	4'
Sousa	Stars and Stripes Forever	4'
Sousa	Washington Post March	4'
J. Strauss Jr.	Perpetuum mobile	3'
J. Strauss Jr.	Pizzicato Polka	4'
J. Strauss Jr.	Thunder and Lightning Polka	3'
J. Strauss Sr.	Radetzky March	4'
Stravinsky	Berceuse & Finale (from the *Firebird*)	6'
Stravinsky	Greeting Prelude	1'
Tchaikovsky	Coronation March	5'
Tchaikovsky	"Dance of the Buffoons" (from *The Snow Maidens*)	3'
Tchaikovsky	"Melodrama No. 1" (from *The Snow Maidens*)	3'
Tchaikovsky	"Trepak" (from *The Nutcracker*)	2'
Verdi	Triumphal March (from *Aïda*)	6'
Wagner	Prelude to Act III (from *Lohengrin*)	3'
Wagner	Ride of the Valkyries	6'
Weber	Abu Assan	4'
Weber	March to *Turandot*	4'

AUDITION REPERTOIRE LISTS

As a music director of an orchestra, you may be asked to help select audition excerpts for specific instrument openings in your orchestra. Usually, this is done in consultation with the principal player of the section to be auditioned (unless, of course, the opening is for a principal chair). It is useful for a conductor to be familiar with the most commonly asked for audition pieces according to instrument. From these pieces, there are specific "excerpts" that can be selected from excerpt books, or by just identifying the harder, more exposed passages. Most of these excerpts have become standard on a national level. When you post audition lists, it is normal to define the exact measure numbers you would like the candidate to prepare. However, if you choose, you also can just identify the pieces and announce the exact sections at the audition itself. Most audition lists include about eight pieces from which the excerpts will be drawn. This list identifies some of the most commonly asked for audition pieces by instrument.

Strings

Violin

Beethoven	Symphony No. 3
Brahms	Symphony No. 1
Mendelssohn	*A Midsummer Night's Dream*
Mozart	Symphony No. 39
Rimsky-Korsakov	Capriccio espangnol
Rimsky-Korsakov	*Scheherazade*
Schumann	Symphony No. 2
Smetana	Overture, *The Bartered Bride*
R. Strauss	Don Juan
R. Strauss	Ein Heldenleben

Viola

Beethoven	Symphony No. 5
Berlioz	Roman Carnival
Brahms	Symphony No. 3
Mendelssohn	*A Midsummer Night's Dream*
Mozart	Overture, *The Magic Flute*
Ravel	*Daphnis and Chloé*
Rossini	La Gazza Ladra
Shostakovich	Symphony No. 5
R. Strauss	Don Juan
R. Strauss	Don Quixote

Cello

Beethoven	Symphony No. 5
Beethoven	Symphony No. 9
Brahms	Symphony No. 2
Debussy	*La Mer*
Mozart	Overture, *The Marriage of Figaro*
Rossini	William Tell Overture
Smetana	Overture, *The Bartered Bride*
R. Strauss	Don Juan
Tchaikovsky	Symphony No. 4

Bass

Beethoven	Symphony No. 5
Beethoven	Symphony No. 9
Brahms	Symphony No. 1
Mahler	Symphony No. 1
Mozart	Overture, *The Marriage of Figaro*
Mozart	Symphony No. 40
Shostakovich	Symphony No. 5
R. Strauss	Don Juan
Tchaikovsky	Symphony No. 4

Woodwinds

Flute

Beethoven	Leonore Overture No. 3
Brahms	Symphony No. 4
Debussy	Prelude to the Afternoon of a Faun
Mendelssohn	*A Midsummer Night's Dream*
Prokofiev	*Peter and the Wolf*
Ravel	Daphnis and Chloé
Saint-Saens	*Carnival of the Animals*
Stravinsky	*Petroushka*

Piccolo

Bartók	Concerto for Orchestra
Beethoven	Symphony No. 9
Brahms	Variations on a Theme by Haydn
Prokofiev	*Lieutenant Kijé Suite*
Ravel	*Daphnis and Chloé*
Rossini	La Gazza Ladra
Tchaikovsky	Symphony No. 4

Oboe

Bartók	Concerto for Orchestra
Beethoven	Symphony No. 3
Brahms	Symphony No. 1
Brahms	Violin Concerto
Debussy	*La Mer*
Ravel	Le Tombeau de Couperin
Rossini	La Scala di Seta
R. Strauss	Don Juan
Tchaikovsky	Symphony No. 4

English Horn

Berlioz	Roman Carnival
Berlioz	*Symphonie Fantastique*
Debussy	Nocturnes
Dvořák	Symphony No. 9 (New World)
De Falla	Three-Cornered Hat
Wagner	*Tristan and Isolde*

Clarinet

Beethoven	Symphony No. 6
Brahms	Symphony No. 3
Mendelssohn	*A Midsummer Night's Dream*
Rimsky-Korsakov	Capriccio espangnol
Rimsky-Korsakov	*Scheherazade*
Schubert	Symphony No. 8
Sibelius	Symphony No. 1
R. Strauss	Don Juan
Tchaikovsky	Symphony No. 5

Bass Clarinet

Grofe	*Grand Canyon Suite*
Prokofiev	Symphony No. 5
Ravel	*Daphnis and Chloé*
W. Schuman	Symphony No. 3
R. Strauss	Don Quixote
R. Strauss	Til Eulenspiegel
Stravinsky	*Le Sacre du Printemps (Rite of Spring)*

E♭ Clarinet

Berlioz	*Symphonie Fantastique*
Ravel	*Daphnis and Chloé*
Shostakovich	Symphony No. 5
R. Strauss	Til Eulenspiegel
Stravinsky	*Le Sacre du Printemps (Rite of Spring)*

Bassoon

Beethoven	Symphony No. 4
Berlioz	*Symphonie Fantastique*
Brahms	Symphony No. 3
Dukas	*The Sorcerer's Apprentice*
Mozart	Overture, *The Marriage of Figaro*
Ravel	Boléro
Rimsky-Korsakov	*Scheherazade*
Stravinsky	*Le Sacre du Printemps (Rite of Spring)*
Tchaikovsky	Symphony No. 4

Contra-Bassoon

Beethoven	Symphony No. 5
Brahms	Symphony No. 3
Mussorgsky/Ravel	*Pictures at an Exhibition*
Ravel	*Mother Goose Suite*
Ravel	Piano Concerto for Left Hand

Brass

French Horn

Beethoven	Symphony No. 3
Beethoven	Symphony No. 9
Brahms	Symphony No. 4
Mahler	Symphony No. 1
Mendelssohn	*A Midsummer Night's Dream* (Nocturne)
Shostakovich	Symphony No. 5
R. Strauss	Don Juan
R. Strauss	Til Eulenspiegel
Tchaikovsky	Symphony No. 5
Wagner Siegfried	Rhine Journey

Trumpet

Bartók	Concerto for Orchestra
Beethoven	Leonore No. 3
Mahler	Symphony No. 5
Mussorgsky/Ravel	*Pictures at an Exhibition*
Ravel	Piano Concerto in G Major
Respighi	*The Pines of Rome*
Rimsky-Korsakov	*Scheherazade*
Stravinsky	*Petroushka*
R. Strauss	Don Juan
Tchaikovsky	Symphony No. 4

Trombone

Berlioz	Rákóczy March
Brahms	Symphony No. 1
Mozart	*Requiem*
Ravel	Boléro
Rossini	*William Tell*
R. Strauss	Till Eulenspielgel
Wagner	Die Walküre

Bass Trombone

Berlioz	Rákóczy March
Brahms	Symphony No. 1
Kodaly	*Háry János Suite*
R. Strauss	*Also Sprach Zarthustra*
R. Strauss	Ein Heldenleben
Tchaikovsky	Symphony No. 6

Tuba

Berlioz	*Symphony Fantastique*
Bruckner	Symphony No. 7
Mahler	Symphony No. 1
Mussorgsky/Ravel	*Pictures at an Exhibition*
Prokofiev	Symphony No. 5
Stravinsky	*Petroushka*
Wagner	Die Meistersinger

Other Instruments

Harp

Bartók	Concerto for Orchestra
Berlioz	*Symphonie Fantastique*
Ravel	Le Tombeau de Couperin
Rimsky-Korsakov	Capriccio espagnol
R. Strauss	*Death and Transfiguration*
Tchaikovsky	*The Nutcracker*

Piano

Bartók	*Music for Strings, Percussion, and Celesta*
Copland	Appalachian Spring (chamber version)
Stravinsky	*Petroushka* (1947)
Stravinsky	*Song of the Nightingale*

Celesta

Holst	*The Planets* (Mercury)
Mahler	Symphony No. 6 (mvt. 1)

Organ

Saint Saëns	Symphony No. 3
R. Strauss	*Also Sprach Zarathustra*

Timpani and Percussion

Timpani

Bartók	Concerto for Orchestra
Beethoven	Symphony No. 1
Beethoven	Symphony No. 9
Brahms	Symphony No. 1
Hindemith	Symphonic Metamorphosis on Themes of Weber
R. Strauss	*Death and Transfiguration*
Stravinsky	*Le Sacre du Printemps (Rite of Spring)*

Bass Drum

Berlioz	*Symphony Fantastique*
Mussorgsky/Ravel	*Pictures at an Exhibition*
Prokofiev	Symphony No. 5
Stravinsky	*Le Sacre du Printemps (Rite of Spring)*

Cymbals

Mussorgsky	*Night on Bald Mountain*
Rachmaninoff	Piano Concerto No. 2
Rimsky-Korsakov	Capriccio espagnol
Tchaikovsky	*Romeo and Juliet*
Tchaikovsky	Symphony No. 4

Mallets

Dukas	*The Sorcerer's Apprentice*
Gershwin	*Porgy and Bess*
Kodály	*Háry János Suite*
Shostakovich	*The Golden Age (ballet)*
R. Strauss	Don Juan
Stravinsky	*Petroushka*

Snare Drum

Bartók	Concerto for Orchestra
Prokofiev	*Lieutenant Kijé Suite*
Ravel	Boléro
Rimsky-Korsakov	Capriccio espagnol
Rimsky-Korsakov	*Scheherazade*
Rossini	La Gazza Ladra

Tambourine

Berlioz	Roman Carnival
Bizet	*Carmen*
Dvořák	Carnival Overture
Rimsky-Korsakov	*Scheherazade*
Tchaikovsky	*The Nutcracker*

Triangle

Berlioz	Roman Carnival
Brahms	Symphony No. 4
Liszt	Piano Concerto No. 1
Rimsky-Korsakov	*Scheherazade*

Sample Contracts and Résumé Format

As you apply for various conducting jobs, you will become familiar with the posted job announcements. These list the details regarding the position and the skill set required. Here is a sample job posting, a standard job description for a regional orchestra, a "guest conducting" contract similar to what might be used for your audition engagement, and an industry standard music director contract. All of these might appear in various forms and with alterations depending on your specific circumstance. I also have included an overall format for organizing the information on your résumé. A clear and precise résumé will be a great asset in moving your application to the top of the list.

Music Director Job Posting

Duties and Responsibilities

The Music Director will serve as a leader, both on stage and in the community. The Music Director is responsible for developing and enhancing the artistic vision and quality of the orchestra. They are responsible for musical decisions including the planning and supervision, preparation, programming, rehearsing, and conducting of all scheduled concerts. They are responsible for functioning within the orchestra's Policies and Procedures for selecting new players, disciplining players, and determining seating within sections.

The Music Director also will participate in fund-raising and promotional activities in the community to help encourage business and individual support. They should guide and help to expand the educational outreach initiatives of the orchestra. It is important that they establish a vital presence in the cultural community.

The Music Director works closely with the Executive Director and the Personnel Manager. They report directly to the Board of Directors.

Requirements

Exceptional musicianship and conducting skills; innovative and thoughtful programming style; strong skills in interpersonal relations, leadership, and communication.

Music Director Job Description

The Music Director is responsible for the artistic operation and development of the orchestra. He/she exercises authority in artistic matters according the guidelines and budgets established by the board and in accordance with the terms of the working agreement with the orchestral musicians.

Musical Responsibilities

Assist in the development, implementation, and monitoring of artistic objectives for the orchestra that ensure high levels of artistic quality.

Determine all repertoire to be performed by the Orchestra and submit these programs to the Executive Director according with an established time schedule (subscription concerts, educational concerts, special concerts, chamber ensemble programs, pops concerts, etc.).

Select Orchestra Members and Guest Artists

Within the terms of the working agreement with the musicians, select and approve playing personnel, conduct auditions, hire musicians, dismiss musicians, select principal players, determine seating within each section.

Consult with the Executive Director, Finance Chair, and Board President regarding the budget.

Nonmusical Responsibilities

Attend Board meetings whenever possible, and specific committee meetings when appropriate.

Assist in public relations functions to maximize the recognition and appreciation of the orchestra.

Represent the Orchestra at official functions and receptions.

Become a visible and active part of the community.

Help to develop educational materials and programs for educational activities and youth concerts.

Develop a strong working relationship with the music educators in the community.

Work with the Board, the Volunteers, and committees to help with special projects designed to help the Orchestra.

Reporting Relationship

The Music Director reports directly to the Board of Directors through the President of the Board.

The Music Director should maintain a close working relationship with the Executive Director in all matters.

The Music Director will serve as a nonvoting member of the Board of Directors.

Sample Guest Conducting Contract

AGREEMENT, made this _____ day of _____, 20____ between the
_____ (ORCHESTRA) and _____ (CONDUCTOR)
for the rehearsal(s) and performance(s) with the ORCHESTRA for the following dates:

	DAY	DATE	TIME	PLACE
REHEARSALS:				
PERFORMANCES:				

REPERTOIRE TO BE PERFORMED:

IN CONSIDERATION of the agreements specified above, the ORCHESTRA agrees to pay CONDUCTOR the sum of _____ U.S. dollars. Payment will be made by ORCHESTRA check payable to the CONDUCTOR following the final performance.

ADDITIONAL: (*to be negotiated*)

The ORCHESTRA will also provide:

Roundtrip airfare between _____ and _____

Transportation to and from the airport, and to and from rehearsals and performances

A rental car for the duration of the guest conducting engagement

Mileage reimbursement at _____ per mile

Hotel accommodations for _____ nights

FORCE MAJEURE: In case of delay or detention in transportation or the inability to fulfill this contract through illness, accident, action or ruling of governmental authority or other legitimate cause, it is agreed that there shall be no claim for damages by either party against the other:

THE _____ ORCHESTRA   CONDUCTOR: _____

BY: _____   BY: _____

Executive Director   Conductor

Conductor's Social Security Number

_____

Sample Music Director Contract

This Agreement is made and entered into this _____day of _____, 20_____
between _____ ("ASSOCIATION") and _____("CONDUCTOR").

WHEREAS, the Association requires the services of a Music Director/Conductor who can continue to enhance the artistic growth and reputation of The _____ Symphony Orchestra.

NOW, THEREFORE, in consideration of the mutual promises herein contained, it is agreed as follows:

I. *Engagement:* The Association hereby engages said Conductor as Music Director upon the terms and conditions set forth.

II. *Term:* This contract shall be for the term of ____ years, beginning on _____, ____ and ending on _____, _____. The term may be extended by mutual agreement of the parties following written notice delivered by either party to the other not later than _____, _____.

III. *Duties and Responsibilities:* The Association hereby empowers the Conductor with such authority, functions, and duties as are usual and customary to the position of Music Director/Conductor as listed in Exhibit "A." The Conductor is responsible for the artistic leadership of the Orchestra and for the ongoing improvement and upgrading of its musical standards. The Conductor is also specifically employed:

   A. to supervise, select repertoire, prepare, rehearse, and conduct all concerts (subject to paragraph VI) given by the Association during the term of this agreement as set forth in Exhibit "B." Proposed repertoire for each season will be submitted to the Executive Director by _____ of the previous season.

   B. to recommend the engagement of guest artists for performance with the Orchestra.

   C. to recommend to the Executive Director the engagement and termination of Orchestra members according to the terms defined by the Orchestra policy, to determine seating, and to attract and retain quality musicians within the budget restraints.

   D. to devote time and conscientious effort to the overall artistic direction, public promotion, and financial development of the Orchestra, in cooperation and coordination with the Executive Director and the Board.

   E. to devote time and conscientious effort to the overall planning and implementation of the educational programs in cooperation with the Education Staff, Education Committee, and the Executive Director.

   F. to work with the Executive Director in establishing rehearsal schedules, terms, and conditions for any of the concerts.

IV. *Presence and Availability:* It is understood and agreed that Conductor shall at all times further the best interest of the Association and will actively participate in Board meetings, specific committee meetings as necessary, development activities, meetings with media, visits to civic and cultural groups, and other similar activities designed to improve the financial base and the public recognition of the Orchestra. In scheduling these activities, the Association agrees to utilize reasonable efforts to avoid conflicts between the dates of these activities and the Conductor's pre-existing obligations.

V. *Publicity:* The Association will show the name of the Conductor as Music Director and Conductor in all printed material, announcements, general advertisements, programs of concerts, broadcasts, and television performances. The Conductor, in turn, will list their position as Music Director/Conductor of the _____ Symphony in all of their personal promotional materials.

VI. *Outside Activities:* It is understood and agreed that Conductor may conduct and participate in musical engagements and services for orchestras and other musical groups which do not interfere with their performances and the planning and execution of activities to be performed for the Association under the terms of their Agreement listed in Exhibit "B." Both parties shall use every reasonable effort to resolve conflicts of schedules. In addition, the Association reserves the right to hire ____ guest conductors per contract year at their expense. Recommendations for these guest conductors will be provided to the Association by the Conductor.

VII. *Compensation:* The Association agrees to pay Conductor an annual fee of _____ for the first year, beginning _____ and commencing _____; _____ in the second year (_____ to _____) and _____ in the third year (_____ to _____), all payable in *monthly/semi-monthly* installments.

Other Clauses that can be used as applicable:

Employee: It is understood that the Conductor shall be serving as an employee of the Association, and not as an independent contractor, and as such, the Association shall be withholding from the monthly pay all legally required payroll deductions. Conductor shall also be entitled to the benefits of Association's employee health care plan.

Independent Contractor: It is understood that the Conductor is an independent contractor and, as a result, the Association will not (i) make any payroll deductions, (ii) make contributions to any benefit program on behalf of Conductor, government-sponsored or otherwise or (iii) extend any other benefits whatsoever such as paid leave or health insurance.

Expenses: The Conductor will be paid or reimbursed with respect to any and all reasonable and necessary expenses incurred in the performance of their duties according to the policy established by the Association upon submitting the appropriate documentation and receipts.

The Association will provide suitable accommodations for the Conductor for all scheduled trips.

The Association shall provide a vehicle or pay for a rental car for the duration of the Conductor's stay for performances.

The Association shall reimburse the Conductor at the automobile mileage contribution rate allowed by the Internal Revenue Service upon timely presentation of an invoice with appropriate backup.

The Conductor shall be reimbursed for _____ toward attending enrichment seminars and conferences such as the ASOL National Conference, the Conductors Guild National Conference, and/or conducting master classes or workshops.

The Association shall reimburse the Conductor _____ per month toward long-distance phone expenses related to Symphony business.

VIII. *Contact Renewal:* Providing both parties have performed this contract in accordance with its terms and conditions, this contract can be extended for _____ years under the same terms and conditions provided herein, and provided that the Base Salary for the additional year(s) is increased ___% over the Base Salary for the current fiscal year. The offer to extend shall be made in writing by the Association to the Conductor _____ months before the expiration of the existing contract. The Conductor shall have _____ months to accept or decline the offer. Should the offer not be extended or accepted as provided herein, either or both parties are free to negotiate with each other or with others.

IX. *Disability, Death, Force Majeure:* In the event of the mental or physical incapacity of the Conductor or other events beyond Conductor's control which renders Conductor unable to perform any of the services hereunder for a period of sixty (60) days or more, then the Association shall have the right to terminate this Agreement by notice to Conductor. Termination shall be effective ten (10) days following notice to Conductor. In the event of termination under the provisions of this section, Association shall be obligated to pay Conductor accrued and unpaid compensation, prorated to the effective date of such termination.

In the event of the death of Conductor, this Agreement shall be automatically terminated, and the Association shall be obligated to pay Conductor's personal representative accrued and unpaid compensation prorated to the date of death.

It is expressly understood and agreed that performance by Association may be affected by strikes, act of God, weather conditions, inability to secure labor services, fire regulations, restrictions of any kind imposed by any government or governmental agency, or other similar circumstances beyond the Association's control. Upon any such event or events, or other circumstances beyond the control of Association, which results in the inability of Association to produce the majority of Subscription Series Concerts for any Year, then Association may terminate this Agreement, and shall thereafter be relieved from any other or further obligation to Conductor under the terms hereof; provided, however, that in the event the Agreement is terminated under the terms of this section, Association shall pay to Conductor all sums accrued and prorated to the date of such termination, plus compensation equal to _____. Should Association resume normal operations during the period covered by this Agreement, Association shall provide notice to

Conductor not less than _____ days in advance of such resumption of its intention to so resume operations, and once again offer to engage Conductor's services if available, under the terms of this Agreement.

X. *Unique Nature of Services:* It is expressly understood and agreed that by reason of the unique and special services to be performed by Conductor, in the event of Conductor's default or refusal to perform such services, it will be difficult to determine and ascertain the damages suffered by the Association. For that reason, in addition to such damages as the court may award, the Association shall be entitled to equitable relief to prevent any such default, refusal or breach, including, but not limited to, injunctive relief as is appropriate under the circumstances.

XI. *Entire Agreement:* This document contains the entire agreement of the parties and may not be changed orally but only by an agreement in writing by the parties against whom enforcement or any waiver, change, modification, extension or discharge is sought. This Agreement is made and entered into, and is to be performed within the State of _____, and all of its terms and provisions shall be interpreted, construed and enforced in accordance with the laws of the State of _____.

IN WITNESS WHEREOF, Association, through its officers and the Conductor have executed this Agreement in duplicate the _____ day of _____, _____

THE _____SYMPHONY ASSOCIATION

By: _____
                    President
Address: _____

         _____

         _____

"CONDUCTOR"

By: _____
                 Conductor's Name
Address: _____

         _____

         _____

EXHIBIT "A"
MUSIC DIRECTOR JOB DESCRIPTION

EXHIBIT "B"
SCHEDULE OF CONCERT DATES AND REHEARSALS

Sample Résumé

Sample Resume Format

FULL NAME (In large bold letters)
CONDUCTOR
Address
Phone
Fax
E-mail
Website

"Quote from a review"

EDUCATION

Degree achieved and dates
NAME OF THE COLLEGE OR UNIVERSITY

Degree achieved and dates
NAME OF THE COLLEGE OR UNIVERSITY

CONDUCTING POSITIONS

Name of Orchestra   dates
Title held (most recent first)
Paragraph description of the orchestra: number of musicians, number of concerts, types of concerts, budget size, and what your specific duties were.
  • Improved the quality of the orchestra by...
  • Created innovative programming that...
  • Developed concert partnerships with...

Name of Orchestra   dates
Title held
Same format as above

GUEST CONDUCTING
A list of the most impressive guest conducting engagements you have performed. Do not list church jobs or very small pick-up orchestras.

TEACHERS AND MENTORS
List the names of teachers you have studied with

HONORS AND AWARDS
List between one and five awards that you have received. This could include listing participation at well-respected music festivals.

REFERENCES
List three—include name, title, address, phone number, and e-mail address

Recommended Reading

Becoming a great conductor is a process that will require a lifetime of learning. You should be reading books continually and expanding your knowledge. It is essential to do this, not only in specific areas to increase your musical knowledge but also in the areas of leadership, management, negotiation, and people skills. Here are some books that you may find helpful.

MUSIC BOOKS
Conducting Technique

The Grammar of Conducting, Max Rudolf, G. Schirmer, New York, N.Y. 1950
The Modern Conductor, 7th ed., Elizabeth Green and Mark Gibson, Prentice Hall, Englewood Cliffs, N.J. 2003
The Saito Conducting Method, Hideo Saito, Min-On Concert Association, Tokyo, Japan 1988

Theory—History—Orchestration

Anatomy of the Orchestra, Norman Del Mar, University of California Press, Berkeley, Calif. 1983
Harmony and Voice Leading, Edward Aldwell and Carl Schachter, Harcourt Brace Jovanovich College Publishers, New York, N.Y. 1989
A History of Western Music, Donald Jay Grout, W.W. Norton, New York, N.Y. 1980
Music in the Western World—A History in Documents, Piero Weiss and Richard Taruskin, Schirmer, New York, N.Y. 1984
Partiturspiel, Heinrich Creuzberg, B. Schotts Sohne, Mainz, Germany
The Study of Orchestration, Samuel Adler, W.W. Norton, New York, N.Y. 2002

Percussion Terminology

A Practical Guide to Percussion Terminology, Russ Girsberger, Meredith Music
Publications, Fort Lauderdale, Fla. 1998

Contemporary Percussion, Reginald Smith Brindle, Oxford University Press, New York,
N.Y. 1991

Handbook of Percussion Instruments, Karl Peinkofer and Fritz Tannigel (translated by
Kurt and Else Stone), European American Music Distributors, New York, N.Y. 1976

Music Research Books

American Orchestral Music: A Performance Catalogue, Richard Koshgarian, Rowman
& Littlefield, Lanham, Md. 1992

The Book of Classical Music Lists, Herbert Kupferberg, Penguin, New York, N.Y. 1988

*A Conductor's Repertory of Chamber Music: Compositions for Nine to Fifteen Solo
Instruments,* William Scott, Greenwood, Westport, Conn. 1993

The Da Capo Catalog of Classical Music Compositions, Jerzy Chwialkowski, Da Capo,
New York, N.Y. 1996

International Vocabulary of Music, Stephen Dembski, Gerad Gubisch, Jorge Labrouve,
Patrick Marcland, and Diogene Rivas, Harper Collins, New York, N.Y. 1984

Music Collections in American Libraries, Carol Bradley, Information Coordinators,
Detroit, Mich. 1981

Music Reference and Research Materials, Vincent Duckles, Schirmer, New York, N.Y.
1997

The New Grove Dictionary of Music and Musicians, Stanley Sadie, Editor, Macmillan,
London, England 1998

The New Harvard Dictionary of Music, Don Randel, Harvard University Press,
Cambridge, MA 1986

Orchestral Music—A Handbook, David Daniels, Scarecrow, Lanham, Md. 1996

Pocket Manual of Musical Terms, Theodore Baker, Editor, Schirmer, New York, N.Y.
1975

Private Music Collections, James Coover, Harmonie Park, Warren, Mich. 2001

LEADERSHIP BOOKS

The Art of Worldly Wisdom, Baltasar Gracian (1601–1658) (translated by Christopher
Maurer), Doubleday Currency, New York, N.Y. 1992

Courageous Leadership, Bill Hybels, Zondervan, Grand Rapids, Mich. 2002

Developing the Leader within You, John C. Maxwell, Thomas Nelson, Nashville,
Tenn. 1993

Good to Great, Jim Collins, Harper Collins, New York, N.Y. 2001

The Leader in You, Dale Carnegie and Associates, Pocket, New York, N.Y. 1993

Leadership is an Art, Max DePree, Dell, New York, N.Y. 1989

Leadership Without Easy Answers, Ronald A. Heifetz, Harvard University Press, Cambridge, Mass. 1994

On Becoming a Leader, Warren Bennis, Addison-Wesley, New York, N.Y. 1994

Reflections for Managers, Bruce N. Hyland and Merle J. Yost, McGraw-Hill, New York, N.Y. 1994

Seeds of Greatness, Denis Waitley, Pocket, New York, NY 1983

Servant Leadership, Robert K. Greenleaf, Paulist, Mahwah, N.J. 1977

The Tao of Leadership, John Heider, Humanics New Age, Atlanta, Ga. 1985

ORGANIZATIONAL BOOKS

Management

The 22 Biggest Mistakes Managers Make, James K. Van Fleet, Parker, West Nyack, N.Y. 1973

The Brass Tacks Manager, Pat Kaufman and Cindy Wetmore, Main Street Books, New York, N.Y. 1994

Executive Tune-Up, Karl Albrecht, Ph.D., Prentice Hall, Englewood Cliffs, N.J. 1981

First Things First, Stephen R. Covey, A. Roger Merrill, Rebecca R. Merrill, Fireside, New York, N.Y. 1994

Life Strategies, Phillip C. McGraw, Ph.D., Hyperion, New York, N.Y. 1999

Managing the Non-Profit Organization, Peter F. Drucker, Harper Business, New York, N.Y. 1990

Notes from a Friend, Anthony Robbins, Fireside, New York, N.Y. 1995

The One Minute Manager, Kenneth Blanchard, Ph.D., and Spencer Johnson, M.D., Berkley, New York, N.Y. 1982

Power Lines—What to Say in 250 Problem Situations, Dr. Lynn Weiss and Lora Cain, Harper Paperbacks, New York, N.Y. 1991

The Seven Habits of Highly Effective People, Stephen R. Covey, Simon & Schuster, New York, N.Y. 1990

Stress Management, Edward A. Charlesworth, Ph.D., and Ronald G. Nathan, Ph.D., Ballantine, New York, N.Y. 1982

Success Through a Positive Mental Attitude, Napoleon Hill and W. Clement Stone, Pocket, New York, N.Y. 1960

Working Smart, Michael le Boeut, Warner, New York, N.Y. 1979

Negotiating Skills

Getting Past No, William Ury, Bantam, New York, N.Y. 1991

Getting What You Want, Kare Anderson, Dutton, New York, N.Y. 1993

The Negotiating Game, Chester L. Karrass, Harper Business, New York, N.Y. 1994

Personality Negotiating, Tom Anastasi, Sterling, New York, N.Y. 1993

The Power of Ethical Persuasion, Tom Rusk, M.D., with D. Patrick Miller, Penguin, New York, N.Y. 1993

You Can Negotiate Anything, Herb Cohen, Bantam, New York, N.Y. 1980

People Skills

Bringing Out the Best in People, Alan Loy McGinnis, Ausburg, Minneapolis, Minn. 1985

Conversational Power, James K. Van Fleet, Prentice Hall, Englewood Cliffs, N.J. 1984

How I Raised Myself from Failure to Success in Selling, Frank Bettger, Prentice Hall, New York, N.Y. 1952

How to Get the Best Out of People, Donald H. Weiss, AMACOM, American Management Association, New York, N.Y. 1936

How to Win Friends and Influence People, Dale Carnegie, Simon & Schuster, New York, N.Y. 1964

People Skills, Robert Bolton, Ph.D., Touchstone, New York, N.Y. 1979

Smart Questions, Dorothy Leeds, Berkley, New York, N.Y. 1987

Winning with Difficult People, Arthur H. Bell and Dayle M. Smith, Barons Educational Series, New York, N.Y. 1991

Photo Credits

Index

CPSIA information can be obtained
at www.ICGtesting.com
Printed in the USA
BVHW042256150219
540420BV00002B/3/P